Everything's Gonna Be Alright

Also by

MICHAEL R. MUNDY

Lila The Shepherd and The Wolf

The Love Connection

The Camping Conundrum

I Will Always Love You

Everything's Gonna Be Alright

The Holy Spirit Knows What She's Doin'

Straight Talk about God, Jesus, the Holy Spirit, Religion, Heaven, Hell and about God's Cosmic Plan for the Universe.

Michael R Mundy

First edition published 2020 by Michael R Mundy

NATIONAL LIBRARY OF AUSTRALIA

A catalogue record for this book is available from the National Library of Australia

ISBN: 978-0-9876228-1-5 (paperback)
Interior and Cover Layout: Pickawoowoo Publishing Group
Print and Distribution: Lightning Source | Ingram (USA/UK/EUROPE/AUS)

"That spark of consciousness we are born with, that atom of Divinity that is the Christ within, can be likened to one singular star witnessed at night on a dark cloud filled sky waiting patiently to expand. Comes the removal of that veil of cloud revealing in all its splendour a singular unlimited expanse of sparkling shining light, a star studded sky, a demonstration of the fullness and splendour of our Universal God. This is enlightenment defined, a revelation of the hidden Christ within, and with that an understanding of the unlimited potential of our Soul."

For my daughter Julianna Sexton and son-in-law Richard.
For my son Jason Robert Mundy and daughter-in-law Dang.

Contents

From The Author....xiii

Preface....xv

Introduction....xxxiii

"The Three Mysteries" The Outgoing, the Evolution, the Involution...Creation, Separation, and Return. liii

Chapter 1 The Principle of Separation, The Play of Personhood, The Atonement Process.... 1

Chapter 2 Gnosticism ... A Forgotten Faith. 29

Chapter 3 Truth Versus Belief and The Way of Right Perception....61

Chapter 4 The Biblical Narrative. 85

Chapter 5 Transcendence of Thought from The Ego Mind to The Christ Mind. 109

Chapter 6 The Origins and Nature of Goodness and Evil. 135

Chapter 7 Jung and the Collective Unconscious Archetypes, Myths and Mysteries. 155

Chapter 8 The Evolutionary and Transitionary Nature of Humanity. 177

Chapter 9 The Transitionary Wilderness Experience of Jesus and The Buddha. 197

Chapter 10 The Holy Spirit...The God of Wisdom The Feminine Principle of God....217

Chapter 11 The Holy Spirit the Spirit of Grace Guiding and Leading Us Home. 241

Chapter 12 Life in The Spirit Living a Balanced Life According to God's Universal Laws.................. 257
Conclusion 281
Daily Spiritual Pointers and Practices. 291
Morning I AM Prayer... 295

MICHAEL ROBERT MUNDY

(Taran Nam Singh)

Spiritual Philosopher and Author

Taran Nam Singh

The courageous Lion

who carries others across the perilous oceans

of the material world to spiritual awareness

through

Remembering God's Name

FROM THE AUTHOR

"Wisdom is not a transferable commodity between human beings. Wisdom is the one asset that can be neither bought nor taught. The Holy Spirit alone can birth true Wisdom into one's being. God is the only source of true Wisdom and the Holy Spirit is God's agent, gently delivering that Wisdom as it emanates from the Mind of Christ within us, in those moments in life that we choose as an act of our will, to be still, to be silent, and to listen."

Many times whilst reading a book I have found myself curious as to the author's background, especially those parts of it that may have influenced and inspired him or her to write about its particular subject matter. I have also at times found myself inquisitive, particularly if a book that I am reading is about spirituality, as to what experiential credentials the author may have in the things they are writing about. Have they had genuine life experience in these matters and have they walked the talk as the saying goes? Do they wholly believe in the truthfulness of their work, or do they just have a theoretical or theological understanding of the facts they are presenting? I have always been of the opinion in relation to the things of the spirit, that any new theory, particularly what is described as truth, cannot honestly be proclaimed by the author to be absolute truth, unless it has been tested and authenticated by the author in his or her own personal life.

I believe it is inherently built into our nature to be attracted to the sometimes intriguing and personal aspect of real life stories, whether they are in books, in documentaries, or in movies; an attraction perhaps surfacing out of our subconscious need for truth and reality in our lives whilst we live in world that at times can appear full of falsity and contradiction. Some people with a slightly more competitive bent to their personality, as I had for a great deal of my life, may perhaps also be drawn to real life stories to enable a mental comparison to be made between their own life, the good the bad and the ugly of it, and other people's lives. Drawn to real life stories in a type of ego driven self-esteem road trip, looking for internal validation of their own level of achievement and success in life, thus shoring up psychologically their own feelings of self-worth. For those readers who may have a similar curiosity with regards to myself, I share a few insights into myself in the following Preface.

A Preface at the beginning of a book generally tells the story of how the book came into being, revealing those people who inspired the author to write it, as well as those events that perhaps conspired and certainly transpired to bring the book to fruition. In the following Preface, probably containing a little more detail than the ones usually seen in most books, but all relevant, I share some history about my own life journey, the spiritual side as well as the personal side. Not in any way to shore up my feelings of self-worth, nor in any way as a means of bolstering my ego, and not in any way as a self-aggrandisement or a self-depreciating exercise, but rather to give you the reader greater understanding of what manner of headspace I have been in at various stages in my life as I soldiered on spiritually, some of which you may identify with, and to give you the reader insight into how I arrived at the place I am at now, which hopefully will encourage you to press on.

In particular I share the headspace I was in when I became convinced of the necessity of writing this book. I do this hoping that you may find it helpful and insightful, especially if you see some similarities in your own cosmic life quest, and the stops and starts along the way that you may have experienced as you journeyed through it.

With Grace and Gratitude,

Michael.

PREFACE

All of my life particularly from my pre-teen years, I have been possessed with what might be described as a fascination for the written word, an attraction to books you might call it, all manner of books regardless of what genre they belonged to. Many times during my teenage years I would find myself frequenting bookstores like an obsessed literature stalker, not necessarily with the intent of making a purchase, but merely for the peace and pleasure I felt in browsing the bookstore shelves, and the subtle enjoyment I got in being around books and around my fellow bookworms as they loitered in their chosen section. Even at times as a child on family holidays at the beach, whilst everyone else was interested in going swimming, surfing or working on their tan, I more often than not could be found wandering the street that housed the local Book Exchange, gazing wistfully through the front glass display window, and occasionally with a slight sense of awe venturing inside to catch a closer look at the hundreds of books appetisingly spread out on the trestle tables, or regally standing to attention in the wall stands; looking and longing to find something I could buy, a bargain that I could afford with the limited pocket money allowance my mother had given me.

I am not sure where this passion came from. My father passed when I was 10 years of age so I never had a father figure growing up to influence me in the direction of sporting activities or general father-son things such as fishing and camping. Later in life perhaps to compensate for this, when the subject of sporting interests came up in conversation, I would jokingly say that I preferred to exercise my mind rather than my body. The passion I had for books just seemed always to have been there. I loved the look of the book and the feel of it in the hand. I admired the creative artwork on the cover, and how, if done thoughtfully and cleverly enough, the words on the cover sleeve in an effort to attract me, conveyed a succinct interpretation of the overall content of the writings inside. Occasionally during a browsing session I would buy a book if I could afford it, sometimes not necessarily because of its subject matter, but simply because I was attracted to the title and artwork on the cover.

That book might not be read until many years later when I felt I was in some mysterious way being drawn to its particular content. I remember being very disappointed some years ago when I read an article suggesting that the new age of the digital book, which enables one to read with apps like Kindle, would eventually replace the written word, sadly resulting in the closure of many bookstores. To me curling up with an iPad did not seem as pleasant as curling up with a book. However as yet there have been only a small number of store closures, with digitalised publications seemingly at this stage only complementing the written version of the book giving people an extra variety of reading platforms, which is good.

The first two books that I owned at around ten years of age, after an ongoing fascination with super hero comics and the Secret Seven and Famous Five series by Enid Blyton, were A Tale of Two Cities by Charles Dickens and A Man Called Peter by Catherine Marshall. A Tale of Two Cities was a romantic, adventurous type of story about the lives of a group of people living at a turbulent time in European history, during the French Revolution. Its plot gripped me from the moment I read the first few lines and continued to enthral me as I worked my way through it from start to finish. I read that book three times. A Man Called Peter had a different type of impact on me, in that I marvelled that in such a relatively short lifetime, Peter Marshall passed away at 46 years of age, one man's passion for the things of God, and his dedication towards the welfare of his congregation achieved so much. Whilst I only read the book twice, at ten years of age I did go to see the movie starring Richard Todd and Jean Peters at our local theatre when it was released in Australia in 1958.

Both books were for me the beginning of what you could call a magnificent obsession with the written word for over 70 years. It was an infatuation that saw me in my early adulthood wade into the waters of a variety of different genres, and into a fascinating pool of very talented and gifted authors. The following decades would see me read works of fiction, biographies of influential leaders, books about world history, about health and wellness, about spirituality and religion, and books about the evolution of society over the last two thousand years traditionally, culturally, socially and religiously. Then approximately fifteen years ago something interesting began to happen during my book reading time, which continues to this day. As I was reading a book on spirituality I observed a previously unrecognized phenomena occurring. I say unrecognized, however I strongly believe that it probably had been there all along, but my mind was probably at the time of reading so self absorbed with other things, the many cares of life to be exact, that I was not consciously aware of what was happening. I describe the phenomena here as best I can.

At various times as I was reading a spiritual book, certain paragraphs or sometimes even just a few lines on a particular page would jump out at me, gripping my attention, seemingly in a way separating my attention from the rest of the passage of words around them. You could say that the true spiritual message of what the author was saying in a particular part came alive to my understanding, but more than this many times my mind would immediately align the writer's words with a verse or passage from the Bible that I had read many years before but imagined I had forgotten. The Bible passage was as I see it now being brought back to my remembrance. In a way when these incidents happened, they reinforced to me both the truth of what the author was saying and the truth of that particular passage of scripture. So sudden and so meaningful and intense was the moment, that many times it happened I felt it necessary to write my understanding down immediately so as not to lose this special insight that I had unexpectedly received.

Each time an incident like this occurred, it was like a light had been switched on illuminating my understanding, and then following the incident a deep sense of inner peace would come over me. At times it would deliver a fresh pearl of wisdom, and at other times it would bring clarity to a specific spiritual question that may have been preying on my mind for some time. I remember reading or hearing Oprah Winfrey say that she too often experiences something similar to this when reading spiritual books, referring to it as her having an "ah ha moment." She speaks of it as her moment of enlightenment. Largely thanks to Oprah, Merriam-Webster, America's most trusted online dictionary for the English word, has added that phrase to its latest publication. Its official definition is, "the ah ha moment - a moment of sudden realisation, inspiration, insight, recognition or comprehension." What I did not realise when it first started to happen, but came to realise later, was that each incident was in fact a revelatory experience of the Holy Spirit, a portion of God's Wisdom being imparted to me by God's Spirit.

I also came to realise over time that to receive Divine Wisdom through revelation, which is simply God communicating to us intuitively through the Voice of the Holy Spirit, is certainly not as difficult as many church leaders and theologians have made us believe, nor is it reserved only for the privileged. All you have to do is to be willing, be of right or righteous intent, meaning not asking for anything that will be harmful to another person, things that contain some element of attack or vengeance in them, and then get quiet, ask for guidance sincerely, and continue to stay alert for the answer. The key is in waiting patiently for the answer, it will come. It may take only a minute, it may take hours, it may take days, it may take weeks, but it will come. God does not have a watch or operate according to a diary or a calendar as we do. And do not think that it would never happen to you and that you are not worthy enough. The disciples of Jesus who were present when he spoke of the coming of the Comforter, the Holy Spirit to be with them and teach them all things, were not priests nor members of the clergy; they were ordinary people, living ordinary lives, doing ordinary things, before they gathered up their small personal belongings and followed Him.

The Holy Spirit is fully aware of the pre-destined ongoing script for our lives, whether we are Christian or not, and how that script will be played out at every stage. The Holy Spirit is ever ready to get involved in our lives if we will but ask Her, and She uses a variety of different but easily understood methods to communicate the Wisdom of God to us, and to give us guidance in every situation, including the use of specific passages in spiritual books as happened with me. I say easily understood because the language and methodology the Holy Spirit chooses is entirely user friendly, and is neither religious, nor spooky, nor rocket science. It is not God's intention to make spiritual growth difficult for us; we are perfectly capable of doing that for ourselves.

How did this work for me in relation to books? When I look back on my own evolution spiritually in those 60 odd years of browsing, buying and reading, I see that many times a specific psychological belief took up residence in my mind after reading a certain book at a certain time. In some cases it was an impartation of new truth and at other times it would be for correction of a previously held false belief. Both these processes are vitally important in relation to our ongoing spiritual development. To place these 'moments of enlightenment' in chronological sequence, the first time it occurred was in my early teens after reading A Man Called Peter. The fixed belief formed was that no relationship is more important or worthy of pursuing in this temporary changing earthly life, which too soon becomes as dust, than our eternal heavenly changeless life relationship with God. And that belief has never left me.

Then in my early adulthood after reading The Cross and the Switchblade by Reverend David Wilkinson, the fixed belief formed was that from God's point of view there is not one human being on earth that is not worthy of forgiveness and redemption, no matter how far they have in the eyes of others strayed from the path of right and righteous living; and further to this that the precursor for us personally to receive forgiveness is that we must first forgive those who have trespassed against us, for this is how spiritual law works. The measure of forgiveness we are given is always proportionate to the measure we have given or are prepared to give to others, and this is not just in terms of forgiveness but it applies to everything. Give something and something will be given to you, withhold something knowing deep down that you should give it and something will be withheld from you. That's how spiritual law works.

At around fifty-one years of age I read The Power of Now by Eckhart Tolle, which I came across accidentally whilst roaming around in a bookstore in New York. I believe that it was not a co-incidence as I had never heard of the book or the author, but was intuitively drawn to a large highlighted display of it in the centre of the Barnes and Noble bookstore where I was browsing. I just sensed I should buy it. It had not long been published so had not gained the attention that it has now. The fixed belief formed from reading this book was that this present moment, 'the now' as he describes it, is the only true effective part of clock time we have, for to dwell on the past or to be anxious about the future, both being psychological time zones where our ego prefers to keep us, is totally non-effective and profits us nothing. It is also a principle confirmed over and over again in the Bible with words like "forget those things that are past and press on," and "be not anxious for tomorrow," for it is a truth with great power to benefit us, especially in modern times with the astonishing rise in mental health issues in society.

Lastly a specific belief construct occurred in my latter years after reading The Gnosis or Ancient Wisdom in the Christian Scriptures, sometimes called The Wisdom in a Mystery, written by William Kingsland. This book focuses on the process of Divine Revelation and the role of the Holy Spirit in our lives. Kingsland spoke of an ancient Christian movement known as Gnosticism, which I had never heard of, and after researching it I understood why. Gnostic thought was Christian teaching conveniently left out of the teaching promulgated by the early Catholic Church fathers. They not only vehemently opposed it, but later deemed it heretical, and then with ruthless abandon set about extinguishing all traces of it, as well as any other type of independent spiritual thought that did not fit in with their own church creeds, doctrines and dogmas. The Gnostics believed that God can speak directly to the individual through a visitation of the Holy Spirit and that everyone is able to communicate directly with the Holy Spirit, not just the clergy as the church had long taught. I would say that those four books in particular come to mind whenever I consider what literature has had a significant impact on my spiritual belief system and continues to do so as my spiritual journey unfolds and progresses.

So how in fact did my spiritual life begin and then continue to evolve? I will give you the abridged version. From early childhood I had always felt a pull towards the spiritual aspect of life. This would see me every Sunday morning attending our local Baptist Church, participating along with my sister and other children in what was known as a Sunday School class. It was an innocuous type of Children's Bible Study you could say, focused on the singing of simple Christian choruses and the teaching of easily understood Bible stories. The Sunday School teacher, interestingly always a woman, would use an illustrated picture book held up for all to see, sometimes using felt cut-outs of Biblical characters, posting them on a display board. The stories she shared pertained mostly to incidents in the life of Jesus, but sometimes, probably to hold our interest, she would read adventurous Old Testament stories such as Daniel in the lion's den, or the tale of Joseph and his coat of many colours.

You could say that from a very young age my belief system about God, Jesus, and the Bible was in my own mind, simple and relatively settled. As a child I never felt any need to ask for empirical evidence that everything our Sunday school teacher told us was the absolute truth. I was just happy to know that Jesus loved me, and I was at peace in the simple knowledge that when I died I would be going to this wonderful place called heaven that Miss Green our teacher had spoken of many times. There were no long held belief systems opposed to those of hers lodged in my psyche that had to be dislodged before her simple teaching could take root as a truth filled belief in my mind. I later in life came to see that children accept both truth and falsity equally and effortlessly, for in a child the easily influenced and readily manipulated reasoning aspect of the ego is not as yet fully operational. Religious leaders, particularly those of the two largest Christian churches, are well aware of the vulnerability of a child's thought processes, and the impact of early indoctrination. It was a Jesuit priest from the Catholic Church who famously said, "give me a child for his first seven years and I'll give you the man."

Then in my teenage years, once again it would be this continuous subtle pull towards the things of the Spirit that saw me board a tramcar and journey a short distance to the local showground, to see the world renowned Baptist evangelist, the Reverend Billy Graham, when he visited my hometown as part of his global evangelizing tour. There was no pressure from my mother for me to go; I just intuitively felt that I should go.

As an adult when I looked back later on that crusade experience, I concluded that it was indeed a spectacular well planned and well intentioned beautifully choreographed event, but that it would have borne no resemblance at all to what history tells us were similar crowd drawing events that Jesus was involved in during His earthly ministry. I had missed the first tramcar and consequently entered the showground only minutes before the crusade was scheduled to start, and by that time there was standing room only. The seats in the grandstands were full to overflowing with thousands of people standing to their feet as the rousing sound of the hundred strong choir accompanied by the booming base baritone voice of George Beverly Shea burst forth singing the age old hymn, "Then Sings My Soul My Saviour God To Thee How Great Thou Art." As the hymn had almost finished the choir on the conductor's cue hushed to a whisper, and to the applause of the crowd the fiery evangelist strode onto the stage up to the lectern Bible in hand, and commenced preaching emotively and passionately about the evils of sin, war, racism, and spiritual and physical poverty.

He preached for around thirty minutes and finally settled into a slow conversational tone as, with his voice lowering in volume to a soft gentle level, the choir members once again on cue took their places on the stage and softly sang as a background accompaniment to his voice, "Just as I am without one plea but that thy blood was shed for me, O Lamb of God I come." He continued speaking softly, probably for about another ten minutes, almost at times in a whisper, about humanity's need for God's love and His saving grace, strongly encouraging all who were present to believe, or as he put it, 'make a decision for Christ.' He concluded his sermon with an impassioned plea, "only believe, only believe, all things are possible if you only believe," and the words "will you come...will you come," as hundreds of people began leaving their seats, and walking across the arena to the stage area. His part in the crusade was then finished as he handed things over to the church representatives who were surrounding the stage waiting to greet those who came forward to take their names and addresses and direct them to a church they should attend.

Now once again, similar to the child in Sunday School, I didn't question the veracity of what he was saying as he enthusiastically encouraged all who were present to believe his own set of personal beliefs. I didn't analyse what he was saying to gauge if it was truth, nor did I call out for proof as to the accuracy of what he was saying. Presumably like the hundreds of others who also came forward at his call, I was for some unknown reason simply drawn to accept his words, and to believe his belief system. As I looked back later in life, I realised that whilst some of the motivation in my response may have come from an emotional reaction to what he was saying midst the very emotional atmosphere of the meeting, I also later realised that this life experience too was a part of a greater plan, and that it wasn't just a co-incidence that I had found myself there. You see emotions good and bad, surfacing out of love or out of hate, borne out of an unconscious desire to either create unity or to engender separation, are indeed a powerful influencer in our daily lives. They can bypass truth and our inherent need for truth.

From my mid-thirties my reading habits changed and I found myself only interested in reading books dealing with specific subject matter. Mostly they were books written about things pertaining to the cosmology of the universe from a scientific and a spiritual perspective, and those writings dealing with what I would describe as the operational aspects of a person's inner life; anything I could find on the metaphysical, psychological and spiritual aspects of a human being's makeup. I sought out books on new age philosophies, mystic religious thought and practice, the history of religion over the last 2000 years, mythology, and those books written about different religious customs and traditions; including a variety of different writer's perspectives on the spiritual nature of the universe, and our relationship to it as understood and taught in Eastern religion. I also became very interested in books about the psychological workings of the ego and the projections and multiple facets of the mind, at one time delving into the writings of Carl Jung and Sigmund Freud.

During my exploration into religious groups I commenced reading the sacred writings of the largest religions in the world; the Bible of the Christian faith, the Quran or Koran of the Muslim faith, the Bhagavada Gita of the Hindu faith, commentaries on the Tao of Confucianism, and with Buddhism as much as I could find on the teachings of Gautama Buddha. In relation to the Bible I read the Old Testament twice and read and studied the New Testament four times. I also explored different types of yoga and meditation. In an attempt to gain a deeper understanding of the things of God of the Bible and of the Christian faith, as a regular disciplined routine, I would retire to bed at 9 p.m. and arise at 3 a.m. to read study and contemplate the scriptures and to meditate for a few hours in the quiet and solitude of early morning. Then it would be back to bed for an hour or two before it was time to get up and ready myself for my day job. My reasoning for doing this was based on the Hindu philosophy that speaks of the amrit vela or the ambrosial hours just before dawn as being the best time to wake up and to practice things of the spirit in order to maximize the potential for spiritual awakening. This time of day is said to be the time when the veil of the ego is thinnest, offering fewer of the distractions that are present through the rest of the day.

The more closely I looked at all these Holy books, the more I saw similarities or parallels in much of their religious thought, particularly in the meta-physical area; similarities about God's plan for the universe, about mankind's relationship with God and the unified relationship or oneness of mind that God desires for all human beings to have with each other. I also saw similarities between the process and outcomes of the Atonement experience, as it is described in Christian teaching, and the Pathway to Enlightenment, which you could say is the Atonement experience of Eastern religion.

In my mid thirties I left my chosen secular work and entered into full time work in a Christian community. I was ordained as a Pentecostal Pastor shortly later. However as my time in that role progressed, I began to feel increasing disquiet with some elements of the town's religious community that I had become ensconced in, as I witnessed what I felt was the hypocritical nature and behaviour of some of my fellow Christian ministers and priests. Whilst trying not to mentally judge them I was starting to feel a certain amount of discomfort when we met at the monthly minister's fraternal meeting. I felt that something wasn't right. It was hard to describe my feelings. Perhaps you could say that as time went on I started to develop a case of progressive disillusionment with church organizations in general because of the religious hypocrisy I witnessed.

The fraternal meeting was a monthly gathering where the ministers and pastors heading up the local congregations of the Catholic, Anglican and denominational churches got together for fellowship and discussion. Many times during the meeting I would find myself watching closely as several of my fellow ministers appeared to be jockeying for position to see who could sound the most pious, religious and knowledgeable. To my mind these particular representatives of Christ were all seemingly suffering from a mental condition that manifested in one being unable to control hypocritical displays of misplaced virtue, arrogance and self-grandeur. The Bible records Jesus in his day witnessing behaviour something similar to this in a Jewish religious group known as the Pharisees. Over time since nothing meaningful seemed to come out of these meetings I began to question my personal motivation for attending them, and also question myself as to whether or not I was a good fit for the ministry. This ongoing disillusionment culminated in my making the difficult decision to resign from my role of Pastor and head back to the city, back into my role as a senior business executive, a position which I stayed in until around my sixtieth birthday at which time I retired.

In my retirement I took up writing, knowing that there were things I wanted to creatively express, but being unsure of my ability to do so I starting writing in the first instance purely as a hobby, something to keep my over active and inquisitive mind occupied. All I knew was that I had this deep unquenched desire to put down in writing certain things that were hovering in my mind waiting to be creatively expressed. Over the next number of years I wrote much, filed away a lot, and had four books published as I intrepidly stepped out into the sometimes murky waters of book publishing. Then fourteen days after I turned seventy years of age something totally unexpected happened which changed my attitude to spiritual things in a dramatic way, causing me to re-evaluate the direction of both my spiritual life and my personal life. My friends had jokingly remarked at the time of my impending 70th birthday, "Michael, the big 70 hey, you know it's all downhill from here." I appreciated their humour and joined in the laughter. Then seemingly out of nowhere, with no prior symptoms of sickness, in mid 2018, just over two years ago, I suffered a stroke.

In the immediate aftermath of that event, a week spent lying on my hospital bed gave me ample opportunity to seriously reflect on what had happened. I realised that over time I had become a little spiritually blasé you could say, in that whilst I was consciously aware of my own mortality, I was sub-consciously living with the attitude that I was invincible and that physical death was a long way off for me; thinking also that I had the afterlife thing well under control too, because when I die, everything's going be alright, I'm off to heaven, just like my Sunday School teacher Miss Green and Dr. Billy Graham had said. Now, in that moment, lying there in my hospital bed, contemplating my near miss, I started to question in my mind how secure my eternity really was. "What if Billy Graham had got it a little wrong, not totally wrong but perhaps a little wrong or even a lot wrong, then that means I've got it a lot wrong. I mean the way he put it, it almost seems too simple, almost too easy I thought. Just say I'm sorry, confess that Jesus died for my sins and bingo heaven will be my home. You know, expect everything having given very little in return. I wonder have I got it right?"

Midst daily nurse visits and physio sessions, I began in my mind to critically examine and sometimes question the outcomes of my spiritual journey thus far. If I had been wrong about my state of physical wellbeing, perhaps I was also wrong about my state of spiritual wellbeing? My brush with my own physical mortality caused me to rethink my understanding of spiritual immortality. I found myself doing a mental spiritual stocktake you could call it on everything I had come to understand over the years regarding the ministry of Jesus, the message of salvation, the work of the Holy Spirit, and the whole heaven and hell end of life scenario that Christianity had taught me from a very early age. "Was all this the truth, the whole truth, and nothing but the truth?"

On the day after my discharge from hospital, whilst sitting on my balcony at home, I starting re-reading one of my favourite books, The Gnosis or Ancient Wisdom in the Christian Scriptures by William Kingsland. As I touched on previously, in his book Kingsland describes how the fundamental teaching given to the world at the beginning of the Christian era was derived at the outset from the Gnosis or Ancient Wisdom of those who had lived before the time of Christ as well as during the time of Christ. He went on to say that over time these teachings on the Christian faith had become so perverted by the dogmas and doctrines of the ecclesiastical church hierarchy, that the modern interpretation of this Ancient Wisdom, as taught in the modern church, represented merely their debased survival. The book had intrigued me so much when I had first read it that I decided that now, post hospital, I would read it again.

Kingsland spoke of how many adherents to the early Christian faith in the post crucifixion era communicated with the Holy Spirit through regular lifestyle disciplines of intuitive contemplative prayer, and through visions and dreams. Their justification for this came from the Gospels where Jesus, knowing His crucifixion was imminent, told his disciples that when He was gone He would send the Comforter, the Holy Spirit to them, who would be with them and in them and teach them everything they needed to know. The Gnostics as they came to be known were in their own minds simply Christian believers acting on that promise of Jesus during their daily spiritual practices; and it simply involved getting quiet and being open to the Holy Spirit's Voice, as She spoke to them, not audibly but intuitively in their contemplative stillness of the moment.

For whatever reason I put the book down, picked up my iPad to surf the internet, and came across the following story about the Buddha, which whilst differing in phraseology was remarkably similar in circumstance and intent to the words of Jesus. In the Buddha's dying moments, as he was giving final guidance to his companions in relation to their ongoing spiritual lives, perhaps he was sensing their fear of being left alone without him, the Buddha said to them, "Do not believe it, meaning the way of enlightenment, because I told you it was so, or because you read it in a holy book, or because some supposedly wise person said it was so, but believe it when you know in your heart that it is true"; the word heart meaning the innermost spiritual core of one's being, our true reality.

The Buddha's words jumped out at me, perhaps because he was encouraging his followers to prioritise the process of inner knowing in preference to the supposed wisdom of man. The Buddha was saying to his followers, stop relying on what others have said about God and what others have said about the way to enlightenment, you must come to an understanding in your own heart about the plan and purpose of God for humankind's collective salvation. He was directing his followers to rely only on their inner connection to the true source of Wisdom, rather than deliberately seeking to gain spiritual wisdom from another person or from some book or some book described as being holy. Jesus similarly, knowing His crucifixion was imminent, and with his disciples fearful of being left alone questioning Him as to what they were going to do for guidance after He was gone, told them that he was sending the Comforter, the Holy Spirit, the Spirit of Truth who would speak to their hearts, who would teach them everything they needed to know and who would bring all the things of God they had forgotten back to their remembrance.

I realised that in some ways whilst not entirely wasted, I had spent most of my life searching for Absolute Truth in the wisdom of man; from other people, from books, from spiritual teachers, from seminars, from conferences, from retreats, from study, from research, from personal practices, and from different types of religious ritual. It came like a bolt of lightning. All I had to do to obtain God's Truth and Wisdom was to ask and patiently wait for an answer. The Holy Spirit, the spokesperson of our inner Christ mind, had been there all the time silently directing and redirecting my decisions waiting for me to stop searching, to stop reading, to stop all the mental gymnastics and all the psychological and physical wellness programs, and to be silent and still and start to listen to that inner voice.

I realised also that yes, the Holy Spirit might direct us to a specific teacher, or specific book, or a specific spiritual practice or philosophy, and that this is okay because it is the Holy Spirit doing it and not our finite mind which has a history of making wrong decisions particularly when the situation is clouded by emotional influences. It is the Holy Spirit directing us to the revelatory knowledge or understanding received intuitively by someone else in the past, and revelatory knowledge, which is the Wisdom of God, fortunately does not have a use by date.

In my post-hospital recuperation I also came to see that all human beings have an inherited subconscious sense of psychological separation from God, a sense that we are all alone on this earth and it's just survival of the fittest and the fastest. All human beings have an inherited bad case of spiritual separation anxiety; an anxiety brought about by the original psychological disconnect of humankind that occurred in the Garden of Eden incident. I realised that we are all in this semi-restless mental state continuously looking to fill that loss of connection, to close the gap between time and timelessness, and that contrary to what many believe, neither religion, nor the church is the ultimate prescriptive medicine to cure spiritual separation anxiety. There is only one cure for this. The parting gift that Jesus bequeathed to humanity for this purpose was not the church, not the Bible, not the minister, not the priest. His parting gift to every human being, His panacea for all of society's ills and humankind's thoughts of alienation from God, was the Holy Spirit, the Comforter, and the Spirit of Wisdom.

From this more enlightened headspace I rethought my intention as to the content of this book, as there were many things I intended to share that I now see as neither being absolutely necessary to a person's spiritual wellbeing, nor would they lead anyone to a greater understanding of God's mysterious plan for all of humanity, the mystery of the Atonement. It would all be just more clutter for the human mind already overcrowded with irrelevant things and fodder for the ego ever seeking to distract us away from the purpose and plans of God. I am trusting however that what I have shared in this book, obtained under the guidance of the Holy Spirit, will be both of benefit and blessing to you the reader, and that as you progress with an open mind through its pages, you will realize that as we play our part, as we display a willingness to do what's necessary to fit in with God's cosmic plan for the redemption of humankind, then our life eternal will indeed work out as intended, for it is God's ultimate intention that no person gets left behind.

"I am fully cognizant of the fact that the information I am offering, a deeper knowledge of the mysteries of the cosmos, cannot be fully released by the universe to the individual unless they have denied their ego and recognized and acknowledged the limitations of the knowledge they already possess."

INTRODUCTION

"It was the best of times, it was the worst of times, it was the age of wisdom, it was the age of foolishness, it was the epoch of belief, it was the season of darkness." So said Charles John Huffman Dickens in the opening paragraph of his classic serialized novel A Tale of Two Cities. Dickens, the much-celebrated English writer, social critic, and creator of some of the world's most lionized fictional characters, including Oliver Twist and David Copperfield, had chosen the late 18th century as the timeline for this epic novel, the storyline being set during the time of the French Revolution, with those opening words in the very first chapter depicting amongst other things, some of the social and behavioural characteristics of that time. It was a momentous time but also a frightening period in European history that ushered in a season of far reaching social and political upheaval in France, the course of which witnessed the overthrow of the monarchy and the establishment of a dictatorship under the rule of Napoleon Bonaparte, a French military leader and statesman.

The French Revolution was a watershed episode in time that saw French citizens, in order to 'save' their country, rise up against the establishment and set about razing and redesigning their political landscape in a dramatic way. During a reign of terror carried out in a most barbaric manner, to supposedly ensure the political and economic salvation of the majority, some 300,000 citizens were arrested, 17,000 officially executed and around 10,000 people died in prisons. But there was more, the French Revolution also oversaw the reclamation of massive amounts of land and monies held by the Catholic Church, the subsequent termination of Catholic religious practice, and eventually through new laws the discontinuation altogether of the religion in France.

Although all social classes and professions were targeted, the death by guillotine method of retributive justice that was implemented was especially high in numbers for members of the clergy and those of the aristocracy. The guillotine, a new invention designed to end a human being's life efficiently and effectively, was presented as the only quick, visible and rational means for doing so. Those who were selectively chosen as being in the way of progress were ceremoniously marched to their death, whilst hundreds of French women in an obscene act of indifference sat in their chairs for hours on end, watching, knitting, jeering and clapping as the life of each accused person, man woman and child, was abruptly and unexpectedly taken from them.

Time and time again throughout history, the world has witnessed the rise and fall of kings and kingdoms, of despots and dictators, and of tyrants and tricksters, all hell bent on bringing to society their own particular ideological philosophy for the salvation of the human race, whether that be political salvation, economic salvation, or spiritual salvation. More often than not the outworking of these philosophies quickly turn into hate filled agendas, that witness mass atrocities and unspeakable acts of cruelty being committed against those deemed not suitable for inclusion in the particular new world order that the perpetrators are insanely intent on establishing. Hate filled agendas carried out seemingly with little regard for the sanctity of life, nor for the innocence or guilt of those chosen for elimination.

For the most part, except perhaps for occasional small pockets of resistance, the rest of the citizens, conscripted and carried along in the deadly wave of violence, fearful for their own safety, sit silently, passively accepting what is in reality just another self-serving brutal agenda masquerading as the necessary means to an end. In doing so their act of passive acceptance through non-resistance, their "I'd rather not be involved attitude," gives the originators and perpetrators of the particular uprising a conscience cleansing mental justification for their maniacal self-interested ego driven behaviour.

In the 19th and 20th centuries we were led to believe that the means of humanity's salvation would come as we embraced specific socio-economic doctrines, for we were told that it would be through these ideas that our world would become a better place. Karl Marx, the German philosopher, sociologist, economist, and revolutionary socialist, the man whom historians would say contributed more than anyone else to the Labour belief that life is basically a class struggle between the opposing forces of the haves and the have nots, said that he had the answer, "just wed politics to economics."

Others that followed him, those of a more evil nature, said yes, but we need to separate the wheat from the chaff, separate the valuable members of the community from those viewed as valueless in terms of the ideological agenda. Thus the world bore witness to the emergence of some of the most effective terminators of human life that had ever graced the evil annals of history. People like Stalin, Mao Tse-tung and Pol Pot, and Adolf Hitler the German politician and leader of the Nazi Party, whose deranged theory that the salvation of the human race could only be achieved by cleansing the world of all ethnicity through the use of superior military might, brought suffering and death to some fifty million people including many of his own countrymen and women. Not forgetting the Gulags, a system of forced labour camps established by the Russian dictator Joseph Stalin, which over time incarcerated some 18 million people. Run in a brutal manner they forced prisoners to work 14-hour days often in extreme weather, which resulted in hundreds of thousands dying due to starvation, disease or simply exhaustion.

The Gulags were the destination for the spoils of Stalin's great purge, his campaign to eliminate dissenting members of the Communist Party and anyone who openly disagreed with the government. It was a campaign that was eventually extended towards anyone who expressed freedom of thought, including doctors, writers, intellects, artists and scientists. Similar to Hitler who came the decade later, all done to uphold an insanity coming from the ideological obsession of one man, Joseph Stalin. Aleksandr Solzhenitsyn, the Russian novelist, himself a former inmate of the Gulags wrote this about ideological insanity. "The imagination and spiritual strength of Shakespeare's evildoers stopped short at a dozen corpses because they had no ideology. Ideology, that is what gives evildoing its long-standing justification and gives the evildoer the necessary steadfastness and determination. (The Gulag Archipelago, Chapter 4, Page 17).

In more recent times we have seen the appearance of another ideologically insane group in the guise of Isis, a Salafist-jihadi organization whose adherents interpret the religion of Islam as a struggle against anyone who they decide has corrupted the ideals of Islamic governance. Their method of dealing with those supposed betrayers of the faith? Eliminate them all by starting a holy war, the leaders brainwashing the followers into believing that this supposed God given calling they have received is in fact Divine permission to embark on the violent overthrow of all that is wrong with society by whatever means it takes, to create a proper Islam and with that a more orderly world. The leaders believing in their own deluded self-serving minds that the only true religion is Islam and that the world's only hope of salvation is its complete conversion to the Islamic faith. They would not be the first group of religious zealots who have used the God is on our side deceptive religious premise, as a counterfeit salvation of the masses message, when in reality it is just another self-serving ideological agenda being used to justify their own personal evil, greedy and hate filled intent.

We live in a world that in various ways and in different forms still continues to deny the true message of salvation and the true pathway to humanity's freedom and unification, that being the existence of a Light, the Light of God, or as Jesus described Himself the Light of the World, that shines from beyond to hasten us all to our individual spiritual purpose, and ushers the whole of humanity into its pre-ordained cosmic destiny. Through the use of human willpower the deniers of the existence of this Light set about their task, their method always assuming the shape of some type of social, spiritual or materialistic ideology, its emergence and outworking further delaying society's introduction to the only true and predetermined pathway of salvation and the inevitable maturation of every human beings cosmic destiny. A predetermined pathway that is in accordance with God the Creator's will, rather than in accordance with a particular person or group's ideologically inspired will.

We live in an age populated with leaders of both the religious, political and business persuasion who are concerned or you could even call it obsessed with their own power base. They are known as numbers people; continually measuring their success by the amount of followers they have who will agree with their fixed mindset. They are leaders, or those who see themselves as potential leaders, always having their own emotional and material success hovering in their subconscious, driving them and pushing them forward, always wanting to feel good about themselves, with many having little or scant regard for the purpose and will of any power other than their own as they pursue their thought based agenda; unless however that agenda seriously impacts on their existing power base. Then you can be sure they will compromise it even in a small way.

One could fairly ask the question, "Well at any time in the history of the world has it ever been any different?" And if we look closely at world history the answer would be no, not really. To use Shakespearean type phraseology, "for such as is now, as such has always been," and such was indeed the way at the time of the French Revolution. Charles Dickens' opening words in his book A Tale of Two Cities could easily have been applied as a preface to many a historical tale and many other tumultuous times not only socially and politically in humanity's history, but also very much so in the combined arena of religion and politics.

One particular period of political interference in religious freedom that stood out in history for its depth of intensity more than others commenced during the reign of the Roman Emperor Nero in 64 A.D. and continued up until the time of Emperor Constantine's conversion to Christianity in 313 A.D. Constantine's conversion was the catalyst for what is known as the Edict of Milan, a proclamation that permanently established religious toleration for Christianity within the Roman Empire. You see prior to Constantine's conversion, with Rome under the reign of Nero and others, the Christian faith was by law officially regarded as *religio prava,* an evil or depraved religion detrimental to society. Religio prava was a governmental ruling as was the Edict of Milan but one of a different kind entirely. It was a proclamation that enabled the early Christian community to be repeatedly persecuted in unspeakable acts of violence, with full immunity from prosecution granted to the instigators and perpetrators of that violence.

Amongst the many barbarous acts committed and perhaps the most depraved and treacherous one was when the Emperor Nero, increasingly threatened by the popularity and continuing growth of the Christian movement, shamed, blamed and framed Christians for a fire in the City of Rome that became known as the Great Fire. It occurred in July 64 A.D. and burned for nine days, the aftermath of which saw two thirds of the city of Rome totally destroyed. The truth of the matter was that the fire had in fact been started deliberately on the orders of Nero himself as an excuse for his troops to round up all the Christian believers in order to "legitimately" kill them. Some were fed to wild dogs to be torn apart as a spectacle for public viewing, others were nailed to a cross and set alight, the crosses so positioned to be used as human torches to illuminate Nero's royal gardens at night.

Subsequent persecutions by Emperors Decius and Diocletian Galerius saw Christians fired from public office, church buildings destroyed, and church leaders arrested and mercilessly tortured to try to get them to recant their faith. But whilst one could describe this pre-Edict of Milan period as one of darkness similar to Dickens quote about the French Revolution, if we look closely at history we can also describe it as a time of light, in that the ongoing penetration of the Christian faith was so particularly persuasive before during and after this, that the Christian Church itself, in spite of the continued attacks upon it, was never totally obliterated, and so continues to this day.

Over these last few decades, in order to come to a greater understanding of this aspect of religious faith, namely its seeming indestructibility, I have studied and researched the spiritual practices and history of the major religions in the world to gain a deeper understanding of this and other mysteries of the universe. In the last few years I have sought the insightful guidance of the Holy Spirit for a greater understanding of God's true plan for us as a collective society, coming to see afresh new spiritual truths many of which you could say rattled in a good way the cage of my mind, the cage containing my inherited belief systems and all my past experiences.

This book is not meant to be contentious but I fully understand that some will find it so. I am totally aware that as it was for me in the past so it may be for you in the present, that the belief cage of our mind can be easily rattled when introduced to new truth that contradicts some long held beliefs we hold. Neither is it written with the intention of upsetting the faith and long time spiritual practices of any person or to convince or convert anyone to my viewpoint. But it certainly is written to give you the reader amongst many other things, a more accurate glimpse of religious history than you previously had, an evidential account you could call it, which for some will be a validation of what you currently believe and for others a disconcerting invalidation of what you have believed all your life.

If you have purchased this book looking for stimulating theories or interesting ideas, or intellectually inspired religious debate or discussion, or a new serious set of practices you can implement into your life, you will not find them here. The words in this book are really no more than signposts. However I am hoping my words will point you in the direction of what practices are in the best interests of your attaining a higher level of conscious awareness and what are not, and similarly which beliefs that you currently hold are in your best interests and which beliefs may simply have been a waste of time for quite a period of time. You could say that a primary purpose of this book is to help you remove from your thinking that which separates you from the truth of who you really are and what you already know in the inner depth of your being, but have forgotten that you know it.

In order for every human being to come to a truth filled understanding of God's plan for humanity and thus for their own personal life, two things must happen. The first is correction. Mind correction is the most important component of our spiritual journey. Simply said our minds need to be corrected, released and renewed from many wrongful constructs, from wrongly accumulated belief systems built up over the years that obstruct, hinder and crowd out any new truth, preventing it from entering. When we embark on a process of mind correction blockages to truth are removed like a log jam in a river, allowing the rivers of life, the truth of the Spirit to flow freely. The second thing that needs to happen is that we must acknowledge that this new tenant in residence in our Soul, this Holy Spirit, has made Her home there and desires to establish a communication dialogue with us.

Over the centuries of Christianity's existence the church has dumbed down one of the key purposes of Christ's life on earth, which was to introduce the Holy Spirit to humanity. Perhaps it has done this in a way to make this Christianity thing a little more palatable to our minds, or perhaps just through ignorance. Here's the thing. The Holy Spirit was given to us all to be the teacher who replaced Jesus. The Holy Spirit is that part of the Trinity, of the Father, Son and Holy Ghost that has an active participating function directly in the spiritual progression of a human being's life. Therefore if we want to grow in spirituality, and in the Spirit led life, and come to a deeper understanding of life as it is from God's perspective, and to also understand God's cosmic plan for humanity, we must establish a relationship of engagement with the Holy Spirit. In the Bible the Holy Spirit is referred to as Wisdom, Truth, Healer, and our Guide and Comforter. It strikes me that on that basis alone She is worthy of getting to know. More importantly however in terms of our individual spiritual evolution She is also God's answer to the psychological separation we all have from the Creator, and the means through which the Atonement purchased by Jesus on the cross is fully activated in our lives. She is the God given post-Jesus mediator between God and us.

We have all been freely given an opportunity through Christ's gift of the Holy Spirit to come to a perfect understanding of what human existence, our life as we call it, is all about, and to be gently and patiently guided to our ultimate eternal destiny. She is our true guide in all of this and we have a choice to make, which the Book of Deuteronomy in the Bible refers to as a choice between spiritual Life and spiritual Death. The Voice of the Holy Spirit is the voice of spiritual Life, and the murmuring and disruptive mental interference of the Ego Mind is the voice of spiritual death. If we are listening to both, which most people are, Christians and non-Christians alike, it is in Bible terminology known as being in a state of double mindedness, which generates an emotional lifestyle alternating at various levels of psychological or mental disturbance, distress and unrest, which is then reflected in our physical life at various levels of anxiousness, ranging in intensity from mild anxiety to off the charts extreme depression, depression in its clinical reality being a state of mental isolation or separation from the rest of society.

Contrary to the voice of the Ego Mind the voice of the Holy Spirit does not command, does not demand, and does not reprimand. If you are experiencing difficulties in life the Holy Spirit will not condemn you or seek to control or attack your sense of self-worth or make you feel guilty. If that is going on rest assured it is not God trying to teach you something. We are given the Holy Spirit for edification and ongoing enlightenment. The Comforter, the Holy Spirit gently leads you to the right choice. We must arrive at a point of knowing Her, not just knowing about Her, including how She moves about doing what She does, and God's real purpose in sending Her to be with you and in you. And to do this we have to have what I mentioned before some sort of communicative relationship or engagement with Her. I have included in this book all that I see as both relevant and necessary for both of these things to happen, both correction from common long held beliefs as well as a greater understanding of the functioning of the Ego Mind and the Holy Spirit, which is discussed in more detail in Chapter 6, The Battle of Two Minds, the Ego Mind and the Christ Mind.

I remember reading a poem by Margaret Jang a Reiki Master Teacher and inspirational spiritual poet some years ago and one part of it intrigued me so I noted it down. It said, "to know your future you must know your past, each stepping stone that has been cast, remember the good as well as the bad, and feel the emotions of happy and sad." To complete our "need for correction" from wrongful religious belief constructs thoroughly, to clean out the cage so to speak, it is necessary that we come to a greater understanding of Christianity past, both the good and the bad of it, the happy and the sad of it. We need to be aware of certain historical aspects of the post Jesus early Christian Church era, not only how it developed, but also how it fragmented, and how in the midst of all this a true understanding of the purpose and work of the Holy Spirit got lost along the way. This is important so that we gain clarity as to how the religion of Christianity, in particular as practised in the biggest Christian churches on earth, for the most part has become a religion of form and ceremony only, almost of Old Testament style, rather than one of true power and blessing, a religion of New Testament style.

In addressing this component of the book I will share the history of one particular group of early Christian believers, the Gnostics, who did attempt to hold on to the reality and true purpose of the Holy Spirit, the one whom Jesus sent to replace Himself, but had little support in doing so and were opposed at every turn by those who assumed leadership of the early Christian Church. We will look at the rise and subsequent disappearance of the Gnostic church at the end of the third century, the role of the established church in its disappearance, and its subtle rise again in this the 21st century, as fresh information about its existence has been obtained, particularly through archaeological discoveries. We will with all simplicity explore its belief system and its teachings and practices, its lack of relationship with the Orthodox Church and the reasons for it, and the parallels between Gnosticism and the true message of Jesus Christ, mysteriously embedded in analogical form in the New Testament.

Historians and theologians throughout time have vehemently argued about the religious status of Gnosticism. Are the teachings of Gnosticism true or false, heretical or not? Was the Apostle Paul a Gnostic or was he not? Did Jesus come from the religious tribe known as the Essenes who were basically a Gnostic Jewish group of believers or did he not? Be guided by the Holy Spirit as you read this book and you will come to your own truth filled conclusions. In a chapter titled The Biblical Narrative, I will explain in some detail the role of the early Catholic Church fathers in collaboration with the Roman Emperor Constantine in the construction of what we now call the Bible, what they included in it as well as what they chose to leave out. And why the secret writings that the original Gnostic community revered, the secret gospels, ancient wisdom, mystical thought, the teachings of Jesus and His disciples after his resurrection, all of which whose existence the Vatican hierarchy were fully aware of, were deliberately excluded from that canonical collection that finally became known as the Bible.

You will find that at times in referencing specific Biblical stories such as Adam and Eve in the Garden of Eden I may refer to these stories as being in the form of parables or in the likeness of myth. Just be aware that Jesus spoke in parables in much of His teaching. A parable is simply a made up story told to illustrate a moral or spiritual lesson. To some readers who have lived their lives believing that every single thing written in the Bible is absolute literal truth this may be disconcerting. Please do not be concerned or let it throw you. There is no need for you to do a sudden about turn and start thinking or worrying that some stories such as Adam and Eve in the Garden or Noah on the ark may be a myth or a parable to illustrate a specific spiritual truth. There are far more important things to focus on in the first instance.

I am also aware that certain readers with a specific ingrained doctrinal thought pattern, and yes I am referring mainly to members of the Catholic Church, may find some of the detail I present confronting, and subsequently reject it due to their long time personal religious beliefs and fixed mindset. That is why I spend some time in the early chapters dealing with the psychological aspect of our mind and our nature, how the mind works to create belief systems, how the mind's chief manipulator the ego works, and linking what Jesus and the Bible have to say about all this. I also make reference quite often of the absolute necessity for mind renewal to occur, which I describe also as mind correction, if we are ever going to progress forward in the plan of God and in our capacity to hear the voice of the Holy Spirit in our daily lives. Humanity's greatest enemy has always been and still is the illogical ramblings of a confused mind.

I will also explain how the Holy Spirit's involvement in mind renewal is vital in order for us to successfully extricate ourselves from all those mind paralysing beliefs that we vigorously guard and defend, beliefs that seek to prevent us from obtaining a full, meaningful, and purposeful understanding of God's plan for us as individuals and subsequently for the whole of humanity. I will detail all you will need to know about how our rational mind works and entraps us so many times, stifling our spiritual growth, and all you will need to know in order for you to use it rather than it continually using you.

I am fully cognizant of the fact that the information I am offering, a deeper knowledge of the mysteries of the cosmos, cannot be fully released by the universe to the individual unless they have recognized and acknowledged the limitations of the knowledge they already possess. You've got to want it to get it, you've got to welcome it to receive it, and certainly not fear it, for fear, a tool of the ego, is the greatest obstructer of all good things coming into your life that you will ever encounter. The information I present does also require of the reader, like all types of esoteric writings, a subtlety of thinking and a proclivity for intuitive perception. I ask that your reading of it be slow and deliberate so that those parts of it that need to be intuitively understood are not too soon hastily passed by and their true meaning missed. In order to get maximum benefit from the information provided in this book one needs to pause occasionally when reading certain parts and ruminate. For with rumination comes revelation and subsequent illumination.

It is not my intention to put down or invalidate anyone else's spiritual path or approach, for in the final analysis all the words in this book are just that, words, providing a window for some and an open door for others. Spiritual teachers of all ages would put it this way. "We can unlock the cage, and we can open the door, but in the end it is only the individual who can step on through it and find their way home." However there is one starting premise we need to have. We need to accept that there is an egotistical component of our nature that exists to obstruct and hinder our spiritual evolution, and that it is a powerful influencer on the direction our everyday spiritual life takes. This will be discussed in more detail in Chapter 1 and Chapter 6, so I simply say the following as a short but necessary precursor to your reading of the book, since you will see me referencing the terms ego, ego self or ego mind at various times in the book before and after you get to these chapters.

In using the term ego or ego self or ego mind I am not using it in the way that most of us would at some stage have heard the word ego being used, as in 'he's got a big ego', meaning he has an overinflated sense of his own importance. From a spiritual perspective whilst it does include the personality pattern of an inflated attitude of self-importance, in its spiritual context it holds a much deeper meaning. The ego's outworking or communication process manifests as that little voice in our head that quietly opposes every new truth that comes across our mind that it, the ego, hasn't thought of first. It appears as that little voice in our head that says things such as "naaa, that can't be right" or "can't be, that's not what I was taught," or "that's not what my church teaches," or phrases similar. We must believe that the ego aspect of our mind is real, that it is alive and confrontational and that it continually seeks to control our every move. This is a spiritual warfare we are involved in. Does that sound spooky? To some maybe. But it's true. The ego is like a psychological stalker always attempting to hinder right thought processes.

Call it an entity, call it Lucifer, call it the deceiver, call it the devil, call it Satan, call it an energetic life force, call it an illusion creator, but recognize and accept that it is there, that it is real, and that its sole aim is to create some type of disruption in your thinking or disunity in your interaction with others, and to maintain the unconscious sense of separation from God that all human beings are born with and journey through life with; its mission being to keep you from progressing in the things of God and coming home. We may call the ego what we want but must understand that as the Holy Spirit is the guiding light of our ongoing potentially enlightened reality, so this entity called the ego is in fact the guiding darkness of our existing unenlightened and false reality, and darkness always causes disorientation.

The ego has a purpose in you just as the Holy Spirit has a purpose in you. That's the warfare. It's a war of two minds, the Christ Mind and the ego mind. The ego mind is the faulty compass that deliberately and in a cunning manner steers our ship of life in the wrong direction sending us straight onto the rocks. The Holy Spirit, the voice of the Christ Mind within is our lighthouse, warning us of the wiles of the ego and giving our ship of life the means of safe passage. Be aware of the ego's existence but be not afraid of its persistence. The biggest weapon the ego has in its artillery is doubt, as demonstrated in the "hast God said" conversation that occurred in the Garden of Eden story. Doubt is a spiritually energetic force and it is the enemy of truth. Doubt brings about distrust, which causes division, which promotes or leads to some form of retreat from an objective or connected relationship. Doubt induced distrust working with fear can become, if embraced, responsible for a lack of progress in any aspect of our lives where we allow it to encroach. It is equally at home working in the spiritual dynamic, in our relationship with God, as it is in the personal dynamic, in our relationship with a human being.

Remember the ego is the spokesperson for and the enforcer of the illusionary subconscious belief human beings have that they are separated from God, and it is an entity that wants to keep it that way. And if the ego is the symbol and active agent of the principle of separation, which it is, it is also the symbol of guilt and as such its actions become an attack on God, because it is attacking the Atonement principle of Christ's crucifixion which saw Jesus in His substitution role remove all psychological guilt from humanity. The ego's principal aim is always to attack God and to do that it always uses a human being as its vehicle of expression. But as mentioned before more will be discussed on this in Chapter 6.

In summary I have written this book in the hope that its content will encourage you the reader to push on past an intellectual understanding of Jesus the Christ, or a vague knowledge of Him you may have through Christmas and Easter celebrations, and stir you into undertaking an experiential journey with the Holy Spirit. A journey enabling your earthly walk to be as a heavenly walk baring witness to everyone you meet of the availability of the prize of a truly resurrected life, an enlightened state of being, a heaven on earth experience, right here right now in the present moment; to be transported from a life of personhood into a life of purposeful presence. I have presented the overall contents of this book as a mixture, each chapter containing historical truth, spiritual truth, psychological truth, and my own personal revelatory truth.

I am trusting that blended together they will give you greater insight into the mysteries of God, and the ancient wisdom of the ages, the wisdom of the masters who have gone before, masters in both Eastern and Western religion who have understood these mysteries and lived their lives accordingly.

As the book cover states, Everything's Gonna Be Alright is straight talk about God, Jesus, the Holy Spirit, about Religion, Heaven and Hell, and about God's cosmic plan for the universe. It is written to help you the reader arrive at a greater understanding of the Holy Spirit's presence in your life, Her role in the Atonement process, and Her intended purpose as She carries out Her role of the Voice for God and the communication agent of the Christ within you. We are all living at a time in the evolution of humanity when an enlightened state of being should no longer be regarded as an alternate state or even a spiritual luxury, rather more a spiritual necessity. We are living in a time I think it is correct to say when much of humanity is hell bent on self-destruction, so consequently there is an even greater urgency for all to rise to higher levels of God consciousness.

Be blessed in knowing that regardless of the chaos and confusion that you witness increasingly around you, and the accompanying discouragement and disillusionment that may come with it, there is no reason to be concerned for God's Spirit of Grace is sufficient. So be not dismayed or fearful in any way, rather rejoice and be comforted in the knowledge that **Everything's Gonna Be Alright, the Holy Spirit Knows What She's Doin'.**

"Humanity is faced with a stark choice: Evolve or die. If the structures of the human mind remain unchanged, we will always end up re-creating the same world, the same evils, the same dysfunction."

A New Earth by Eckhart Tolle

The Outgoing, The Evolution, The Involution, Creation, Separation and Return

"THE THREE MYSTERIES"

Human beings everywhere love mysteries. There is something fascinating about the hidden, secret, sometimes startling truth that needs to be discovered and revealed. God knows this, understands this, and I believe to accommodate this has hidden mysteries in every area of the cosmos, in a way you could say almost challenging scientists as well as everyday people to attempt to discover some of them. We do not know anything fully. The Bible speaks of God's Wisdom before the ages being hidden in a mystery and also of it being hidden in the coming of Jesus Christ. There is always an element of life we don't understand. For example we know one can fall in love but we do not fully understand, the why or in fact the how of the equation. We just know that people do fall in love. Such is the mystery in everything.

Physicists will tell us that hidden away in every physical manifestation in the universe around us is mystery. Quantum theory upon which much of modern physics is based, theory which has unleashed the whole realm of nuclear fission, has at its heart, say the physicists, a principle of indeterminism, a hidden principle. It states that we never can discover fully the truth about anything and that there is an element of hidden information about every subject we go into. However in terms of the spiritual God says it differently, for when speaking about that which appears to be hidden in a mystery, whether in the Bible or just in the spiritual life generally, God through Jesus said, "seek and ye shall find, knock and the door shall be opened unto you, for everyone who seeks shall find."

Life you could say is an ongoing confrontation with mystery, and it is the mystery that makes life entrancing and fascinating. I believe that God, whilst delighting in mystery, does accommodate our hunger for a revelation of truth about that which is a mystery, for we read in one of the Wisdom of God books in the Old Testament, the Book of Proverbs the words, "it is the glory of God to conceal a thing: but the glory of kings to search it out." The Apostle Paul spoke of the mystery of life itself when in addressing the people of the City of Ephesus he said that the mysteries of God were revealed to him by revelation, revelation simply being Divine Knowledge and Divine Truth given to one in intuitive thought by God's Spirit.

You will see me at various times in this book use the expression, "the mystery of God's Cosmic plan for the universe," and very likely may at some stage ask yourself well what is that? What is this mysterious plan that God has set in place for the universe? It is very important for us to understand the following because the Atonement process, and the transitionary journey of humanity that I reference deliberately and sometimes subtlety throughout the book all comes out of it. The answer to this question in brief is this.

God's Cosmic plan for the universe, the primary essential teaching of the ancient masters since the beginning of time, the same teaching which for the most part was systematically removed from the original text in the construction of the Bible or if not totally removed then the parts remaining were selectively and carefully over written in an attempt to hide their true meaning, was all about **"three mysteries,"** three mysteries that are the major cornerstones of God's Cosmic plan.

Jesus makes reference to these mysteries when He said to His disciples as we read in the Book of Luke, "unto you it is given to know the mysteries of the Kingdom of God, but to others it is given only in parables." A parable is a simple story used to illustrate a moral or spiritual lesson. He explains further in the scriptures that the reason for this was because the others were not mature or willing enough to hear straight talk. Similarly as just mentioned, the Apostle Paul speaks of hidden mysteries being revealed to him when he was caught up into heaven during what is known as the Damascus Road incident at the time of his conversion to Christianity, and references these mysteries as the "meat of the Word" that some were not spiritually ready or willing to receive.

There are three mysteries that form the basis of God's Cosmic Plan for the universe and I share them with you here. Mystery number one is the cosmology of an Outgoing, mystery number two is the cosmology of an Evolution, and mystery number three is the cosmology of a proposed Involution or Return. Cosmologies refer to the origin and development of the universe.

The **first mystery** contains information relating to the **Outgoing**. It speaks of how the universe was created by the Outgoing of God into manifested form, the Outgoing of God's creative life stream into the void that existed, which saw the creation of this universe, as we now know it. That life stream or energetic force or substance that created the universe is referred to in the book of Genesis as "the Word." It says, "In the beginning was the Word, and the Word was with God, and the Word was God." It's not talking about the Bible, which is sometimes described by the church as the Word of God, because the Bible did not exist in the beginning. The Word that Genesis refers to is the spoken creative life stream of God.

The **second mystery** contains information relating to the **Evolution** or journey of the universe. The main thrust of it centres on the psychological separation that came about after that manifested universe, that Outgoing that came from God, stepped out from being under the umbrella of God and repositioned itself under the umbrella of Lucifer. The second mystery centres on what came after the universe stepped out from being under the umbrella of Light and repositioned itself under the umbrella of Darkness. The only slight reference to this mystery that survived in the Catholic construction of the Bible is what we see in the Garden of Eden story, which really only takes the form of a sort of mythical or archetypal explanation on how sin came into the world. That story is historically referenced only as "the Fall," and that's all that most Christians know about it; that the story of Adam and Eve in the Garden of Eden is all about the fall of humankind out of a life of grace and into a life of sin. It is much more than that.

The second mystery, the Evolution of humanity, does involve a type of fall, but it involves a fall from a psychologically connected state, a state of one mindedness between the Mind of God and the Mind of Humanity, into a state of psychological separation, a separation of the human mind from the God Mind, or you could say a separation of the human thinking process from the God thinking process, and the resultant imbalanced thought processes and subsequent behaviours that came out of it. The second cosmological mystery then details the commencement of the journey out of that fallen state back to God and the process on how it would happen, namely through the appearance and activity of Him who would lead humanity out of it, the man Jesus, God in flesh.

The **third mystery** pertaining to God's Cosmic plan for the universe references the Involution of everything, the return to God of all that was manifested in the first mystery, and all that evolved over time in the second mystery, back to that from which it originally came out of, the Word, the creative source or life stream of God. The Involution can be likened in a physical sense to the return of the uterus to normal size after childbirth. The Apostle Paul spoke of it albeit in a mystery in his Letter to the Romans where he said, "I consider our present sufferings," meaning this evolutionary life on earth, "insignificant compared to the glory that will soon be revealed to us," referring to the final stage of the third mystery, the Involution or Return of all our Souls to the bosom of God.

He then went on further to say, "we know that the whole creation has been groaning as in the pains of childbirth," referring to the ongoing evolution of humanity, the second mystery, and continued, "as we wait eagerly for our adoption to sonship, the redemption of our bodies." The redemption of our bodies that he spoke of is that third mystery, the Involution or Return; it's the return of our Soul to the universal source from which it originally came in the beginning. There are numerous stories in the Bible about this separation and redemption principle at work usually centred on the alienation of a singular human or a group of humans from God and the redemptive process that restores them to their original state. We see it in the story of Adam and Eve, we see it in the story of Moses and the Israelites, and in the story of Joseph, and we see it in the story of the prodigal son in the New Testament.

Concerning these three mysteries what is self-evidently true in this ancient wisdom of a variety of different faiths, is that when the universe has completed its Evolution, mystery two, which is the stage in which the universe is progressing through right now, then all of humankind will ultimately return to its source, and regain its oneness with God, its oneness with Universal Consciousness, its oneness with the life stream of God, the Word, from which it originally came out of. That is when as the Bible expresses it those who are living will be caught up in the clouds and the dead "in Christ" shall rise. Not all the dead, only the dead in Christ, those who have completed the Atonement process, the complete redemptive process, that part of mystery number two. That will be at a time of God's choosing and will initiate the end of this world, as we know it.

What comes next after the end of this world as we know it? As the beloved Apostle John a man of mystic disposition who more than any other Apostle understood the three mysteries of God said, as we see written in the Book of Revelation, "then I saw a new heaven and a new earth, for the first earth had passed away." Meaning that when this earth and these heavens as we know them have gone, a new earth and new heavens will manifest. That then becomes the beginning of a new manifestation of mystery.

What all this simply means is that every individual, during this time of Evolution that we are in now, this second mystery that we are participating in, many unknowingly, must recover from this state of psychological separation that occurred in "the fall' and remerge as a new creation manifesting in their life the attributes of the Divine nature that was given to the universe at the beginning of its existence during the Outgoing; that same spiritual nature that has sustained it with conscious life since the time of its birth. The longer this takes in terms of chronological time then the longer the cycle of birth and death will continue in the world for all those who have not yet reached an individual readiness to cross over, who have not made karmic restitution, who have not reached the point of Atonement, who have not completed the transitionary journey.

Jesus himself had reached that point of readiness to cross over hence the resurrection. Jesus had completed the first two stages or passed through the first two mysteries and as such He returned to the Father leaving His earthly life as an example for us to follow. I discuss this further, Jesus' example, His transitionary journey, in Chapter 9, but for now we look at the separation principle, the psychological fall, and how it all works.

Personhood from a secular aspect.

"The state of being a person and existing as an individual, having human characteristics and feelings and having a material presence and identity."

Personhood from a spiritual aspect.

"The state of being an individual person living life with an attitude of psychological separateness from God and from our fellow human beings. Also known as identity, it is a compilation of those facets of our body and mind that we totally identify with and accept as our true self, when in reality this is not so, but nevertheless we continue to live this life of personhood being influenced by these illusionary beliefs."

The Principle of Separation, The Play of Personhood, The Atonement Process

From the Author.

During the course of this chapter you will see different words and terms used for the human mind, for what the average person would simply describe our one single mind, our thinking rational mind. Historically certain religious thought of most Eastern and some Western religion has spoken of a human being having not one mind but two minds, an upper mind and a lower mind. Traditionally both the upper and lower minds have been called different names in different spiritual writings and religions.

So as not to confuse the reader I have outlined below the words and terms I use in this chapter in reference to the two minds we possess, our upper mind and our lower mind.

When I talk about the Upper Mind and its workings I will refer to it in either of the following ways:

As the Upper Mind, as our Higher Nature or Higher Self, as the Mool Mind, as the Christ Mind, as our Intuitive Mind, as the Voice of the Holy Spirit emanating from the Christ Mind, or as Conscience.

When I talk about the Lower Mind and its workings I will refer to it in either of the following ways:

As the Lower Mind, as our Lower Nature or Lower Self, as the Maya Mind, as the Ego Mind, as our Intellect or Rational Mind, or as the Voice of Ego at work in our minds.

I trust this brings clarification.

ONE

Rene Descartes was a French philosopher, mathematician and scientist, who lived in the 16th century, a man widely regarded as one of the most important founders of modern philosophy. In some of his more notable writings in the early 1600's Descartes presented a formulation for *dualism* that gave rise in most parts of the Western world to a philosophical approach to the association of the body and the mind in how they relate to each other.

In simple terms *dualism* is the state of something having two main and separate aspects. Dualistic thinking for example is to take the approach when observing a subject matter that it has two separate and different realities to its existence. These realities can be subjective or objective, subjective meaning based on personal interpretation or objective meaning fact based, measurable and observable. They are also usually seen to exist as opposites and in some cases live in an ongoing confrontational mode with each other, or as a minimum, functioning in an ongoing state of opposition to each other. A prime subject for the exploration of *dualism* with writers over the centuries has always been that of the inherent nature of humankind and the perpetual conflict that has always existed between the good and evil sides of human nature.

Descartes approach to *dualism* predominates still in this modern world we live in, its basic premise being that there exists two kinds of 'things' that make up this world. There are thinking feeling things, subjects, and non-thinking feeling things, objects. Subjects include the human soul and God, objects being material things or inanimate objects; and both exist separately from each other. The 'dual' in dualism means two. So in dualistic situations we find that two things are set up in opposition and are separate in some essential irrevocable way. A religious concept following along the same lines as Descartes formulation, also known as Dualism, is to be found in Eastern Religion. It is a concept that has been taught throughout the ages, long before Christianity came into existence, and long before Descartes scientific work was published. But it only talks about the 'duality of the mind' we possess, not the duality of our existence with God, and basically teaches that we have two different operational aspects of our mind, two separate minds you could say. Two minds that not only continually seek our attention but also influence and seek to control our behaviours and who also live in a state of opposition to each other.

One of these minds is described as the lower mind or lower self of the body-mind-intellect persona, and it is a mind that spends all of its functioning time continually focused on the past, on the future, and on present moment experiences, activities and achievements. Over time this lower self entraps our thought processes causing us to continually psychologically attach ourselves in our thinking to things of the past, usually regrets or pleasurable events, to objects and forms in the present, usually relationships, achievements, and material possessions, and to things in the future, mainly dreams and desires that we believe will bring us happiness, peace and contentment. Things that make us feel better. The consequence of this lower mind's onslaught of activity is that it continually fills in and absorbs all of our thinking time, thus distracting us and diverting us away from any interest or involvement in gaining understanding of our higher self, the higher spiritual aspect of our nature. It keeps us separated from our Divine self.

The lower mind in its functional aspect is connected to *Maya*, a concept of "personhood," Maya in Hindu philosophy meaning illusion. Maya connotes a type of magic show; an illusion where things appear to be present but things are not what they seem. It is a spiritual concept connoting that life as it exists visibly to the senses is constantly changing and thus is spiritually unreal; consequently it has no reality, because the true invisible things of Spirit are changeless. But more so Maya is the power or the principle at play in life, which I like to call the play of personhood, that conceals from us the true character or nature of the spiritual reality of our being, by placing what you could call a psychological veil between God and us. The play of personhood, the illusionary life of Maya, separates us psychologically from God.

It is a constant distracter, and a constant enabler, and the chief advocate for an illusionary, ever changing and uncertain type of lifestyle. A lifestyle full of attachment to things in the present and full of attachment to things of the past as in memories, and full of desires for things in the future; things that will create even more ongoing attachments. This Maya mind principle is like an actor on the life stage of a human drama playing a role and not sticking to the script, but rather adlibbing as they go. It attaches itself to whatever comes its way whether it is matter or thought. Shakespeare, a seemingly enlightened man, described this illusionary life full of illusionary things in this way in his pastoral comedy As You Like It. "All the world's a stage, and all the men and women merely players."

Then, further to this we have the second mind, known in Eastern philosophy as the higher mind or higher self. In its functional aspect this upper mind is connected to Mool, which is a concept centering on creation's origins, God's Spirit. In Christianity it is referred to as the creative voice of the Mind of Christ, also known as The Word. We see examples of this in the Old Testament where it is written, "in the beginning was the Word, meaning the creative aspect of God, the Mind of God, and the Word was with God, and the Word was God," and in the New Testament where we see the Apostle Paul telling the people of the City of Corinth that they had been given the Mind of Christ, meaning the creative thought processes and perceptive abilities of God. This Mool Mind or Christ Mind is invisible, pure, and the observer from within of all things within and without. It is the energetic force that guards our heart and our mind, our emotions and our thoughts, ever seeking to comfort us and teach us the things of God. It is the observer of all thought, all matter, and all activity; the observer of all things both Mool and Maya in our lives.

Now these next few sentences are very important for us to grasp. The Mool Mind or Christ Mind psychologically connects us to the thought processes of God. You could describe it also as the creative influence and watchman of our lives. In its active or functioning mode the Mool Mind is in fact the Holy Spirit, for the Holy Spirit is the Voice of the Christ Mind within, and the Christ Mind within is the God Mind, which is the creative Mind of God, the source of all things. In the Book of Genesis in the Old Testament where it says, "in the beginning was the Word, and the Word was with God, and the Word was God," the "Word" is in fact God's Spirit known as the Holy Spirit.

Eastern religion teaches that those people who are attached to Mool alone, a non-dualistic state of mind, are in a state of full enlightenment, a state of total presence, of being in God's Presence, tuned in to the Mind of God continually. To this enlightened person the past is totally gone and the future is of no relevance. The slate of the past has been wiped clean and the Mool Mind sees no necessity in worrying about the future. The errors or mistakes of the past, which were really only illusions, are gone. Consequently in a person's daily life, thoughts of regret about the past and thoughts or worries about the future all fall on deaf ears. Because the enlightened person's inner ear is tuned in to the thoughts of God only, and those types of thoughts, the thoughts of the lower mind are non-existent to God, or you could say they play no part in God's thinking processes.

For someone who is totally attached to the Mool Mind, the Maya side of the persona no longer has any power or influence in their lives, it is still there, but has no power to influence behaviours. However this is not the case if they welcome it, this Maya side of the persona, and entertain it, similarly as in a physical sense the local gossip in our neighbourhood has no opportunity to influence our thoughts about or reactions towards our neighbours unless we invite her or him in for a cup of tea and a chat, unless we entertain their presence. If we resist the Maya side of our persona, it will flee from us in the moment, and with continued diligence eventually disappear altogether. The Bible in the Book of James succinctly puts it this way, "resist the devil and he will flee from you." It doesn't come any more straightforward and simpler than that.

The Maya Mind itself can be likened in a physical sense to a gun that has the capacity to wound, in this case wound us emotionally or mentally, but a gun with the bullets removed. However if we choose to load the bullets of unhealthy thinking back into the gun it rearms it. There is a distinct parallel or correlation between this Hindu philosophy and the Christian message, where in the Book of Corinthians we see the Apostle Paul saying, "if any man be in Christ, meaning living in a Mool state of mind, he is a new creation, old things are passed away, meaning the old Maya Mind things, and all things have become new." In other words the slate of the old way of thinking, the old way of the Maya Mind becomes psychologically wiped clean once we start living out of the Christ Mind's way of thinking and perceiving. After this it is up to us to keep that slate continually clean by not entertaining unhealthy thinking.

Most Christians are dualistic in their thinking to some greater or lesser degree, meaning they fluctuate between the Maya Mind and the Mool Mind, depending on their circumstances. They fluctuate between personhood and presence, or between non-enlightenment and enlightenment, with most unfortunately leaning more towards a Maya Mind way of thinking as the cares of life ensnare them. Not so the non-Christian, who with little or no interest at all in the things of the Spirit, usually becomes fully attached to the Maya Mind way of life. Consequently physical things that bring some sort of emotional satisfaction such as people, possessions, relationships, activities and pleasurable experiences become their primary point of interest and involvement.

For the Christian the more one is attached to the Maya Mind, the stronger is the emotional attachment to past doubts and regrets and future hopes and dreams. Their Maya Mind is always tempting them to either totally ignore or override through logic and reasoning what their inner Mool Mind the Christ Mind within is trying to tell them. The Maya Mind in fact chokes off the Voice of God, the Holy Spirit, silencing it. Jesus references this play of personhood in a parable in the Book of Matthew, where He talks about the good seed in the garden that is choked by the thorns or weeds. A parable is a simple story designed to illustrate a moral or spiritual lesson. His teaching was in fact a perfect example of Eastern Religious thought aligning itself with Western Religious thought.

This choking off process could be likened in a physical sense to a person continually talking over the top of you in an attempt to drown out your words. But in this case it is drowning the Holy Spirit's voice out because our old nature will always preference logic and reasoning over intuitive thought until we train it not to do so. The thought process of the Christ within, the way of thinking of the upper mind is then veiled through a person's deference or bowing to the will and to the reasoning and supposed logic of the lower mind, the Maya Mind. There is an obedience shift in relation to the things of the spirit.

This ancient Hindu belief in the dualistic nature of the mind is completely in line with the New Testament teaching of the Apostle Paul where he speaks of us having two minds; in one place he speaks of us having a mind that needs transforming and renewing, which is the Maya Mind, and in another place where he tells us that we have been given the Mind of Christ, which is the Mool Mind. Dualistic thinking, leapfrogging between the Maya Mind and the Mool Mind, when continuously active in a person's life is aptly referenced in the Book of James as being in a state of double-mindedness causing much instability in life. People even unconsciously use the phrase, "I'm of two minds about this" or "I don't know whether to go with my head or my heart" when thinking about making a decision, not really understanding that probably their whole life is in fact one of two mindedness, or double mindedness or dualistic thinking.

The only thing that enables dualistic thinking to maintain its grip on one's life, the only thing that enables this constant movement or travel back and forth between the Maya Mind and the Mool Mind, between the Ego Mind and the Christ Mind to continue, is in fact us. We are the enablers. It is not some sort of secret spiritual power the Maya Mind possesses that enables it to distract and divert us away from the thoughts emanating from the Mool Mind or the Christ Mind within, it happens because we allow it. We as an act of choice consciously or unconsciously allow the dominant nature of our Ego or Maya Mind to continually fill our cup with physical, emotional and material desires in thought form, and in doing so continually reinforce to our thought processes, even subconsciously, a belief in the incompatibility of a spiritual life with those desires. We reinforce in our thought system a strong sense of individuality and identity, what I would call the "I" factor; it is an attitude of complete focus on what "I must do", on what "I must have," and on "this is who I am."

An ancient prophet once said, "we all like sheep have gone astray, each of us has turned to his own way," referring to the tendency for humanity when convenient, to wander like sheep far away from the truth of our being, our true individual and universal purpose and cosmic destiny, thus self-creating a psychological spiritual void in our lives. Consequently in this mind vacuum that we have self-created through neglect of the invisible things of the Spirit, in an attempt to fill that vacuum or void we seek out and embrace things of form. We seek out all things visible, new possessions, new relationships, things which appeal to our mind's carnal senses, to the visual sense realm and to the mental and emotional sense realm, things that appeal to our feelings, things that make us feel good. We may search out a new relationship, we may go for a holiday, change jobs, join a club or organization where we can connect with like-minded individuals. We hunt down sensory visible things to fill that spiritual void in our lives.

This in the present gives us a momentary sense of being worthy and a common sense of connection. We become part of the system and perhaps even part of the problem that the world finds itself in. An unenlightened person will always tend to favour the Maya over the Mool, the ephemeral over the invisible, for as life unfolds, in the pursuit of happiness and peace, most people will tend to move in the direction of what they can physically see, as in material possessions or in the direction of what they can physically participate in, as in relationships and pleasurable experiences, or what they can psychologically regurgitate from the past, such as pleasurable memories. Always looking for some sort of connection that makes them feel good.

> "The tendency of the lower human nature is always to move towards that which is mortal and perishable because it believes it is just human, rather than move towards that which is immortal and imperishable, its true Divine nature."

Non-duality or non-dualistic thinking is as mentioned previously, duality's opposite. Whilst the literal meaning of non-duality is 'not-two,' it is also what might be described as a philosophical and spiritual approach in understanding who we are in relation to the universe and to each other. For instance, as the philosophy of yoga has as it's main aim the unification of body, mind and spirit into one, the word Yoga meaning *union*, so the philosophy of non-duality espouses the opposite. It believes that since there is no such thing as duality in the first place, no joining together from two or three into one is necessary, for everything that exists, in non-dualistic reasoning, is already in a state of oneness.

Non-duality's spiritual philosophy is expressed in its basic form as a belief that the whole universe and everything in it, human and non-human alike, share a common source, an energetic creative life force, known in Christianity as the Word or the Mind of God and known in Eastern Religion and spiritual psychology as Universal Consciousness. It is a creative life force and reality that emanates from God, which is in fact God's Spirit, and which is shared by all; and because of this no individual thing can or ever will be separated from the whole. We are all one in Spirit. I share a short story at the beginning of Chapter 10 about the renowned singer songwriter and activist of the sixties Pete Seeger, whose underlying attitude in all he said and did was centred on a non-dualistic way of thinking.

Jesus in his time on earth demonstrated a non-dualistic attitude in all He said and did. We read in the Bible in the Book of John Jesus saying, "I and my Father are one." Further to this, described as the Trinity in theology is the Christian concept of the three persons of the Godhead, the Father, the Son and the Holy Spirit, sharing the one substance, the one life source. The meaning of the word trinity is, "the state of three things being as one thing." Which is in fact an expression of a non-dualistic nature. But this is where the early Church fathers, the founders of the faith so to speak, put a stop to it. They were prepared to accept that Jesus in human form lived in a unified state with God, they were prepared to accept the concept of the Trinity, but they would not accept that we human beings in human form also live in a unified state with God. They would not totally embrace the concept of non-dualism. And this became one of the major points of difference between Western Religion and Eastern Religion.

Why would the early Church fathers not accept this? Because if we human beings are formed from the same substance of God as Jesus was, it puts us in a spiritual position of equality with Jesus, and that goes totally against the Catholic position that only the Catholic Bishops and priests have permission to access God and to access God's creative power, as Jesus did; and if any one else wants to do so they can only do it through a priest. It is a doctrine the church purports stemmed out of a dogma, which is a Divinely revealed truth. The church fathers say that God revealed this to them. But one would have to believe it came rather from the power-crazed control driven ego minds of the senior bishops of the early church who were looking to form an all powerful universal religion, which is where the word Catholic came from. It means universal.

Consequently, as Christianity rapidly spread during the centuries following Christ's crucifixion, the doctrine of duality, a doctrine of God and us existing as separate things, spread with it. Except for those Christian churches of a mystical nature that sprang up through disillusionment with that Catholic doctrine, including a group known as the Gnostics. Now with regards to what I have shared about the concept of dualism, here is what I have been getting to and this is very important. Whether or not a religious organization is dualistic or non-dualistic in its philosophical outlook and subsequent beliefs, makes a significant difference in how it formulates it's teaching with regards to the meaning of life and our relationship with our God and with other human beings.

So in the world of religion, in relation to which religions are dualistic and which are non-dualistic in their philosophical approach, to put it simply you could say that all Western Christian organizations adopt a dualistic attitude to their respective charters apart from the odd breakaway ones such as Christian Mysticism, and those of Gnostic or Theosophical leaning, who take a non-dualistic approach, and the philosophy of non-dualism in Eastern Religion is mostly embraced by those of the Buddhist and Hindu faiths, two of the largest Eastern Religions. To put that in even more simple language we could say that Christianity supports the belief that God and man are cosmically separate, whilst Buddhism and Hinduism and Christian Mysticism believe that God and humans both emanating from the same life source, in reality are cosmically a whole, united as one, even whilst the human in the cosmic equation is still alive on earth.

The belief of the Hindu and the Buddhist of our existing oneness or cosmic connection with God in the present life is a similar thought process to that of the Apostle Paul when he spoke of us being one in Christ and being one in the Spirit. So by extrapolation that means that the Apostle Paul is in disagreement with the Catholic Church's teaching on the dualistic nature of Christianity. You may be thinking well if this is true, why did the Catholic Church continue to follow along the path of Dualism since they appeared to regard Paul very highly? Here is why, and please read this thoughtfully.

In Descartes writings on Dualism he would speak of thinking feeling things, subjects, being able to experience non-material things, objects, but that the opposite was not possible. Meaning we human beings can have the experience of tasting an ice cream, but the ice cream cannot have the experience of being tasted by us. His idea broadly speaking was that matter exists separately from and is devoid of Soul or Spirit or a life giving force, but the following is what is very important for us to understand. Descartes belief or teaching on the Dualistic nature of the world provided what was seen at the time as a reputable confirmation to the Catholic Church hierarchy of his day, as it still does to this day, that their theological mandate to teach the dualistic nature of Christianity, a type of God up there in heaven and human beings separated down here on earth physically and psychologically, is the correct approach to take in our attitude and actions regarding our relationship with our creator.

"Why was Rene Descartes concept of dualism embraced by the Vatican?"

Descartes dualism theory was both welcomed and embraced by the Vatican because his theory promoted a God and us philosophy, a separation of spirit and matter philosophy, and by implication, since the Catholic Church had designated the Pope and the bishops as God's only legitimate earthly representatives, it fitted together nicely with the established church doctrine that promoted what I would call a hierarchy of separation between the church and the laity, between the priests and the congregation of believers. To put this doctrine in analogical story mode to help us understand it, let's put it this way, for this is the way the Catholic Church sees it and has taught it, and it is highly unlikely that this will ever change whilst the universe as we know it exists.

"If a priest came knocking at God's front door the priest would be allowed in. If a member of the priest's congregation came knocking by herself or himself shortly afterwards, the door would not be opened, they would not be allowed in. However if a priest escorts the congregation member to God's front door, the congregation member would be allowed to enter, but only with the priest leading them in a display of having initiated and given authorisation and permission for the congregation member to the enter God's presence."

This doctrine of priest and laity separation also gives supposed legitimacy to the Church's teaching on the distribution of God's power, meaning which people in the church are given which particular Godly powers and gifts, such as the gift of healing, power to forgive, gift of working of miracles, and the power to exorcise. In the Catholic Church all Godly power is given to the Pope, bishops and priests, and absolutely no power has been bestowed on the rest of the congregation of believers. But you may well ask. Did not the Apostle Paul as recorded in the Book of Acts when speaking to a gathering of all Christian believers say, "but you shall receive power when the Holy Spirit comes upon you?" Yes he did, but the Catholic Church has conveniently ignored that because it conflicts with their established church doctrine.

Further to this by embracing the concept of Dualism it accommodated the following church teaching. If there is a spirit or soul in a human being contained in a body that is distinct and totally separate from God, then there must be two separate worlds or kingdoms where both these 'things', God and human beings, permanently reside. For God it became a place called heaven and for human beings it meant earth. This further sought to legitimise church teaching that when the physical body died the soul or spirit would go either to live with God in the Kingdom of Heaven as a reward for being a good Christian on earth or alternately go to hell the lake of fire, the residence of the enemies of God, as punishment for not being a Christian, more particularly not being a Catholic Christian, because the Vatican believes that only Catholic Christians will go to heaven, such is the spiritual arrogance of the Vatican.

However it is not only in Catholicism that this dualistic thought process occurs. It was then and still is now the driving force in what you could call evangelical Christianity's recruitment programme, being used very effectively to influence the minds of many people into a type of non-questioning passive acceptance of the dualistic approach to Christianity. In most Western Christian organizations that are based on Descartes duality theory, it is implied and taught that when we are born we emerge from the womb in a state of singularity, a state of separateness of soul and body from God, and that whilst we are able to ask God to come into our heart whilst we are alive here on earth, we will only become reunited, more so in a physical sense than a spiritual one, and at one with God when and if we get to that distant place called heaven after we die. In the meantime we are encouraged to live the Christian life of kindness and compassion, carry on with our lives as best we can, be a good person, and try to keep in touch with "Our Father who art in heaven" by attending church and by praying as the need arises.

This type of teaching always reinforces in the mind of the hearer a thought pattern shrouded with a continuous subconscious sense of separation and alienation from the creator. A type of thinking that God is way out there in the cosmos somewhere, and we are far away from Him, way down here on earth. Thus in this life a human being knows of God, has heard about God, believes that God exists, thinks about God occasionally, but because of this mental or psychological sense of separateness only expects to get to meet God and be in the presence of God when they die and go to heaven, having never come to truly know God, to achieve an enlightened state of existence in this present lifetime, right here right now on this earth.

Very little instruction has ever been given in the Christian Church on the existing oneness of God and humanity, the non-duality of the Christian faith rather than the duality, for reasons that I have outlined; instruction that is paramount to a believer's working relationship with the Holy Spirit. Both Jesus and the Apostle Paul taught that regardless of our religious status, whether we are a priest or a parishioner, regardless of our personal status, whether we are a prince or a pauper, that the Kingdom of God is within us all, and that all human beings have been given the Mind of Christ, which is the thought pattern and the perception processes of God; that all human beings have been given the ability to see life from God's point of view rather than the egos, to see life from the Mool Mind point of view rather than the Maya Mind point of view.

Further to this both Jesus and Paul taught that a person's life could be transformed now in the present moment through the renewing of the Ego Mind, by renewing the Maya Mind that took over our lives after the original psychological separation. It is a renewal of the rational mind that corrects our thinking process, re-aligning our perception with God's, perception being our way of thinking and interpreting things that happen to us in life. We then start looking at life from God's way of thinking rather than the ego way of thinking. How does that happen? By initiating a working relationship with the Holy Spirit we begin as a deliberate act of our will to perceive, filter and interpret the happenings of life through the Christ Mind rather than the Ego Mind. We begin living our lives looking at life deliberately from God's point of view, which brings a tremendous peace into our lives. The Bible describes it as the peace that passes all understanding guarding our heart and mind, meaning it is almost unfathomable how good it is.

Unfortunately though this gap of psychological separation that the church reinforced through neglect by not teaching the God ordained process of mind renewal, has been filled by the ego in its role as the deceiver using a secular almost religious type of teaching that is commonly known as new age philosophy or new age thinking. The intent of the deceiver being that if it can't stop a person from searching for the God way of thinking, the Christ Mind way of doing things, then give them some type of secular thought process that they think is God but really isn't. Perhaps something laced with a little spiritual terminology, and this will keep them happy. And the bullet that the ego mind loads into the chamber to fulfil its mission is simply the energetic thought force known as "lack," and its co-conspirator the energetic thought force known as "desire." I discuss this further on in this chapter.

And so enter into the lives of humanity all types of books to accommodate this new age philosophy, two of the original ones being Norman Vincent Peale's The Power of Positive Thinking and Napoleon Hill's Think and Grow Rich, both books which I read in 1966 at around eighteen years of age. These teachings were reinforced in the decades following by the publication of thousands of books with similar themes. The deceiver had stepped into the gap, taken the Spirit based mind renewal process that God ordained and that does in fact work if applied correctly, because it is Universal Law, and handed it over to the world but with one major difference. The Ego Mind is still overshadowing the Christ Mind in the thinking process and maintaining a person's sense of separation from God. And when the new age philosophy for many fails through lack of willpower, the psychological state of the participant is worse that it was before the attempt, because many people just give up on any further attempts at finding something of a spiritual nature that will fill the void and complete their lives.

We even saw many well-known ministers in the Christian Church fall as prey to these deceptive practices preaching what was known as the prosperity doctrine, which they used to intentionally influence peoples propensity to give financially to the church. In doing this they built not only many of the largest church organizations in the world numerically and financially, but spent fortunes of other peoples money on their own lavish lifestyles in the process. But in the end, for the most part, these religious empires came to a crashing end either after internal power disputes or after allegations of sexual impropriety and financial fraud came to light. The prince of egos working through the individual Ego Mind had in the process however fulfilled its primary intent of distracting and subsequently destroying lives to maintain what it feels is its rightful place of rulership above God and its ownership of creation.

"Why is there very little teaching given to Christians on this subject matter, the renewal of the mind and the Christ Mind within?"

The reason is mostly due to hereditary religious influences, going back to the post-crucifixion era and the early establishment of the Christian church. And as I touched on before, for religious leaders to teach on the reality of our earthly existence as children of God at one with God, being led by the Spirit of God and having the creative powers of God within us, would contradict the doctrine of the church. Which doctrine? The doctrine that originated from early Catholic Church founders who had from the get go set about indoctrinating believers, that it is only through God's legitimate representatives on earth, their own bishops and priests, that we have access to God, and that only through our allegiance to the dogmas and doctrines of the Catholic Church and our support of it, will we receive the reward of a front row seat in that faraway and separate kingdom called heaven in the afterlife.

"What is indoctrination?"

Indoctrination is simply the process of creating a fixed belief in the mind of a person through repetitive suggestions or practices. From early childhood through the teachings of the church and perhaps with parental reinforcement we commenced our spiritual journey thinking of the God of this universe as a judgemental but benevolent type of character; a God who punishes bad people and rewards good people, and someone we can turn to in prayer when we desperately need help, when nothing else has worked. In our imagination God is pictured as an old fatherly patriarchal type of person, dressed in white robes, perhaps with a white beard who lives in a magical place called heaven which is geographically located far away somewhere out there in the cosmos; an old man who sits around waiting for us to ask for something or looking for ways to punish us for doing something wrong. I am sure as children we would all have heard that threatening parental statement, "God will punish you if you keep being naughty." I know as a child I did.

Ask a child the question "where do you go when you die?" or "what happens when you die?" and you will surely get the answer, "you go to heaven of course." Ask a child "where does God live?" and the answer will probably be "up there in heaven of course." Ask a child "what is hell?" and you will probably get the answer, "that's where bad people go when they die." The underlying thought process being one of God is up there and we are down here. It is the 'separation principle' cementing its place in our thought process from the very beginning of our lives. The problem is though that if we wait twenty years and ask the same child who has grown into adulthood the same question, we more than likely will get the same answer albeit expressed with a slightly lessened tone of innocence.

Midst all the clutter and haste, midst all the strife and sadness we have in this world, there exists a society of souls desperately needing to know this Supreme Being we refer to as God, rather than just knowing of God, and in doing so witness the gap of separation closed and thus be reunited with Him, our source of being, the life force within. This is the ongoing plan of God for humanities cosmic evolution. To bring humanity to a point of knowing God is all part of the Divine Wisdom of God as witnessed in the going out process, the original separation incident as analogised in the Old Testament story of Adam and Eve leaving the garden, and in the coming home process, the return, as analogized in Christ's parable of the prodigal son in the Bible's Book of Luke. It is the closing of the gap of psychological separation, and we are home, back home with God, and this is the important part, we are in fact back home with God whilst we are still here on earth if that makes sense.

"So how does this principle of separation become established in our lives, and how does this singular identity based life, this life play of personhood function?"

From a very early age in our search for happiness, contentment and fulfilment, to restore the peace filled state, that peace of God that passes all understanding that was lost in the separation, we join the world of achievers, of collectors, of futurists and of becomers; earnestly leaning forward towards the next acquisition, experience or pleasure and ever seeking to obtain more than our fair share of the success, happiness and riches that the unseen ego forces of the world temptingly beckon us toward. This then progressively strengthens our individuality and our sense of separation from God, our independent nature, whilst subconsciously continuously reminding us that this is what life is all about, we are all on our own, this is reality so make the most of it, go for it.

We are born into this world as either a male or female with absolutely no psychological baggage at all, save perhaps the odd genetic influence, but certainly born with no self-inflicted mind baggage. From that moment on we start collecting what we could call 'thought things', thought things that will eventually turn into mind memories, which will either continue to influence us throughout our life, if they are of value to the ego, or be discarded from our memory bank if they are of no value. One category of memory that you can guarantee the ego will choose to hold on to in your mind is any experience that can be grouped under the category of fear. The Bible tells us that this was the first non-pleasurable emotion that Adam and Eve experienced in the Garden after initiating the process of separation. Fear caused them to hide from God's presence. Why is fear important to the ego? Because fear is the one emotion that the ego mind can use again and again in a variety of different circumstances to influence or disrupt our lives. We see fear manifest in every area of people's lives, even in its most subtle forms such as anxiousness, worry, anxiety or depression.

So throughout our life, perhaps more intense though in the first half than the latter, this process of thought collecting and the depositing of each one into the memory bank of our mind continues, contributing to our sense of individuality, our identity, and our sense of differentiation from each other, whilst strengthening our subconscious sense of alienation from God and from the rest of the human race. At the beginning of our life we are given a name, John Smith or Mary Jones or whatever, to identify us as a separate or individual person, and with that comes the impartation of the belief that this is who I am, I am Mary Jones, this is my true self. It is a name that is then used continuously throughout our life, as a reference point to distinguish us from other people and to keep the separation principle alive.

We inherit a nationality and a particular language that differentiates us geographically, socially and linguistically from other societies on earth and for some we are upon our arrival into the world embedded into a specific culture which can be visually identifiable as different from others in certain areas of lifestyle such as in religious practices, in dress, in dance, in music and in culinary choices. Our culture then influences our lifetime habits and to some extent our relationships, accentuates our differences and demonstrates our independence from other cultures on earth, thus taking away any desire or notion of embracing the spiritual universality of humankind that is our cosmic destiny, or as the Apostle Paul put it, "coming to the unity or universality of the faith."

In terms of the spiritual life children born into some cultures are directed towards a particular religion, taught to preference its belief system and shown how to participate in its rituals from a very early age. This is usually a hereditary bequeath, handed down either by the parents or through cultural influence. We find this happens more so in the East than the West, and for many people in the East this culturally inherited religious belief system becomes sole spiritual truth to them, and remains a person's only spiritual perspective as they move through life. They are never really exposed to any other alternative religious viewpoint save their own inherited beliefs.

In Western society however, whilst there is no specific cultural influence directing a child towards a specific religion, there is a generalised misleading belief that Western cultures are all Christian societies but this is not correct. However many people who have no understanding or knowledge of the Christ within or of the Christian faith itself, save for the Easter and Christmas celebrations, will when asked about their religious beliefs, describe themselves as a Christian. I'm a Christian; my parents were all Christian they can be heard saying sometimes almost defensively. It is also common practice in Western Christianity for allegiance to a particular Christian denomination to be handed down from generation to generation, more so with those of the Catholic faith, so effective and focused is the indoctrination process of their brand.

Over time, as part of the play of personhood, we will accept certain 'thought things' as truth, and they become our reality, including numerous false assumptions about ourselves and about our fellow human beings, about the rightness or wrongness of individualised cultures and religious beliefs and most importantly about who this person 'this identifiable me' really is. Most of these assumptions about our personal self are linked to the physical, mental and psychological aspects of our person; I'm good looking, I'm plain, I'm hot I'm not, I'm clever, I'm dumb, I'm good at Math, I can't do Math, I'm shy, I'm quite confident. Thus the firming up of what is known as our identity, including aspects of our personality noticed and recognizable by other people, such as she's a bubbly person, he's a moody person, she's funny, he's dour, all continue to grow and solidify as we and those around us acknowledge that this is who we are.

It is a personal identity being continuously shaped and reinforced through relationships, through our body mind experiences, the good and the bad of them, through our obsession with objects and forms meaning the material world, and through the continuous introduction into our minds of a conglomerate of supportive 'thought things,' for our ego mind is always on the lookout for thought things that more often than not reinforce our negative opinions about ourselves rather than the positive aspects of our identity. Together all these thought things merge into our own personal identity, a fixed and hard to change belief system about ourselves, seemingly set like cement. It is a personal identity that, having been seared into our minds, will go on to influence the direction of the rest of our life in a positive or a negative way, whilst continuously reminding us that this is who we really are, and that this is all there is to life, there is nothing else and we must live with that, you can't change it.

Thus a platform for an ongoing self-absorbed, self-willed and self-determined life, a life lived solely in personhood has been established by early adulthood, with our day to day attention span completely focused on all manner of things that affect or influence us personally. Focused on all manner of visible material things, including experiences and achievements, on other people such as family and friends, and on interpersonal relationships. More particularly focused on relationships that will make us feel loved, boost our self-esteem, and shore up our inner feeling of worthiness, thus delivering a sense of fulfilment and completeness to the emotional side of our Ego Mind.

"So does that mean that a successful material life is not compatible with a successful spiritual life?

No of course not. The problem is that as Jesus alluded to, the nature of the physical self is to lean towards that which is visible, that which is time bound, that which is continually changing, as in new experiences, new achievements, new relationships, whereas our true Self, our true nature invisible to the eye leans towards that which is timeless and everlastingly unchanging. This conflict is what causes the stress. None of these things, neither new possessions, new experiences, new achievements, nor new relationships, all present moment life things, have any value in God's spiritual purpose for us as individuals or for humanity universally. They profit us nothing in our journey to an enlightened state of being. Jesus said in the Book of Mark, "for what shall it profit a man, if he should gain the whole world and lose his own Soul."

There are now around 7.6 billion inhabitants on the earth every single one born with the nature of God buried within them, many of whom will never discover or know anything more about themselves during their lifetime other than their own interpretation of their bodily appearance, their mental capabilities, their material successes, their likes and dislikes, and their manner of responding to life's events, which at the end of their earthly life will all become as dust and be quickly forgotten or very rarely acknowledged by those who were close to them. They have not in the present moment of their existence and perhaps will not in this current life, simply because of neglect, ever come to understand the eternal Atonement process lying dormant within their being waiting to be acted upon that will change their lives completely and secure their eternity.

"What do you mean by the eternal Atonement process?"

The word Atonement means "undoing", and in terms of humanity it is the undoing of everything that is not of God but of the ego self. It is not a physical undoing it is a psychological undoing. It is about detachment. We psychologically detach ourselves from an existing state of psychological attachment to the things of the ego, whether they are physical things, mental and emotional things or spiritual things. Yes it does involve spiritual things because religious practice itself can also become just another manifestation of the ego mind. It involves the undoing of everything that is of our lower nature and the appropriation of everything that is of our higher nature. It is a process which when completed in the life of a believer closes the psychological gap of separation that was created in the Garden of Eden scenario, and in doing so releases the power and peace of the Godhead back into the earthly life of the person who undertakes to go on that transitional journey.

The Atonement process is in fact a healing event, a complete healing of the body and the mind brought about through the renewal of the rational mind's thinking process and the alignment of that renewed rational mind with God's thinking pattern. Life then becomes a life led by the Spirit of God, the Holy Spirit. When Jesus prior to His crucifixion said to His disciples greater works than I do shall you do because I am going to be with the Father, the Gospel of John says that immediately after this He said "and you shall receive power when the Holy Spirit has come upon you. " Then still speaking of this Holy Spirit that would come upon the disciples John describes the Holy Spirit as the Spirit of Truth which the world cannot accept and does not know, and he continues to say, but you know Him for he lives "with you" and "will be in you". When he said "with you" he was referring to Jesus in the flesh and when he said "in you" he was referring to the post crucifixion reality when the physical Jesus would be gone but His Mind the Christ Mind, would be in us; and the communicator of the thoughts emanating from that Christ Mind within us is the Holy Spirit.

In spite of all their excesses the Pentecostal religion did get it almost right with their focus on the Baptism of the Holy Spirit as being given to equip a Christian to fight the good fight of faith, but this is where like all others they stopped short. They were so focused on speaking in tongues and striving after the Gifts of the Spirit, which when misused become ego driven pleasurable experiences, that their attention drifted back to the ephemeral, the visually spectacular, what they could see, particularly things like the outworking of the gifts in church services, gifts such as prophecy and interpretation, and healing and the casting out of demons. So preoccupied were they with what was pleasurable to the senses, that they failed to follow through with teaching on the main aspect of the Atonement process, the psychological part, the renewal of the mind and the ascension of the Christ Mind within to its rightful place in the thinking process of a believer.

The Atonement's outworking is the next necessary step after an acceptance of the crucifixion to complete the salvation experience, and is designed to remove the final skerrick of any negative aspects of personhood that are still attached to us and bring us into complete engagement with the Holy Spirit and thus into a Spirit led life. The crucifixion experience of Jesus was a demonstration of a person's denial and rejection of self-will, as indicated by the words of Jesus when he cried out, "not my will but thy will be done Father," and a demonstration also that the surrender of self-will is the first step a person needs to take to press forward into the Atonement or the resurrection evolutionary journey. We consciously make a decision to dissolve the old self or old nature through mind renewal and release the new self our higher nature to be led by the Spirit and not the Ego Mind. We are transformed by the renewal of our mind so that our life is lived in perfect accord with God's will. We become Spirit led people.

The cure for a sense of spiritual separation is not church membership. In very simple terms it is an understanding and acceptance of the following facts. That a state of mind, one of psychological separateness, occurred between God and humanity in the original Garden of Eden incident allowing the ego mind to fill the gap. That God has established the means for the restoration of that sense of oneness with Him that was thought to be lost and in the first instance that happens through the establishment of a working relationship with the Holy Spirit, the Holy Spirit's first focus being to assist us in the renewal of the mind process. She assists us to change our way of thinking and our way of perceiving or seeing things; She helps us to see life from God's point of view rather than the Ego Mind point of view, until eventually as our mind is renewed to a new thinking process we move into a state of continuous knowing. This is what it is to "know God" rather than just know of God. The gap of psychological separation will be finally closed and oneness with Universal Consciousness becomes our new reality.

We must also resolutely understand and believe that the parting gift that Jesus bequeathed to humanity for this purpose was not His own crucifixion, nor the church, nor the Bible, nor the minister, nor the priest. Jesus' parting gift to every human being, and His panacea for all of society's ills and humankind's alienation from God and from each other, that which was given to us to close the gap that separates us from happiness, contentment, fulfilment and a sense of peace and safety, that which takes us from a time bound state into the realm of the timeless, that which takes us from personhood to presence was the Holy Spirit.

The Gnostics were a group of early adherents to the Christian faith who, in their attempt to see the world through the Mind of Christ and to understand and perceive all things that occur from the Holy Spirit's viewpoint, suffered mercilessly for their beliefs at the hands of those who had become the self-appointed custodians of Christianity in the centuries following Christ's crucifixion, the Roman Catholic Church aligned with the ruling Roman authorities. I share their story in the next chapter.

> "The Atonement process, the renewal of the mind process, teaches me how to escape from everything I have taught myself in the past and everything I think about myself in the present, and reveals to me the true reality of who I really was in the past and who I truly am in the present."

“Our intellect has achieved the most tremendous things,
but in the meantime our spiritual dwelling has fallen into disrepair.”

Carl Gustav Jung

Gnosticism ...
A Forgotten Faith

Note from the Author

In this chapter as well as in various other parts of the book, whilst there is a noticeable emphasis on the subject of Gnosticism and Gnosis I am not relating it to the teaching of any particular Gnostic influenced religious group such as Hellenistic Gnosticism or Zoroastrianism, or other Gnostic leaning groups that formed part of the many schools of spirituality that existed in the early Christian era. Neither am I referring to Gnostic groups who in their religious teachings have a blend of Gnostic thought, Greek philosophical thought, Judaism, Greco-Roman mysteries or magic.

Rather when I talk about the ancient Gnostic and the practice of Gnosticism I am talking about those ordinary individuals, perhaps some with a mystic leaning, who lived and worshipped within the orthodox Christian community of the day, but believed in the availability of a higher deeper level of spiritual knowledge pertaining to humankind's origins and humanity's relationship with its creator, knowledge known as Gnosis. I am referring to believers who sought to tap into this knowledge through specific spiritual practices similar to the contemplative prayer disciplines of the Christian Mystics.

When I use the word Gnosis I am speaking of interior, illuminative insight as seen in the ancient teachings of certain Hermetic schools of religious thought such as the Poimandres and the Askeplius. The teaching of these schools was centred on helping humanity come to a deeper understanding of the Mind of God and the Universal Laws that control this world we live in. These were schools of spirituality that focused on empirical knowledge pertaining to the spiritual mysteries of the cosmos.

Most religious institutions have established boundaries, set in place as to what teachings their congregations are allowed to hear and what they are not, many of them seeing themselves as a type of religious gatekeeper, dictating what should pass before the eyes of the believer and what should not. With regards to Gnostic teaching and for that matter all Christian thought, that self-appointed gatekeeper was and is the

Roman Catholic Church. Whilst most congregations are unaware of this it is important to understand that most religious institutions have these what are called gatekeepers whose underlying premise for existing is to keep their followers safely confined within the boundaries of their own religious, philosophical, institutionalised and ideological agenda.

TWO

Edward Norton Lorenz died at his home in Cambridge Massachusetts on April 16th 2008. He was 90 years of age. Edward was a scientist, a meteorologist, and a professor at the Massachusetts Institute of Technology, a man described as a genius with the soul of an artist. In his lifetime he was the winner of many scientific awards including the prestigious Kyoto Prize for outstanding achievement in basic sciences. Known affectionately in scientific circles as "the father of the chaos theory," Edward was lauded by his peers for his many scientific achievements, in particular the theory that later became commonly known as 'the butterfly effect.' In layman's terms it was a concept that explained how small effects could lead to big changes. How something as minuscule as a butterfly flapping its wings in Brazil, could progressively change the constantly moving atmosphere of the universe in ways that might later trigger tornadoes in Texas.

In 1961 Edward in his work as a meteorologist accidentally ran a series of the same calculations through a computer twice, and came up with two vastly different answers. He was utilising a programme he had put together with the help of a reasonably new invention called a computer, to hopefully more accurately predict the weather. He had created a mathematical model, now known as an algorithm, which when given a series of numbers representing the current weather situation, could predict the weather a few minutes in advance. Edward believed that once this computer programme was up and running he would be able to produce longer term forecasts, simply by feeding the predicted and updated weather forecast back into the computer over and over again, with each entry then producing forecasting further and further into the future.

When he investigated the discrepancy between the two results he noticed that a small decimal point difference had occurred, less than 0.0001. It happened because while the computer was printing out the predictions to three decimal points it was actually crunching the numbers internally using six decimal places. The effect led to a significant error which subsequently saw him write a seminal scientific paper, presented in 1963, about 'the butterfly effect' also known as 'the chaos theory', which is a mathematical theory that can be used to explain unexpected changes in complex world systems such as weather, astronomy, and economics. Edward was able to prove that even though many of the world's complex systems appear to behave in a random or chaotic manner, beyond this chaotic appearance, there is an underlying order in the universe that whilst difficult to see is definitely present. However within this order, hidden from physical sight, is a metaphysical influence on the ongoing functionality of complex systems in the universe, which could be described as cosmic interference or perhaps we could even refer to it as the process of Divine intervention.

This chaos theory broadened further some of the long standing views of certain academics and scientists of the day in line with Werner Heisenberg's uncertainty principle, that the long term behaviour of systems cannot be predicted with absolute certainty, and that in order to get close to an accurate prediction it would require a knowledge of the initial conditions with a perfect degree of accuracy, which in itself is impossible. Therefore the possibility of random event interference appears more probable than the pathway of predictability. Could this uncertainty principle equally apply in the area of religious thought and belief and is this why the 'faith component' has been emphatically built into Christian teaching over the centuries thus becoming an integral part, as civilisation progressively gave up in its quest for Absolute truth, the God kind of Truth, and adopted the faith mindset.

Western civilization over the centuries and in particular from the 18th century onwards has witnessed the discovery of a tremendous amount of information, new knowledge you could call it, about the nature of the physical world around us, and about the operation of the psychological and spiritual world within us. Knowledge that has given us greater understanding of this world we live in. Who would have thought that the earth wasn't flat? In the last fifty years it has also begun to understand much more about the metaphysical world through recent discoveries in the field of Quantum Theory and the alignment of that world with certain spiritual principles; Quantum Theory being the theoretical basis of modern physics that explains the nature and behaviour of matter and energy on the atomic and subatomic level.

The Gnostics, followers of the ancient religion of Gnosticism, if present at the time of Edward's scientific experiment, would probably have seen his discovery, this new knowledge, as very exciting and absolutely believable, since it was of a non-dualistic nature and dealt with the interrelatedness and connectedness of all things in time and space in the universe, as well as highlighting the unpredictability and changeful nature of science and scientific knowledge versus their own understanding of the changeless and timeless nature of that which can be received intuitively by humankind through Gnosis.

For the Gnostics the knowledge came first, intuitively, and was followed by personal experiment and experience, whereas with science first came the experiment and experience, and then knowledge manifested out of it becoming self-evident. One of the greatest scientists of all time Albert Einstein, whilst not publicly acknowledging himself as a Gnostic did acknowledge the role of the intuitive thought process in a lot of his own scientific discoveries. He recognized intuitive thought as a sacred gift and spoke of humankind as having forgotten this gift that has by Grace been given.

"So who were the Gnostics, what was Gnosticism, and what became of this supposedly radical offshoot of Christianity in the centuries following its original inception?"

In December 1945 an Arab peasant farmer in Egypt made an amazing find. Muhammed al-Samman and his brother had been out working in the Egyptian desert digging for sabakh a soft soil used by farmers as fertilizer. Whilst digging in the vicinity of the Jabal al-Tarif caves near the small village of Hamra Dom located not too far from the upper Egyptian town of Nag Hammadi, the brothers unearthed an earthenware vessel. It was a large red jar measuring almost a metre high. The story related by Muhammed some thirty years later, was that the brothers were hesitant to break the jar at first to see what it contained, fearing a spirit might live inside it. However after further discussion amongst themselves, thinking that it might contain some gold or precious gems, Muhammad lifted his mattock and smashed it down on the urn. There were no gold or precious jewels inside it. Instead, much to Muhammad's disappointment preserved in this sealed container was a collection of leather-bound papyrus codices.

Papyrus was a material similar to thick paper made from the cyperus papyrus plant. It was commonly used in the day to make boats, mats, rope, sandals and baskets, but also found a great deal of use in ancient times as a writing surface, which could then be rolled up into a scroll once information had been recorded on it. A codice was the name given to multiple sheets of papyrus used to store larger recordings in book format. It was an improvement on the scroll particularly for lengthy writings destined for long-term storage, as it was not as susceptible to cracking as easily as the scrolls were. Thirteen codices were found in this vessel. They comprised a collection of early Christian and Gnostic texts including new and previously unknown Gospels on the life and teachings of Jesus on earth after his crucifixion and resurrection. Many of these ancient texts discovered by Muhammed and his brothers eventually became included in a collection known as the Nag Hammadi Library currently housed in the Coptic Museum in Cairo Egypt.

You see up until this find occurred in 1945 these lost gospels as they came to be known consisted only of a few fragments previously discovered archeologically and viewed by a few scholars and even fewer members of the public. I personally find it interesting that the discovery of both the Nag Hammadi codex and the Dead Sea scrolls came about not long after an event occurred that brought to light the capability that mankind had scientifically developed to totally obliterate the human race from the earth; that being the splitting of the atom and the manufacture of the atomic bomb used in the allied forces attack on the Japanese cities of Hiroshima and Nagasaki. Attacks that saw according to a study carried out in 1998, some 202,000 innocent people killed and many more maimed. It was almost like some Divine force was saying, "you are heading down the wrong path if you think this sort of behaviour is going to heal the world. In order to have lasting world peace each individual in the world must first find inner peace. These texts will help lead the way to this inner peace."

Now whilst a lot of the Nag Hammadi library contains texts that are classed as not strictly Gnostic including some of Plato's Republic, which was a Socratic dialogue written around 375 BC concerning justice, most others could be grouped into a category of teachings and discourse that are decidedly related to the ancient Gnostics. They include the sayings and teachings of Jesus and incidents in his post-resurrection life and are presented in the form of four new Gospels, the Gospel of Thomas, the Gospel of Phillip, the Gospel of the Egyptians, and a treatise named The Gospel of Truth, which contains information on the mission of Jesus as Saviour, and previously unknown truths about his Messianic message. The Gospel of Thomas differs in content from the established and well known Gospels of Matthew, Mark, Luke and John by giving a collection of Jesus' sayings and teachings rather than the mainly historical record of the life of Jesus that the Biblical gospels give.

Some of the sayings of Jesus are almost identical with those in the New Testament, whilst many others have a noticeable Gnostic flavour about them, an essence of myth, mystery and mysticism. It is interesting however that the sayings of Jesus in these Gnostic Gospels, rather than being an exhortation for people to be saved and join a church, are more so an encouragement to seek, to interpret, and to understand the will and ways of God. Most are prescriptions for gaining knowledge so that a person can come to a truthful understanding of their true self, the inner person that is spoken of in other ancient religions as true reality. The writings also include accounts of the creation of the world, including the Adam and Eve story, teachings on the nature of the Soul and its relationship to the world, and most interestingly much about the feminine principle or feminine component of the Godhead.

If one were inclined to go into the deepest depths of the history of Gnosticism with a view to chronicling that history in the form of a stage play, one would discover an unparalleled story full of trials, tribulation and triumph. It would be a tale that would rival many of the most epic exciting and at times tragic works of Shakespeare himself, containing a litany of notable characters of both the religious and political kind, all taking the stage as actors and actresses, and all playing major roles in a storyline encompassing a veritable smorgasbord of plans and plots, and of villains and victors.

There would be a cast composed of all multicultural manner of people and tribes from vast areas of the ancient world. There would be Greeks, Egyptians, Persians, Vikings, Phoenicians, Celts, Jews, Romans and many other nationalities. Their individual occupations would vary from monks, mystics and magicians, to priests, parishioners and the everyday hard working public, all playing their part in this epic play on Gnostic history. The play would feature secret schools of wisdom controlled by the elite, with various priesthoods teaching the ancient way of wisdom and knowledge. Schools that were offshoots of various Grand Orders such as those of Ancient Egypt, the Phoenician Ophites, the Greek Alexandrians, the Platonists, the Valentarians, the Celtic Druids, the Sons of Seth and the Tribe of Levi, with all their secret wisdom and theological argument blending together in a synchronised spiritual cacophony of learning containing both truth and myth, allegory and analogy, parables and poetic verse.

Various religious groups such as Christians, Jews and Muslims would be included in the cast with certain players such as the Pope and his key bishops taking lead roles. There would be secret and mystical societies such as the Knights Templar of Dan Brown's The Da Vinci Code, The Freemasons, the Sufis and the Rosicrucians all playing their respective parts. The sets and the on stage dialogue of the players would contain symbols and secret signs, instruction and initiations, devils and demons, all played out to the accompanying cries of the very vocal, excitable and sometimes antagonistic members of the play's audience yelling "that's hearsay," or "that's heresy."

However as much as that true to Gnostic history Shakespearian type of stage play might generate some intellectual understanding of Gnostic history, Gnostic influence and Gnostic beliefs, and excite and intrigue the imaginative senses of the viewing audience, that is not my intention for this chapter when I discuss Gnostic history. I really only want to centre on imparting to you the reader a greater understanding as to the original spiritual intent of Christian Gnosticism, using as a scriptural umbrella what is regarded as one of the final messages of Jesus to his disciples before His crucifixion, when He said, "It is to your advantage that I go away for when I go I will send the Comforter to replace me, who will be with you and be in you, who will guide you into all truth and bring an understanding of the things of God back to your remembrance."

This offshoot of Christianity that came to be known as Gnosticism is believed to have had its origins in the areas of Syria, Samaria, Palestine, and in the Ptolemaic Kingdom, which was a Hellenistic kingdom based in ancient Egypt. Ptolemy 1 Soter, a Greek who came from Macedon in northern Greece founded it in 305 B.C. The Ptolemaic Kingdom stretched from southern Syria to Cyrene, an ancient Greek and later Roman city near present-day Shah hat Libya. It was a kingdom that over time had been ruled by such notables as Alexander the Great and Cleopatra. From around 180 A.D. Gnosticism also thrived in and around Gaul the Roman province now known as the country of France.

In 1947, some two years after the finding of the Nag Hammadi scrolls, more ancient writings were found by a group of Bedouin goat herders in Qumran, which is an archaeological site located in the West Bank of Israel, about a kilometre from the Red Sea. These texts are known as the Dead Sea Scrolls. When deciphered they revealed that at least some elements of Gnosticism go back to the Essenes, who were a Jewish religious sect. The Essenes were a group who led a strictly communal life often later compared to Christian monasticism. Some historians believe that both John the Baptist and Jesus were part of the community of believers known as the Essenes, simply for the following reason. Long before Jesus' time and continuing into it, all Jews were divided into three religious sects, the Sadducees, the Pharisees, and the Essenes, and Jesus is recorded in the Bible frequently denouncing and rebuking the Sadducees and the Pharisees but never the Essenes. It is believed also that the Essenes were responsible for the writing of those Dead Sea Scrolls unearthed in Israel.

Most original adherents to Gnostic teaching remained as part of the established Christian church, followed the teachings of Jesus Christ and partook of the sacraments during the church services. However they added to the church teaching their own particular type of revelatory spiritual knowledge about the things of God, knowledge received by individuals intuitively during meditation and in dreams and visions. In the daily life and activities of the Gnostic community it was recognized however that this new knowledge was only discernible by those who were spiritually ready, who were spiritually mature.

The Gnostics were never completely satisfied with the quality or depth of the established church teaching, which virtually came straight from selected scriptures. They viewed a lot of what they were hearing as simply a transfer of historical information passed down from various sources who had trod the Christian path before them, which in a lot of ways it was. And whilst they were very much persuaded that apart from the historical events presented, other writings and teachings in the Scriptures were in fact Gnosis in their original form, to them it was still someone else's Gnosis, someone else's revelatory experience from another place and time. You could call it second hand Gnosis. They believed that much more Gnosis was readily available to all Christians if they deliberately sought it, in moments of reverential contemplation through intuitive dialogue with the Holy Spirit. The Holy Spirit referred to by Jesus in his discussions with His disciples as "the one who will come after me who will teach you all things and bring all things to your remembrance."

They also rejected the introduction into the church of man-made dogmas creeds and doctrines based purely on a literal or in some cases what they determined was a false interpretation, perhaps even a deliberate misrepresentation of the scriptures. These things amongst others caused them to become increasingly frustrated with the uncompromising determination of the early Catholic fathers to ignore the allegorical, mystical and Gnostic (revelatory) nature and meaning of the scriptures. They strongly believed that religion was not just a matter of one escaping the fires of hell through a relatively safe passage into heaven if one obeyed the Catholic rules and disciplines. The Gnostics, regardless of the opinions and opposition of those around them, understood in a very real way what really matters in life, and because of this adopted attitudes and spiritual practices that would enable God's reality to become their reality.

They saw the Christian life as a journey of individual spiritual evolution and transformation and in some ways a type of spiritual contest between opposing spiritual forces, its goal being to achieve cosmic unification between God and humankind; this contest to them was a type of cosmic quest that would in victory bring all people into a state of ultimate spiritual maturity or as the Apostle Paul, whose life experience and writings some historians would say had Gnostic overtones, described it, into a state of having attained the complete standard of Jesus, the stature and the fullness of the Christ.

Another thing that the Gnostics differed on from orthodox religion was that they did not accept what they saw as the church's simplistic notion regarding salvation. The church teaching that the totality of the redemptive process was accomplished by the physical death of Jesus on the cross alone. They did not believe that all an individual had to do was to confess a belief in the historical accuracy of the crucifixion and they would be automatically redeemed or saved as is the terminology used in evangelical Christianity. The Gnostic concept of the salvation experience was that it was not just the redemption of someone from past sin, but more so the process of being saved or liberated from the ignorance of spiritual realities of which sin is a continuing consequence. They believed that this could only happen through the process of mind renewal and that for a believer this was not just an automatic thing that occurred when a person decided to become a Christian. For the Gnostics, mind renewal was a matter of choice and a disciplined activity that had to be worked through as part of the Atonement process.

The Gnostics were convinced that behind the doctrinal and sacerdotal form presented by the church in its exegesis of the scriptures lay a series of deeper spiritual truths meant to be available to all Christians, those things referred to by the Apostle Paul as the mysteries of God. Some practitioners of Gnosticism in fact believed that the church fathers were deliberately withholding these truths from them in an effort to maintain their power base in the rapidly growing Christian Church, which in many ways with regards to certain Bishops of the day turned out to be correct.

"So what was Gnosis?"

Gnosis was the term given to these deeper spiritual truths, truths containing hidden knowledge of the mysteries of God that one could obtain through personal acquaintance or what you could call a personal revelatory experience, a mental visitation of the Voice of the Holy Spirit, as well as through psychic experiences such as visions and dreams. Truths that are referred to in the Bible as 'the meat of the Word and not the milk.' The Apostle Paul we read said to the Christians of the City of Corinth, "I have fed you with milk and not meat for you are not yet ready". The word for meat used in the scriptures was *broma*, which in the Greek refers to the more solid complete and deeper mysteries of God and the Christ. Whereas the word milk in the original Greek is *gala*, meaning the elemental teachings of Christianity. You could call gala the birth, life, death and resurrection story of Jesus Christ's life; teachings that give people a historical and intellectual understanding of the mission of Jesus, but do not impart a transformational spiritual experience.

The esoteric (meat) and exoteric (milk) methods of teaching and instruction that were seen being used in early Christianity were originally used by Greek philosophers of the day who would give an esoteric or private teaching, a secret interpretation of certain writings, to an inner circle of followers, versus the public or exoteric version given to the masses. Most of the followers of Christ, save for some of his disciples such as Peter and John, were only able in the first instance to mentally absorb an exoteric interpretation of God's plan for humanity, which was centred on a historical and intellectual understanding of the reason for His incarnation. The esoteric version was destined to come later as the believer matured in their Christian walk.

Jesus is recorded in the Book of John as saying to his disciples that there were things He wanted to share with them but couldn't, as they were not yet ready; meaning not spiritually mature enough. And when asked by his disciples why he only spoke to certain groups in parables he replied, "unto you it is given to know the mysteries of the kingdom of heaven, but to them, the multitude it is not given." So he spoke only to the multitude in parables, which are exoteric and are mostly allegories, stories used to illustrate a moral or spiritual lesson. But God had a plan so that no person would miss out. God's plan is inclusive of all humanity. Jesus said that after he went to be with the Father, after his resurrection, He would send them the Comforter, the Holy Spirit, who would teach them all things, who would start at the level of each individuals point of readiness, and with their willingness and co-operation progressively unfold in their mind through revelation God's plan for them as individuals and for the whole human race.

The Tao Te Ching, the classic Chinese text attributed to the 6th century B.C. sage Lao Tzu says, "when the student is ready the teacher will appear." How and when does the Holy Spirit appear and teach us all things including the mysteries of God? If you asked a Gnostic they would probably answer this way. "When we slow life down, become silent, still, and listen, then we will hear the voice of the Holy Spirit through insight and intuition and in the form of visions and dreams. When we as an act of our will choose to slow down and start living life deliberately rather than accidentally. When we start acknowledging all synchronistic events that occur in our life as having potentially come from the Hand of God, giving thanks at the same time. When we start perceiving life or looking at life from the Holy Spirit's viewpoint rather than our own ego viewpoint, then that is the point when we can acknowledge that the teacher is indeed active in our lives. It is then we can profess to be led by the Spirit of the Lord, to be living in the Spirit."

The process of living a deliberate intuitive in the Spirit lifestyle was the chief rationale behind Gnostic tradition. They lived the scripture that in the Book of Romans says, "For all who are led by the Spirit of God, the Holy Spirit, these are the children of God." However these beliefs of the Gnostics became problematic for the Catholic Bishops, in that they the Bishops had convinced the masses that they the Bishops were the only true representatives of God on earth, which by inference meant that God only spoke to them and through them. Further to this Gnostics believed that the mind exists in, and is largely focused on a self-created world of illusion and error, living in deception you could say, and that it is only through enlightenment coming from Gnosis and a Spirit led lifestyle that one can have a true salvation experience. An experience which is meant to be transformative enabling a complete appropriation of the life changing components of the Atonement, which include a state of holiness and wholeness and a complete healing of the mind as spoken of by the Apostle Paul in the Book of Romans when he said, "let God transform you into a new person by changing the way you think." (New Living Translation)

Interestingly, the Gnostic proposition that the human mind lives and functions in a self-created world of illusion, a state that only enlightenment received through Gnosis can free it from, parallels teaching in the two Eastern religions of Hinduism and Buddhism as touched on in the previous chapter. In that the Upanishads of the Hindu religion speak of this world as being Maya, a world of illusion, whilst the Buddha described the world we live in as one of impermanence, ignorance and lacking in authentic reality. Both Gnostic Christianity and Hinduism believe that the universal life force known as Atman in Hinduism and God in Christianity not only exists but also exists within every human being regardless of religious status, with the ultimate aim of both Gnostics and Hindus being to 'know' this Divine being within and recognize our existing oneness or union with it.

There are also similarities between the teaching of Buddhism and Gnostic Christianity, where both religions teach that the ultimate purpose in life is psychological freedom. Jesus teaching that as you obtain truth you shall obtain freedom. He said, "You shall know the truth and the truth shall set you free." In Buddhism Dharma is a discipline that leads to freedom. To quote the Buddha, "Just as there is only one taste in the ocean, the taste of salt, so in Buddhism there is only one taste, the taste of freedom." So free was the Buddha in his mind, being not bound up by any ego driven preferences, he was able to comfortably encourage his followers that if they so chose, they could examine other religions to compare their teachings against his, and that they were perfectly free to do so. He was not threatened in any way. The ego mind had no power over him.

This is also worthy of knowing. Whilst Orthodox Christianity, Judaism and Islam place much of their teaching emphasis on faith, (I believe and therefore I will eventually see what I am desiring come to pass), the Gnostic Christian aspires not to achieve a certain level of faith but rather a certain level of interior knowing (Gnosis), a knowing that whatsoever they desire they in fact already have, because of the indwelling omnipotent, omniscient and omnipresent presence of the Christ within. It's a psycho-spiritual knowing meant to liberate them from a spiritually unconscious sense of separation from God with its accompanying state of fear and lack, eventually transporting them beyond the boundaries of a manifest existence into the eternal light or oneness with the Godhead.

The word Gnosis itself came from the Greek word *gnostikos*, meaning, 'having knowledge'. It was a word used throughout Greek philosophical writings as a technical term for new spiritual knowledge, in contrast to a different word used for the theoretical knowledge of God, which is knowledge passed down in one form or another over the centuries from generation to generation. The Greek language distinguishes between theoretical knowledge, knowledge that pertains to information gained through learning of some kind, perhaps through a teacher or a book, and experiential knowledge, which is knowledge obtained by self-experience during the process of observational meditation, through the medium of intuition or insight occurring in the area of the psyche, and in other psychic experiences such as visions and dreams.

However for the Gnostics the visionary experience was meant to be one of an internal spiritual transformative nature and one of transcendence past personal desires. The Apostle Paul was highly regarded by the leaders of the Gnostic movement them seeing his personal visionary experience on the Damascus Road as one of redemption and believed that it should not just be classed as a miracle as many churches teach.

Paul had experienced what is known as a Gnostic incident on the road to Damascus where it is recorded in the Bible that he saw a blinding light and heard the voice of God calling to him. For the Gnostics this was a redemptive and transformative moment for Paul where he changed from being a persecutor of Christians to becoming a believer himself and a passionate advocate for Christianity.

It is no secret that there are some distinct Gnostic overtones in Paul's writings, where in talking about this incident on the Damascus road he speaks of having a type of spiritual insight into the hidden mysteries and secret wisdom of God as he was caught up into the third heaven. "Whether in the body or out of it I do not know" he said, and he spoke of "learning things which cannot be told which man may not utter." Obviously as we detect in his later teaching he experienced spiritual insight through Gnosis, which gave him a more truthful and deeper understanding of creation itself, of the mysteries of the Godhead, of the process of redemption, illumination and transformation, and of mankind's necessary willing participation, co-operation and involvement in bringing to fruition God's plan for the spiritual unification of the whole world.

Paul also used the Gnosis term frequently, which is what he was referring to when he said to the citizens of Corinth, "God has shone in our hearts to give the light of the knowledge (Gnosis) of the glory of God in the face of Christ." And to the people of Ephesus where in his preaching he said, "Till we all come to the unity of the faith and of the knowledge (Gnosis) of the Son of God." Meaning to a revelatory understanding of the mission and message of the messiah Jesus.

Gnostics were convinced that the world system was basically flawed with many Christians and non-Christians alike living a meaningless existence focused mainly on matter, on physical things that could be seen, touched and enjoyed, an existence that could only be made meaningful through Gnosis, the revelation of true reality through the discovery of spiritual truth. They felt that the ego part of the human mind creates and promotes a lifestyle that is illusionary, causing people to ignore authentic values in life, favouring instead an obsession with material gain, and that only by reaching a state of enlightenment through Gnosis can one escape this merry go round of an insatiable desire for new things and new experiences. Did that mean that all Gnostics led an ascetic monastic type of lifestyle? No not at all. They married, they raised children, they worked successfully in their chosen employment, but like devout Buddhists they regarded all these things as secondary in importance and always subservient to the inward path of Gnosis, of knowing God, and of knowing His way and His will.

Gnostics argued that the spiritual entity which created and is responsible for the flawed system we live in, and the flawed lifestyle we follow, the entity of spiritual ignorance working through and supported by the ego, is finally defeated once certain Gnosis or spiritual knowledge is accessed and experienced. They believed that the Catholic sacrament of confirmation and the Orthodox born again experience, whilst having some spiritual value and influence, held no power to truly liberate a person, or to be the 'truth that will set you free' that Jesus spoke of. But they reasoned that when a person is spiritually regenerated and re-birthed into the full consciousness of their indwelling Divine nature through Gnosis, which includes accepting as truth that we have been given the Mind of Christ, then the cosmic power to successfully support an overcoming life as a true Son or Daughter of God is fully activated, the Holy Spirit then being enabled to do Her work. This they reasoned was the true overcoming power as referenced in the Bible in the Book of Acts, in the verse, 'you shall receive power when the Holy Spirit has come upon you'.

The Gnostic terminology for what they saw as this flawed lifestyle had two separate components. The sickness of materialism was called *hyleticism,* meaning the worship of matter, and the sicknesses of intellectualism and moralising were called *psychism,* meaning worship of the mind and soul, both conditions being time consuming, energy draining and stress inducing. They believed that the role of Jesus after His ascension, through the Holy Spirit was to deliver people from these conditions by bringing new knowledge, new truth, and a greater understanding of the mysteries of God to the mind, resulting in a transformational life experience, a complete renewal of the mind's functional process, the mind's way of thinking about things or perceiving things. A person is then subsequently liberated from a compulsive and excessive attachment to the material world and reliance on it for pleasure, peace and contentment; then as this mind renewal occurs, as the rule of the soul gives way to the rule of the Spirit, as the ego mind gives way to the Christ mind, a pathway to spiritual and emotional freedom is obtained, releasing into a person's being an outpouring of the peace that passes all understanding that is referenced in the Bible in the Book of Philippians.

The Gnostics saw the resurrection of Christ, Jesus' conquering of death, as being a picture of this renewal of the mind that gives one a capacity for overcoming fear in all its forms, anxiety, worry, depression and the fear of death, taking the sting out of the thought of death, resulting in a peace filled, overcoming, liberated life experience. In many ways the Gnostic understanding of salvation or redemption again aligned itself with the overarching belief basis of both Hinduism and Buddhism, in that a person can be liberated from the shackles of a worldly purposeless or sinful existence, not by sheer willpower, but through an inner knowing of God and God's truth, or as Eastern Religion would describe it, through the process of enlightenment.

For the early Gnostics as seen in the Nag Hammadi texts, the process of self-discovery began when a person's mind contemplated those basic questions all people ask themselves at some time in their lives. What is truth? Why am I here? What is my purpose? Why is their evil in the world? Where does evil come from? Legitimate life questions you could call them that were quickly dismissed by the Catholic Church as they extolled the virtues of the church dogmas and creeds as being the only respite from a questioning mind. From the Gnostics came the retort that no organization can tell a person what spiritual path to take or by enforcing a certain path through institutionalised practices no organization can create a lasting peace for the person.

Gnostics also believed that the message of the cross was not the only purpose in the life of Jesus Christ on earth. Rather that he was also the messianic messenger sent by God to help human beings discover the cosmic and psychological nature of their lives, who they really are spiritually in their inner person, and to re-programme their understanding of their relationship to the universe and the part they play in God's plan for it. They saw Jesus as a messenger who would bring glad tidings of comfort and joy with the good news that all people, regardless of whether they are Christians or not, are in fact primarily a spirit being, temporarily living in an illusionary physical body in an illusionary physical world, and that the spark of God's essence is resident within every mind as the Christ within, wanting and waiting to be activated.

They believed that both Jesus and the Holy Spirit were sent to assist all beings in this journey by overcoming on their behalf the inimical cosmic powers contained in the workings of the ego or lower mind, the powers of self-will, the forces that prevail against all human beings in their quest to know God, thus enabling all Souls to return to the fullness of the Father at the cessation of their earthly life. Cosmic powers in the ego mind that are in fact forces of spiritual darkness, whose sole aim is to prevent the seeker of truth from rejoining the fullness of the Light from whence their Soul or psyche originally came. The Apostle Paul references these cosmic forces in his letter to the people of Ephesus where he speaks of the Christian life being a spiritual warfare, a war not against flesh and blood as for many in his day it had become during the cruel and authoritative rule of the Roman Empire, but against as he puts it, 'the powers of this dark world, the spiritual forces of evil in the heavenly realms.'

As mentioned earlier very few Christian Gnostics in the early church seemed to have any desire to establish their own church, rather they preferred to stay and worship in the traditional churches, intentionally not starting up their own organizations. To the Gnostic it was not a matter of separating themselves from other Christians, as did other groups, the important thing to them was to have a Gnostic nature you could call it, regardless of where you worshipped, a hunger for the revelatory knowledge of the Holy Spirit, who Jesus had promised would teach them all things. Some Gnostics referencing for their belief the writings of the prophet Hosea in the Old Testament, which says, "my people perish for lack of knowledge." The rightness of this decision, of staying within the established church, was perhaps rethought as they witnessed first hand the spiritual and material excesses of the Roman Catholic Church and what they saw as the unchristian behaviour and attitude of the church towards Gnostic believers or anybody else who displayed any interest in any teaching, whether scientific, philosophical or spiritual that disagreed with some aspect of Catholicism.

But nevertheless they stayed for they saw no need for organizational structure, since to them salvation was attained and the Atonement completed through Gnosis, through individualised interaction with the Holy Spirit not through church affiliation. They believed that neither a church organization nor priesthood could authorise or deny access to Gnosis as it was a process coming from the Holy Spirit to each individual's own spiritual mind, part of the ongoing Atonement process which was God's plan for the world, hidden in a mystery.

However whilst they did not see themselves as being incompatible with orthodox Christianity, over time they did begin to feel that orthodoxy through the attitude and behaviour of some Bishops was seeing itself more and more as incompatible with them. This did not deter them. They concluded that the true spiritual life with a fulfilling relationship with God could not be found as a member of a religious organizational structure alone or by adherence to man made doctrines and dogmas, that leant towards unquestioning allegiance to priestly powers in preference to the direction given by the Holy Spirit through the Christ Mind within them. Those same priestly powers of the Catholic Church that were increasingly demonstrating an unholy alliance with the grand nihilistic nature of the Roman Empire, the same empire that was built on the labour of slaves and purchased with the blood of conquered people.

The ongoing difficulty for the Gnostics however was that most of the Church fathers preferred their congregations to strictly adhere to their own Catholic brand of religion and religious ritual, and became vehemently opposed to any believer seen engaging in any teaching other than that sanctioned by the church hierarchy. We must remember that this was a time when many of the Christian Catholic churches had begun to organize themselves into structural ranks of authority, based on the ruling military structure of the occupying Roman forces. A structure with a bishop at the head followed by priests, then deacons, and with the laity positioned at the bottom of the ladder. It was a hierarchy based on the principle of separation as I described in the previous chapter. In some churches the bishop actually saw himself as a type of monarch, meaning he was the sole ruler of the congregation, increasingly demonstrating his self ordained power by being the chief disciplinarian and judge over members of the congregation.

A heretic has long been loosely defined in ecclesiastical circles as a person whose religious outlook or beliefs differ from their own. Heresy is the word used for those beliefs. In some churches for writings to be deemed heretical rather than being totally different from their accusers beliefs, they simply needed to have been assessed to be against the official or popular opinion of that church, and for an individual to be branded a heretic, they simple have to show a proclivity, a leaning towards or an acceptance of those supposed heretical writings or beliefs. The Catholic Church however took the process two steps further. They also branded as heretics anyone who emphasised too strongly in conversation or teaching some point of doctrinal difference from their own. To the Catholic church fathers regardless of whether one called themselves a Christian or not, if they were involved in any diversity of teaching within a Christian group it was the very mark of heretical behaviour. To the Catholic Church fathers the Gnostics fell into that category.

Two of the Catholic hierarchy who more than any others led the charge against so called heretical behaviour with particular emphasis on those of Gnostic inclination, were Bishop Tertullian and Bishop Irenaeus. Supported by the viewpoints of both bishops during the first few centuries after the crucifixion of Christ, the Catholic Church set about with ruthless abandon to declare the Gnostic beliefs heretical and to exterminate any followers of the Gnostic traditions. Since the Gnostics had chosen not to institutionalise their followers as the Catholic Church had, this lack of organizational structure caused them to be easily repressed by the bishops and the supportive Roman troops. The Gnostics were derided and labelled heretics by the Catholic Church, and since the punishment for heresy at that time was a tortuous death sentence, it enabled the church with the help of the Roman authorities to 'legitimately' burn all non-recanting Gnostics at the stake. In addition this period of time saw any spiritual text in relation to Gnostic thought or teaching systematically destroyed by the authorities, except for those writings that were spirited away to secluded monasteries supposedly by monks of a mystic bent, remaining hidden away for centuries until at a time of God's choosing they were rediscovered and revealed to the world.

It was self-evident that the sole aim of the Catholic Church was to create a universal theology and a universal religious belief system, and the only way that this could be achieved was by deeming heretical any other religious or philosophical way of thinking that differed from theirs, and by discrediting or removing those involved. It was an act of arrogance symbolising two things. That only those Christians who belonged to the Catholic Church and adhered to Catholic theology would receive the reward of heaven and that it would be off to hell for everyone else. And secondly making sure that their congregations fully understood that by Catholic law if any Catholic Christian strayed towards any other Christian teaching, God had authorised the Catholic Church to deem that teaching as heretical and exterminate those who chose to follow it; perhaps a way of thinking not much different from the modern day philosophy of radical Muslim extremists.

Consequently no matter how well the Gnostic tradition advanced, it was inevitable that whenever and where it emerged, so did the disdain of the Catholic Church. However every time it became evident that the Catholic Church influence on the government of France or anywhere else for that matter was beginning to wane, so we saw the subtle rise of Gnosticism again, as it, sensing a safe opportunity, came out of the shadows. But it remained out of the shadows only until it was oppressed and suppressed once again by the churches renewed influence on government and subsequent support of government. After the Roman Emperor Constantine's Edict of Milan in which Christianity was you could say legitimised by law, the Gnostic traditions and ways went decidedly underground since the Gnostics were very aware of Constantine's links with the Pope and his bishops. Subsequent to this around the late fourth century in spite of pleas for leniency by many orthodox everyday Christians, severe persecution was rendered upon the Gnostic followers of the Spanish Bishop Priscillian of Avila and others with Gnostic sympathies, making it very hard for them to survive and history did not evidence with any certainty that they did.

That was however until the twelfth and thirteenth centuries when we witnessed the rise of the Cathar Gnostics in Europe. This Gnostic revivalist movement known as Catharism which thrived in some areas of Southern Europe particularly in what is now known as northern Italy and southern France, around the 11th century, interestingly saw a secret organization rise within its ranks of which some readers may be familiar with. Known as the Order of the Knights Templar, it was a Catholic group that gained significant notoriety in the book and movie titled The Da Vinci Code. From the beginning of Catharism's inception in Europe,

Pope Innocent III attempted to obliterate the religion by persuading the local authorities to act against them, to put one last nail in the Gnostic coffin so to speak. When this and other methods didn't quite succeed as planned a military crusade was organized against the Cathars by the Pope.

In 1209 the town of Beziers was set upon becoming the final stage of the Vatican's war against Gnosticism and the Catharists. History records that when Arnaud-Amaury the Catholic Cistercian abbot monk and commander of the Pope's forces, was asked by his troops how to tell a Catholic from a Catharist since many Cathar Gnostics continued to attend Catholic church services, he is said to have replied, "kill them all, the Lord will recognize his own." Consequently in one of the definitive moments of the conflict the doors of the Church of St. Mary Magdalene in Beizers were broken down and the people inside dragged out and slaughtered. Reportedly the Catholic Church forces killed some 7000 men women and children. Elsewhere in the town thousands were mutilated and killed. Those taken prisoner were blinded, dragged behind horses and used for target practice, and what remained of the city was then razed by fire. Arnaud-Amaury later wrote to Pope Innocent III saying, "Today your Holiness, twenty thousand heretics were put to the sword regardless of rank age or sex."

Interesting to note however is that the Gnostic movement, seemingly extinguished, has always returned in some shape or form in centuries since. It was ironical that Pope John Paul 11 in a book published in 1994 admitted that Gnostic ideas were still alive and well, some being hidden under the cloak of the New Age movement. He was partly correct. It is a fact that some of what is known as alternate spirituality in the world today is related to or derives its origin from part but not all of ancient Gnostic teachings. I touched on the self-help movement and the popular discipline of visualisation in Chapter 1, however it would be remiss of me not to mention that there is a real difference between what has been accepted as new age spirituality for many years and true

Gnostic spirituality. The self-help movement is really just a quasi-spiritual supermarket using spiritually based techniques to obtain secular based results.

The new age self-help movement is mainly focused on pushing people into practicing mental processes that supposedly enable them to get what they want and keep it. Its processes are totally of a materialistic nature invoking some sort of materialistic gains. Unfortunately this new age movement teaching is a clever ruse that the ego itself uses to keep people separated from their true spiritual self. The ego's modus operandi centres on maintaining a person's sense of separation from anything Divine by focusing people's attention on an illusionary environment that shifts and changes; the world of materialism. The real you has nothing to do with this temporal changing world. The real you is immortal, invulnerable, constant and unchanging. An experience with the real you is the only thing that can bring lasting happiness and the peace that the Bible describes as a peace that passes all understanding.

Interestingly also in this modern day, in relation to the rise of anti-Muslim sentiment in supposedly Christian societies, and the idea that Christians and Muslims are incompatible, it is worth noting that even though Gnosticism is Christian in its position in the world of religion, it did in fact have a decided influence in those early centuries on the religion of Islam more so in Islamic mystical groups such as Sufism and the Isma'ilism groups. Sufism in simple terms is a way of life in which a deeper or more real identity is discovered and lived. In Sufism this deeper identity, beyond the already known personality or personhood of a person, is in harmony and at oneness with all that exists.

Gnosticism was in fact very prevalent at the time of the prophet Muhammad the founder of the Islamic religion. History tells us that many Gnostics converted to Islam, and perhaps one could relate this to the persecution they were receiving from those of the Catholic Christian faith. Muhammad was the Islamic prophet who said that Christians were responsible for removing the true teachings of Jesus, and replacing them with corrupted teachings, which by inference could refer to the Catholic Church removing the Gnostic gospels, and replacing them with creeds and doctrines. It is also worth noting in relation to this that the great Sufi master Shurawardi freely recognized both Platonism and Gnosticism as sources of his illumination. And to this very day the Gnostic element in Sufism can be clearly seen.

We live in an age when timeless spiritual ideas, which have been submerged and subdued for a long time, are making their appearance once again. Gnostic traditions along with a number of kindred ideas are being reborn at this time and will have a significant influence in the future. When Muhammed-Ali brought his mattock down on the urn that he and his brothers found near Nag Hammadi in 1945, and when the Bedouin goat herders discovered the Dead Sea Scrolls in 1947, I am certain none of those involved in the discoveries ever imagined the tremendous influence these finds would have on the household of the faithful in the decades afterwards. Had the urn been discovered some 1000 years earlier the Catholic Church would have most assuredly deemed these Gnostic texts as heretical and subsequently burned them into oblivion.

But these valuable writings came to light in the twentieth century, when with our more modern and progressive cultural experience and increased scientific and cosmological knowledge we were able to welcome them and to see them no longer as heretical and threatening, but rather esteem them as powerful new spiritual truth, truth of the Absolute kind and not the relative kind; truths that encompass ways to truly know and understand God's ultimate plan for the evolution of the human race. Truth that when appropriated will reveal a new way of thinking and believing, the Jesus way of thinking and believing. Truth that when welcomed, invited in and embraced will transport us all to our preordained cosmic destiny, our eternal oneness with God and with each other. I continue on this theme of God's Truth and what it really means in the following chapter.

"In the physical world illumination occurs as incandescent light dissipates the material darkness, in the spiritual world illumination or enlightenment occurs as the one transcendent light of the Christ transports us thru the veil separating darkness from Light into a true knowledge of himself as the Eternal Light. Jesus put it this way saying, " I am the Light of the world who takes away all darkness."

“It is in accordance with the depth and emotional intensity of a person’s belief in a particular person, circumstance, system or cause, that it, the belief, will ultimately command and control the person’s attention, their intention and move them towards their subsequent responses and actions. There is an inherent power or energy force in belief that influences, controls and directs our conscious decision making process, many times without us even realizing it, we just feel led to make a certain choice or decision.”

Truth Versus Belief and The Way of Right Perception

THREE

Giordano Bruno was born Iordanus Brunus Nolanus in the Kingdom of Naples in the year 1548. Bruno was an Italian Dominican Friar, a priest of that particular Catholic religious order that was founded around 1216. He was also a scientist and a cosmological theorist, which was the name given to a person who studies the philosophical, religious and mythical nature and structure of the universe. So you could say that as a scientist, a priest and a mystic, Bruno being involved in both the scientific world and the religious world, possessed a passion laced with a mixed curiosity for greater understanding as to how these two worlds interrelated, and what, if it exists at all, is the connection between science and spirituality? It was only slightly more than four centuries ago on February 17th in the year 1600, during what was known as the Inquisition, that the Roman Catholic Church put on trial and subsequently sentenced Bruno to death for the crime of heresy.

During the second half of the sixteenth century a series of tribunals were formed by the Catholic Pope of the day. They were formally known as The Supreme Sacred Congregation of the Roman and Universal Inquisition, eventually becoming commonly known as the Roman Inquisition. This part political part religious investigatory office of the Vatican, closely linked to the ruling Roman military, and under the Pope's authority, operated for hundreds of years. It was run by a group of Bishops well known for their cruel persecution of Jews and Muslims, but what is less widely known is that the Inquisition led by Pope Lucius the Third actually had its earliest origins or you could say cut its teeth on the cruel persecution of non-Catholic Christians in 1184, particularly the Gnostics in Europe. The tribunals were responsible for prosecuting individuals accused of a wide variety of offences mostly centred on alternate religious viewpoints, and on spiritual beliefs or scientific theories that were seen to be in any way in opposition to those viewpoints of the Catholic Church.

Historical records reveal that early one morning after eight years of imprisonment, Giordano Bruno was taken from his cell to a rectangular town square in Rome known as the Campo de Fiori, tied to a post, had his tongue laced up so that he could not address the crowd, and ceremoniously burned alive. His crime? He spoke out about the abuse of authority by the Roman Catholic Church, refused to recant his philosophical beliefs even under torture, and dared to espouse and champion the theories of Copernicus the Polish mathematician, astronomer and physician, that the sun and not the earth was at the centre of the solar system. He was executed simply because he held *'different beliefs'* from those of his accusers. In their eyes the truth as Bruno saw it was not compatible with what the church propagated as truth. It would not be until the 19th and early 20th centuries that Bruno's theories came to be celebrated by the scientific world, but not so by the Vatican, for to this day his writings are still on the list of texts that are forbidden by Vatican law to be read by those of the Catholic faith.

Bruno was not the only well-known citizen in those days executed for his beliefs. There were many other notable people who suffered for their supposed heretical beliefs during that period of time, men such as Galileo Galilei an Italian mathematician, physicist, philosopher and astronomer. Galileo was put on trial by the Inquisition in 1615, and found guilty of heresy simply because his discoveries in the field of astronomy contradicted the teachings of the church. Forced to recant his beliefs to avoid execution, which he did, he spent the rest of his life under house arrest, which was meant to limit any supposed subversive influence he might have on church parishioners or the general public. That same entity or energy force of ego driven arrogance, that brought about the deaths of thousands of innocent people during the Roman Inquisition, is still present in many of the Cardinals and Bishops in the Catholic Church today, manifesting in the Vatican in the form of cover ups and lies. It is arrogance birthed out of the Vatican's operational cornerstone, still written in Catholic law, the dictatorial doctrine of Petrine Supremacy.

The doctrine of Petrine Supremacy is a Catholic belief written into Catholic law, stating that Jesus gave the apostle Peter and only Peter, authority on earth to lead the Christian Church, and that this supreme authority was meant to be passed down through successive ages to each subsequent Pope. It also makes reference to the fact that the Pope as Peter's only legitimate successor is not only the final authority on earth, but also considered infallible, meaning incapable of making mistakes or being wrong. One would have to ask the question, "well if the decisions of the Pope are never wrong, if the Pope is infallible, then why is the Vatican in light of recently revealed child sex abuse scandals in the priesthood, currently considering reversing its age old ruling on the secrecy of the confessional and perhaps even the celibacy of the priesthood?"

We live in an age where if we pause for a moment and take the time to contemplate the world as it appears to be, we cannot but fail to come to a particular conclusion; something is wrong, something is broken. I'm not referring to us just taking a superficial glance at the individual horrific and tragic events that we read about in the newspaper daily, or see on television, many of which contain extreme elements of lack of respect and lack of humanity, but I'm talking about us taking time for introspection much more deeper than this. During the thousands of years of humankind's recorded existence terrible things have happened, particularly in these last few centuries, where we have witnessed loss of life in wars on an unimaginable scale and deliberate acts of violence and cruelty being perpetrated in so many situations with complete disregard for the value of human life.

Sadly though in many ways lifetime lessons have never been learnt. From the horrors of Germany's Holocaust to Cambodia's killing fields and Russia's Gulags, the world watched on as all manner of evil deceptively paraded itself as right and true, the world bearing witness of man's callous inhumanity to fellow man, as lives were destroyed in the name of politics, in the name of religion, and in the senseless pursuit of personal power and gain through the greed driven misappropriation of the minds, the livelihoods, and the lands of fellow citizens of the human race.

Somewhere somehow, for reasons that the ordinary person can't explain or understand, regardless of the tremendous amount of new knowledge now available to all, the fabric of this society we live in at the existential level, the basic functionality of this world we live in, seems to have lost its integrity. Without trying to be melodramatic, I believe it is fair to say that we live in a world that is in a progressive dire state of ethical malaise. A world where public trust in the political powers that govern us is waning, and a world that is becoming more chaotic and defective and increasingly insane because of a lack of fundamental integrity and wisdom at the highest levels of power. You only have to look at the various opinions that people are espousing on Twitter to see that much of society is in a progressive state of moral, mental and ethical dysfunction and decline, its thought processes, its way of thinking, functioning in a state of mid to high level ignorance and confusion.

Even in orthodox Christianity, the old behavioural influencers characterised by those religious keywords such as salvation, sin, obedience to God, love of God and love of our neighbour are losing the persuasive power they once had. Whilst for those of the Catholic faith in light of a lifetime of scandals and cover ups in the priesthood being revealed for public scrutiny in recent times, the moral and ethical legitimacy of doctrines and dogmas that have been held for centuries and vigorously defended by the church, are now being increasingly questioned by discerning everyday members of their congregations, who up until this time had been fearful of doing so. But not only this, as new hallmarks in science and spirituality from a metaphysical standpoint are being revealed and further explored, the role and purpose of organized religion itself is now in some quarters being publicly debated and seriously questioned.

We live in a world where the majority of human beings find themselves either totally controlled or at the minimum seriously influenced by potentially soul destroying systems, whether they be religious, philosophical, political or social, with one or more of these systems being involved and active in the lives of all individuals. These are secular and religious systems that in some form or another have always existed and which continue to have one strategic operating component in common with each other in order to achieve their goals. They are all focused on inducing a psychological state called *belief* in their potential followers. One of the most recognizable examples of this in more recent times being the rise of the Jihadist movement, an organization which believes that an Islamic state governing the world must be created at all costs, and that this by necessity justifies violent conflict with those who are deemed to be standing in the way.

A movement that in the first instance focuses on changing the internal belief system of potential recruits, through a network of digital and non-digital means, and having accomplished this then maintains its ongoing psychological and social grip on the recruit through a disciplined process of ongoing mental manipulation. A process that society has commonly termed brainwashing but could be better described as mind washing. The washing out of all that is good and right in a person's thinking and replacing it with all that is evil and wrong. Hitler used this process very effectively in building his Nazi Party. It is an operational platform inextricably linked to the psychological activity of *belief transference,* that centres on isolating the candidate physically and psychologically and then filling their mind with their own propaganda, which basically involves getting the victim to believe the perpetrators belief system and getting them to disregard any opposite beliefs they might have previously held.

"Why do so many people fall victims to these ideological manipulators?"

It is mostly because in general terms there exists in certain areas of society, particularly in places of social disadvantage, a subconscious sense of disconnection from the rest of society. The people targeted usually have an inbuilt subconscious psychological vacuum in their lives; you could call it a vacuum of aloneness, not necessary loneliness, but aloneness, a feeling of being all alone and disconnected from society and for some from the rest of humanity; which in terms of health and wellbeing is a dangerous psychological state of mind to get into. When this state of mind reaches extreme levels it can create a very real mentally tormenting condition commonly known as depression.

"How does this come about?"

I spoke in Chapter 1 about the dominant nature of the Ego Mind or Lower Self and I speak further on this in Chapter 7. Simply to say now that the Ego Mind is isolationist by nature and thus loves creating a feeling of isolation in a person, the "you're on your own now" feeling, which when thought about long enough and deeply enough and when mixed with social disadvantage pushes some people into a mental state that is known clinically as depression. And whilst depression in its mental manifestation is described as severe feelings of despondency and dejection, the root cause for those types of sad feelings surfacing are usually a deep sense of isolation, an overwhelming feeling of being disconnected from society in general, a feeling of being totally alone.

"Where did this psychological feeling of being disconnected that many in the world are experiencing originate?"

It surfaces out of an inherited spiritual condition, an inherited state of mind, brought about by the original psychological separation, the disconnect of the Mind of Humanity from the Mind of God in the early evolution of creation. It comes out of the original disconnect of the collective consciousness of humanity from the universal consciousness that is God, as analogised in the Garden of Eden story in the Bible. After Eden this psychological sense of being separated from the Divine has become an intrinsic part of every human beings nature. I have never really met anyone who deep down desires to be disconnected and who loves long-term feelings of isolation. Yes there are people who appreciate some alone time, but this is usually because most of their waking time is spent with someone in their face as the expression goes, and the human mind needs moments of stillness to rebalance the psyche.

Now in this modern day, in their own personal desire for entrepreneurial achievement and the monetary gain that comes with it, many astute individuals, with the dawning of the digital age, have capitalised on this aloneness or loneliness epidemic, this psychological desire a human being has not to be alone for an extended time, through web based systems such as Facebook, Twitter and even Tinder. Capitalised on a person's propensity for social isolation, for psychological isolation, and for physical isolation. Facebook being the perfect panacea for a person's desire to be socially accepted and to be liked, Twitter being their panacea for a person to be acknowledged as having some sort of societal relevance, something to give intellectually, and Tinder as the panacea for physical, emotional, sexual and relationship isolation.

These websites are not alone in their attempt to fill this psychological, this imagined void of lack that is present in the mind of society and increasing. We live in a world that has become saturated with information availability to supposedly accommodate all our needs and desires for some answers on how to fill that supposed lack, accentuated with the advent of the Internet in the late 1960's. Interestingly though no one seemed to worry too much about it when all we had for intellectual and social fulfilment was the family Sunday roast, the local theatre, the three-channel television, and an Encyclopaedia Britannica sitting on the credenza in the hallway.

Nowadays over 100 million messages are sent every minute through SMS and in-app messaging, over half a million Tweets are sent every minute on Twitter, and Facebook users click the like button on 4 million posts every minute. Along with this dramatic shift over these last few decades for increased societal interaction and connection, an explosion of desire for more knowledge and information about this universe we live in has occurred, and the internet has been right there once again ready to accommodate. Websites such as Google and Yahoo have emerged from the digital information shadows to accommodate and satisfy this hunger for more knowledge and information, where with the simple click of a mouse we can restock our minds with more useful or useless bits of information.

In this current day over 3.5 billion Google searches are conducted worldwide every minute, that's 2 trillion searches every year, and here is the point I am getting to; whilst the quantity or amount of information that we can obtain nowadays with the click of a mouse is unbelievably high, there is no ethical or moral barometer in place to measure the accuracy or truthfulness of that information, for in real time the internet is accountable to no one. It freely distributes information that is unbelievably true and it freely distributes information that is incredibly false or misleading.

Previously before the advent of the Internet, if we needed information about something we would go to the encyclopaedia if we owned a set, to find the truth of the matter, to find out what was deemed to be the *truth,* and we would usually get one or maybe two answers. Now in this current century when we go to the internet seeking *truth* about a particular subject, we find thousands of people in their subconscious desire for societal involvement have thousands of different opinions they want to share as to what they believe is the *truth* of the matter that is being discussed, and most of these internet contributors genuinely believe that their belief, what they specifically are saying is the real truth and the only truth.

"You may rightly ask then how do we differentiate between what is truth and what isn't?"

Well in terms of the ephemeral, due to the differing ideas and opinions that emanate from our individual life conditioning we can't, so I would not waste my time trying. Sure sometimes we can get what is known as a gut feel, which is an intuitive feeling, but in the main most people just fall back on trusting the information to ascertain if something is true and believable. However with the spiritual side of life, and to some degree in politics also, it can be different, because the problem is that in many situations, because of lack of knowledge, we find that people trust the man rather than the message, people trust the person rather than the information the person is espousing. And so the message becomes part of their belief system not because it is necessarily truth, but simply because the person we trust said it was. And that can be a person, or a church, or an organization, or a political party.

"So what is belief exactly? How do I know what to believe with so many things masked as truth being put before me?"

A belief is a mental attachment to some proposition or system. It has also been defined as a mental representation or state of mind positively oriented towards the likelihood of a certain something being true. Not the certainty of it being true but the likelihood of it perhaps being true. So you could say:

"Belief is the state of mind in which a person thinks something to be true whether there is or is not empirical evidence to prove that it is absolute truth with actual certainty."

You see something does not have to be absolute truth in order for you to believe it to be true, for the ego mind is quite capable of making something out of nothing, something right out of something wrong. Belief about something, whether truthful or not, is a psychological state that can be embedded into someone's personhood in a moment in time or over a period of time. This can occur culturally through tradition passed down from generation to generation in either historical or mythological form, or perhaps by simply being introduced into a person's life through exposure to new knowledge. A belief can be formed in the mind in a variety of ways all being a process of information transfer. It can surface from books or from the opinion of a person who we trust such as our early childhood teachers or our parents. A belief can be formed as mentioned previously through some sort of repetitive reprogramming process such as occurs in the Jihadist movement, and it can also be birthed into a person's mind through some sort of traumatic emotional experience.

Many of the beliefs we now hold as adults came into our lives through our parents and our teachers in our early school years. As I mentioned in the Preface it was a Jesuit priest from the Catholic Church, who famously said, "give me a child for his first seven years and I'll give you the man," meaning I will embed into his untainted mind a set of beliefs so deeply that they that will carry on and influence his actions and decisions throughout his whole adult life.

The purpose of inducing a state of belief in a person if done deliberately, particularly as pertaining to religious or political beliefs, many times can be one of complete self-interest on the part of the inducer, usually centred on their need for either personal egocentric power or personal financial gain. To cement a particular belief in a person's psyche the process usually involves targeting a need in the person's everyday life, the belief being the supposed panacea for that need, like a psychological paracetamol, helping a person to get relief and to feel more satisfied or whole in life, whether it be in the area of the physical, the emotional, the spiritual, or the social. This is the way much television and in store advertising works. It is called audience targeting, where the sales pitch targets a particular demographic in society according to what it sees as their need, a particular sector of society, either a geographical demographic, a psychological demographic, a cultural demographic, a social demographic or a gender based demographic.

Here is a simple but noteworthy example of it being used in a societal gender based demographic. Most of us would have heard that old saying, "blondes have more fun," its been around for decades. Many young women hold this as a fixed belief. Yes they may jokingly reference it in conversation, but rest assured for some it is still embedded in their psyche causing many young women to wonder if blondes do have more fun, and causing others to dye their hair blonde to try to find out. This belief came about through a woman called Shirley Polykoff. In 1955 Shirley was working at an advertising agency called Foot Cone and Belding as a junior copywriter, and as its only female employee, when she took over the Clairol account. Up until World War 11 a woman who dyed her hair was considered 'fast.' Hollywood depicted blondes as being dumb, naughty and immoral, and because of this supposedly having much more fun in life than their brunette counterparts. Successful Hollywood movies such as Gentlemen Prefer Blondes and Some Like It Hot, both starring a very blonde Marilyn Monroe, brought the movie moguls great success and of course got certain female patrons curiosity juices flowing. They were thinking, "well do they, do blondes really have more fun. Are men more attracted to blondes than brunettes?"

Shirley Polykoff had blonde hair. After meeting Polykoff for the first time, Shirley's future mother-in-law took her son aside and asked him about the true colour of his girlfriend Shirley's hair. Does she or doesn't she dye it she asked. Although Polykoff did colour her hair, the practice was not one to which women readily admitted to during the Depression, which is why the mother-in-law asked the son and not Shirley herself. The son took his girlfriend aside and told her of his mother's question, "does she or doesn't she?" and this gave Shirley a thought for an advertising campaign for Clairol. Through Shirley's provocative use of the question, "well does she or doesn't she?" and the slogan, "if I've only one life to live let me live it as a blonde" in her advertising campaigns, that featured attractive girl-next-door blonde models accompanied by children with the same hair colour, within six years 70% of all adult women were colouring their hair resulting in Shirley's ad campaign helping Clairol achieve fifty percent market share in the industry, and cementing her name in the Advertising Hall of Fame. And she did it simply by creating the belief in the minds of millions of women that "yes blondes probably do have more fun," so go out and buy some blonde Clairol hair dye and see for yourself.

Now what I say next is very important. Please think about it carefully and perhaps repeat it to yourself and dwell on it a moment:

"It is in accordance with the depth and emotional intensity of a person's belief in a particular person, circumstance, system or cause that it, the belief, will ultimately command and control the person's attention, their intention and move them towards their subsequent responses and actions. There is an inherent power or energy force in belief that influences, controls and directs our conscious decision making process, many times without us even realizing it, we just feel led to make a certain choice or come to a certain decision."

This is why belief manipulation is the major weapon in the arsenal of the adversary, the ego in the cosmic warfare that exists in life. If the enemy can convince you to believe that what you see is all there is, or what you see is reality, and that there is nothing else, you become trapped in the separation mindset that the ego wants to keep you in, preventing you from pressing forward and discovering not only the truth of how this universe works, but also the truth of who you really are and your function in the ongoing evolution of this universe. When someone attaches themselves to a particular belief or belief system over a long period of time, particularly in the area of politics or religion, the fixed mindset can become so strongly entrenched in them that for some people, even when faced with empirical evidence that contradicts the belief they accept as truth, their attitude will remain unchanged; their mind is closed to receiving new truth. We have all heard the saying 'he's got a closed mind' or 'she's got a closed mind'. There certainly is such a thing. It's a mind that has separated itself off and closed itself to anything that would attempt to interfere with its fixed belief.

"So what exactly is truth and how to we differentiate between truth and illusion?"

It is a simple fact that truth and illusion cannot be reconciled regardless of how hard we try. They are both separate components of this world of opposites this world of dualism we live in. There is no point where they can meet, blend into each other and become a combined lukewarm version of what something is. Something is either true or untrue. There is no such thing as a love hate relationship regardless of how often we carelessly use that expression. We either love or hate. We don't half love someone and half hate someone. Sure we may like or dislike some particular aspect of a person's personality or their actions, but with regards to the totality of that person's being we either love them or hate them. We are either evil or good, kind or unkind. We cannot be a half kind person or a half evil person.

The same principle applies to information. It is either true or false. No singular piece of information can be either or. It must be one or the other. The saying people use that someone is telling half-truths is wrongly expressed. A component of the whole may be true or untrue but when combined the totality must be said to be untrue not true. The totality of two parts will always be aligned with the negative aspect of the two components. Once even the slightest element of untruthfulness enters into a situation the whole situation morphs into the negative. In a relationship a person cannot be half unfaithful. They are either faithful or unfaithful. No matter how many faithful acts they have committed in a relationship once one unfaithful act occurs, in that moment, then the whole relationship becomes an unfaithful one.

Let me say unequivocally. The reason there is so much confusion in the world of religion with regards to what is truth and what isn't is because there are in fact two kinds of truth. There is *absolute Truth* and there is *relative truth,* and if we don't learn how to correctly discern between the two it can bring about poor discernment and misguided perception, leading ultimately to a lifetime of potentially wrong spiritual choices, choices that are certainly not in our best interests. Jesus, God in flesh, described Himself as the Way, the Truth, and the Life. Please be willing to dwell on the following to help you grasp it for it is very important. Absolute Truth is in fact God and only God, or you could say absolute truth is only that which proceeds from the mouth of God, that which emanates from the Christ mind within us, which is in fact God within us. Everything else is relative truth. Everything else belongs in the realm of *relative truth* because it is subject to and influenced by human ego, by human conditioning whether that be cultural or educational, by human opinion and by human belief, and in terms of religion that includes the concept that to be a member of a certain religion is the only true way to know God. Most people live lives consumed and directed by relative truth and not absolute Truth.

"So how do we find absolute Truth?"

We don't find absolute Truth, absolute Truth finds us. Let me repeat that. We don't find absolute Truth; absolute Truth, Divine Truth finds us, and that is the only sure way to obtain absolute Truth. It appears not of our own unregenerate rational mind's making. You seek it and you shall find it or more the point is that if you seek it, "it will find you". You knock and Truth opens its door to you. If we demonstrate an attitude of willingness to embrace absolute Truth, absolute truth will come to us. The Bible simply puts it this way, with God saying, "draw nigh to me and I will draw nigh to you." The Holy Spirit is the bearer, the communicative agent for absolute Truth. If we show a willingness to allow the Holy Spirit to remove untruthful beliefs from our minds, a willingness to be open to what you might describe as an ongoing process of thought correction, or Mind renewal, then God's truth, the truth that transforms will find us and set us free.

The truth that the Holy Spirit brings is the truth that Jesus was referring to when He said; "you shall know the truth and the truth shall set you free." As an act of our will if we choose to embrace only absolute Truth that proceeds from the mouth of the Holy Spirit, it does not in fact create truth but rather tears down the veil of untruth or relative truth that has kept the absolute Truth of the ages hidden from all of humanity's sight since the original psychological separation of our mind from the Christ Mind. That tearing down the veil process is referred to in the Bible in the Book of Romans as the renewing of the mind and elsewhere as the process of tearing down every argument, every opinion, and every presumption of the ego set up against the knowledge of God and bringing every thought captive to Christ's thoughts. Christ's thoughts naturally reside in the Christ mind within us.

Every thing that happens to us in life is the result of our individualised perception. Perception in simple terms is how we see things, how we look at things. All of the decisions we make in life, all the responses we make to life, all come as a result of our individualised perception or interpretation of all things brought to our cognitive sense realm, our sight, our hearing, our touch, our taste and our sense of smell. Whether or not we make the right response or the wrong response is dependant totally on how we perceive a situation. And simply said if we see things from the Holy Spirit's point of view based on the absolute Truth of God as it is, we will make the right response. If we see things from the Ego Mind's point of view we will ultimately make the wrong response.

However as we all know we don't always get it right, but if we with right intent attempt to make a response from the Holy Spirit's point of view, but in our response we have misinterpreted the way to go, there is a way out that God has by Grace provided, and it is in the following Bible verse in Romans 8, "and God will cause all things to work together for God for those who are living according to God's purpose." What does living according to God's purpose mean? It means living by every word that proceeds from His mouth, the voice of the Holy Spirit. Jesus put it this way in the Book of Matthew, "people should not live by bread alone, but by every word that comes from the mouth of God," meaning the Holy Spirit. (New Living Translation)

We are all determining what is truth and what is falsehood in every aspect of our lives on a moment-by-moment basis and we mostly don't even realise it. We all unconsciously or consciously make an immediate decision to accept something as truth or to reject it as false. Perhaps an incident, a conversation, something we read in a book or see on television, or just some advice from another, and we do this mostly in the moment, but for some with a more questioning or you could call it doubting nature, it can require more thought. We all have heard that expression, "let me think about it." The potential danger in this however, in "over thinking" something, is that the time lapse gives the ego extra time to influence our perception, to cause doubt. For it is at the time this new knowledge is in the moment entering one of our God given perceiving faculties or sense realms, truth or lack of truth consciously or sub-consciously is established.

Truth dawning on us through Divine means is the only real answer to the ego's antics. The ego has no problem with people finding intellectual answers to their questions or problems, in fact the ego thrives in the combative nature of intellectualism, the puff your own chest out way of, "well you may believe that, but this is what I think," with an emphasis on the "I". For to the ego it reinforces the principle of mankind being separated from God's truth and thus only having one way to turn, to a fellow human being's opinion or if not this then stick to his or her own opinion as to what is truth. But it is the experience of God's truth that renders the ego ineffective because it renders the principle of separation meaningless.

"So in terms of religion then, who can we trust you may rightly ask?"

The Gnostics, adherents to the ancient religion of Gnosticism, believed they had found the answer to that. They trusted that which the Holy Spirit confirmed in their heart through intuition and insight, similarly as the disciples had trusted Jesus on earth prior to His crucifixion. The Gnostics trusted the teachings of Jesus, but not necessarily all of the church's interpretation of those teachings, unless it was confirmed as truth intuitively to them by the one who Jesus said would replace Him, the Holy Spirit. To the Gnostics, communicating with the Holy Spirit intuitively was the same as having Jesus in the room. The Secret Book of John, also known as The Secret Revelation of John, is a second-century Sethian Gnostic Christian text of secret teachings. It describes Jesus appearing and giving secret knowledge or gnosis to John the Apostle. The author describes this having occurred after Jesus "had gone back to the place from which He came."

There are four separate surviving manuscripts of The Secret Book of John, three of these were found in the Nag Hammadi codices in 1945, while the fourth was found independently 50 years earlier from another site in Egypt, and all four versions date back to the 4th century A.D. The book in part tells of how Jesus' disciple John, while grieving after Jesus' death, felt the earth shaking beneath his feet and saw a brilliant light with the voice of Jesus coming forth from the light saying, "John, John, why do you doubt, and why are you afraid, for I am the one who is with you always: I am the Father; I am the Mother; and I am the Son." John then spoke of how in this comforted state he felt free to ask Jesus all the questions that had been weighing heavily on his heart and to receive consolation from this Divine Presence, which had revealed itself as the original trinity: the heavenly Father, the Son, and the heavenly Mother, the Holy Spirit.

Am I saying that according to these Gnostic writings the third member of the trinity, the Holy Spirit, is of the female gender and not the male gender as the church has long taught us? Well that is what we read in the Secret Book of John, but as we know it is not revealed in the Bible gospels, which the early Catholic Church selected to be the sole writings about Jesus to be included in the construction of the original Bible. So you intuitively be the judge. Kind of makes sense to me though seeing that Jesus referenced the Holy Spirit who He would send to replace Himself, as being "the comforter who will teach you all things." No disrespect to the male species, but that to me, the word comforter, sounds much more female than male. Women are blessed with more nurturing and comforting and instructional instincts than males, that's a fact. For the inherently curious however and others, I will talk about this in more detail later in the book in Chapter 10 The Holy Spirit, God the Mother, and the God of Wisdom.

So going back to the question who can we trust? If the Apostle John in these Gnostic writings referenced the Holy Spirit as God the Mother and the church has always followed the line that all three members of the trinity, Father, Son and Holy Spirit are male who do we trust and how can we discern truth from illusion? With so many people offering different revelations how do we know what we can trust to be truth? How can we tell truth from lies or from deliberate or non-deliberate scripture misinterpretation? Adequate knowledge, wisdom and experience are important parts of the equation but there is an added extra which one can develop and utilize.

When there is a difference of opinion between what the church historically says and what is actual truth, yes sometimes it can be difficult to discern which is correct, but it is in situations like this that the Gift of Discernment given by God to believers can help. We read in the Book of Acts that every believer has been given by the indwelling Spirit of God externally operating gifts of God' cosmic power. The Holy Spirit can manifest any one of these gifts through a believer any time She wants to. Each of these gifts are major power gifts, and the one gift that has been given to discern what is truth and what is false is the Gift of Discerning of Spirits. It is an intuitive impartation of the Wisdom of the Holy Spirit to our mind telling us what is right and what is wrong. People who know little of spiritual things are aware of its existence but will commonly refer to its manifestation as conscience, that little voice in the head that attempts to keep us on the straight and narrow. All Christians are encouraged to seek earnestly the Gifts.

More than a decade ago I visited the Island of Patmos located in Greece amongst a group of islands in the Aegean Sea near the west coast of Turkey. Patmos houses the grotto type small cave home where John the Apostle spent the last years of his earthly life, the place he did most of his writing. John, the beloved Disciple of Jesus, was banished to Patmos during the latter years of his life. When the Roman authorities exiled him to Patmos he was the last remaining member of the twelve disciples of Jesus. To enter that cave, to see the simple surroundings that bore witness to the life changing teachings written by him, to feel the intense presence there, that was enough to intuitively point me towards the likelihood of his words in reference to the motherhood of the Holy Spirit being correct, as against the words of the patriarchal Bishops, who, in true Abrahamic tradition from the get go of the formation of the Catholic Church saw no place for women except to sit in the pews, keep their heads covered and keep quiet.

With situations like the banishment of such a well respected Apostle such as John to an isolated cave home occurring, one can certainly understand at this time of extreme persecution why certain monks of a mystical disposition hid themselves in monasteries and caves in the hills, at the same time taking with them these secret writings and practices that eventually came forth through the discovery of the Nag Hammadi Codices, for what mattered most to these monks was not doctrine or creed but rather God's truth. They were not judging the value of sacred writings by whether or not they conformed to Catholic dogma, or judging Christian character by the measure it conformed to church doctrine. Christian Mystics and monks were only interested in openly exploring other traditions other than their own, to see what truth could be ascertained from them. For the same reason we see today's monks in monasteries around Europe, include in their libraries works of Buddhism and those of other religions, which I observed when I spent time in the library of the Eastern Orthodox Meteora Monasteries on top of the mountain in Central Greece some years ago. The monks were less concerned with whom to believe rather more concerned with deepening their spiritual practice and experiences similar to the Gnostics.

This arrogant self-righteous attitude of the church however, that they had it all and knew what was best for all believers, would eventually see the Catholic fathers decide it was necessary to put some rules in place in writing to keep the masses in line and hold them in a cohesive state of Catholic belief. But they reasoned, the rules and disciplines would have to be based on the word of a higher authority than their own, one that the people would not be bold enough to dispute, meaning God. And so came the catalyst for a reference book that was simply known as the Bible, the name coming from the Greek word Byblos meaning papyrus plant and the Latin Bilia meaning a collection of works and writings constituting the sacred text of scripture. But a century or more would pass without an officially recognised Bible, until the Emperor of the day Constantine began to get involved, for he too was looking for societal cohesion but his desire was politically based.

Constantine as Emperor of Rome had many things he was dealing with in his reign over the Roman Empire. He was an astute politician, a statesman of sorts, diplomatic but with a warrior's instinct, ruling over a massive conglomeration of different people of different races, different political aspirations and different religious perspectives. He realised that he needed to have a greater measure of social order and cohesion in his Empire if he was to maintain control of his position as Emperor, to ensure his political longevity so to speak. From a religious perspective there were differing Jewish groups, there was diversity of Christian groups with breakaway sects who had different ideas on how to live the Christian faith, and of course a wide variety of pagan groups. You could be a Jewish Christian; you could be a non-Jewish Christian or a Gentile, as they were known. You could be a Gnostic Christian, and you could be a Christian Mystic, or you could be just a good old-fashioned pagan.

Consequently there was no shortage of writings and religious commentary to choose from to create a "Book" that Constantine felt could be used universally by the Christian Church to subtly influence and subsequently control the masses, on his behalf, creating the long term social and political unity he was so desperately trying to achieve; and his theory was correct. So enter the Bible into the spiritual lives of humankind, the book that has more than any other been used throughout the centuries to influence and control the belief systems of humanity, not always for the right or righteous reasons, and to create or maintain a greater measure of social cohesion.

Being a book of life influencing proportions it is important that we who might look to it or parts of it for guidance and inspiration have a truth filled clear understanding of how it came into being. The following chapter The Biblical Narrative, a type of semi historical tale, will reveal to you only a small part of history's record of the evolution of the Bible, but a necessary part which I hope will provide some sort of clarity for you. For in order for humanity to have a truthful and unbiased understanding of the present, it must have a cognitive based understanding of the past.

Revered by millions, referred to as the Holy Word of God and the primary handbook for the largest religious institution in the world, the Christian Church, the Bible has a far longer evolutionary history than the space in this book permits. Nevertheless I have included all the detail that I feel is necessary for you to come to a greater understanding of this book's journey and those parts of it that are relevant to living an authentic Christian life. The historical detail in this chapter, laced with my accompanying commentary, is also given to provide some sort of guide to those who may be seeking guidance as to the legitimacy of much they have been taught in the past in the institutionalised church. I believe you will find it both interesting and enlightening.

> "We are all determining what is truth and what is falsehood in every aspect of our lives on a moment-by-moment basis and we mostly don't even realise it. We all unconsciously or consciously make an immediate decision to accept something as truth or to reject it as false."

“In order for humanity to have a truthful and unbiased understanding of the present, it must have a cognitive truth based understanding of the past. Throughout history, in terms of stifling an individual's spiritual growth, the one great weapon in the arsenal of the adversary has always been the deliberate deception of the mind, brought about by a systematic manipulation and dilution of truth to change it into ego acceptable knowledge and teaching.”

The Biblical Narrative

FOUR

Lucius Mestrius Plutarchus, was a Greek biographer, essayist, philosopher and priest, who lived in the first century A.D. In his essay The Symposiacs, he was the first person ever to pose the question that most of us would be familiar with having heard it or perhaps even having asked it ourselves during the course of our life. It was a question centred on an oft-discussed philosophical dilemma, and asked that age-old question, "which came first, the chicken or the egg?" This dilemma of course originally stemmed from the realisation that all chickens are hatched from chicken eggs and all chicken eggs are laid by an already living chicken. The chicken and the egg scenario was originally used as a metaphor, describing situations that occur in life where it is not entirely clear to the finite mind which of two associated events came first, or which sequence of actions came first.

It was a question that was quite often posed and usually associated with philosophical discussions amongst the leading minds of Lucius's day centring on the origins of mankind. The dilemma seemed to be conveniently solved to the satisfaction of most of them in the 16th century, with the Christian church's teaching on the origins of creation, in which it was suggested and accepted, that as with all other animals created by God the chicken was just one animal of the many. So therefore in the first appearance of a chicken no egg was needed. God said, "let there be a chicken," and a chicken came into existence. However, even then, supposedly enlightened philosophers and scientists of later generations felt this suggestion did not quite suffice.

In theological discussions a similar question has also been posed with regards to the collection of miscellaneous writings that came to be known as the Holy Bible. A collection of writings that you could say became a type of reference book for the early church fathers for use as supportive evidence and justification for the formulation and implementation of the doctrines, creeds and dogmas of the Catholic Church. The chicken and egg implication posed here is this, "What came first? Were the carefully and specifically select group of writings that would become the official Canon of Scripture, the Bible, chosen first, with the formulated creeds and doctrines coming out of these writings, or did the already formulated dogmas and doctrines of the Catholic Church, designed to underpin the organizational structure of the church and to control the religious agenda of the parishioners, dictate to those tasked with the construction of the Bible which writings should be included, and which writings should be rejected?"

This chapter has not been written in any way for the purpose of questioning the authenticity of those writings that were included in the book we know as the Bible, rather to look at how the Bible was put together in terms of the writings that were selected to be included, and the reasons behind some of these inclusions, and also to look at the various spiritual writings that were perhaps worthy to be included and the reasons why they were rejected and left out. Most certainly as verified by archaeological discoveries and through research over hundreds of years, the authenticity of the books that make up the Bible cannot be questioned.

Archaeologists have consistently discovered the names of government officials, kings, cities and festivals mentioned in the Bible, sometimes when certain historians and intellectuals didn't think such people or places existed. For example the Gospel of John Chapter 5 tells of Jesus healing a cripple next to the Pool of Bethesda. The text even describes the five porticoes or walkways leading to the pool. Scholars of the Bible didn't think that the pool existed, until archaeologists found it forty feet below ground, complete with the five porticoes. The Bible has a tremendous amount of historical detail included in it, and whilst not every significant place mentioned in it has been found, for those that have been found, not one as with the Pool of Bethesda, has conflicted with Biblical records.

I had the privilege some years back of visiting the ancient ruins of the city of Ephesus located in Turkey as referenced by the Apostle Paul in the Book of Ephesians. Seeing the ruins of the foundations of one of the most marvellous constructions of the Hellenistic Age, the Temple of Artemis, known as one of the seven wonders of the ancient world, brought home vividly to me the reality of Biblical history. In stark contrast news reporter Lee Strobel in commenting about the Book of Mormon wrote: Archaeology has repeatedly failed to substantiate the Book of Mormon's claims about events that supposedly occurred long ago in the Americas. I remember writing to the Smithsonian Institute to inquire about whether there was any evidence supporting the claims of Mormonism, only to be told in unequivocal terms that its archaeologists see no direct connection between the archaeology of the new world and the subject matter of the book. Archaeologists have never located cities, persons, names or places mentioned in the Book of Mormon, whilst many of the ancient locations mentioned in the Book of Acts in the New Testament have been identified without error through archaeology; in all being thirty-two countries, fifty-four cities and nine islands.

Archaeology has also refuted many ill-founded theories about the Bible. For example a theory still taught in some theological colleges asserts that Moses could not have written the first five books of the Old Testament, or the Pentateuch as they are known collectively, because writing had not been invented in his day. Then archaeologists discovered what is known as the Black Stone Stele which was a massive finger-shaped black stone pillar that had Hammurabi's Code etched on it. Hammurabi was a Babylonian king who reigned from 1792 to 1750 B.C. Hammurabi's Code was a code of laws that established rules and standards for commercial transactions and set fines and punishments applicable to anyone who breached these standards. It preceded Moses' writing by three centuries. Writing had indeed been invented. So the authenticity of Moses authorship can no longer be questioned.

For centuries and centuries books have served as not just one of the central forms of entertainment for humankind, but also as one of the most central forms for influencing and changing the belief systems and behaviour of humankind, whether socially, politically or religiously. The annals of history are littered with evidence of how certain books have reached out and impacted many lives ranging from individuals, to large groups of people, to whole nations, so that many people by reading certain mind influencing content contained in a specific book have become psychologically or philosophically changed forever. Books such as The Republic, a Socratic dialogue authored by Plato around 375 BCE, The Communist Manifesto by Karl Marx, Brave New World by Aldous Huxley, an English writer and philosopher, and On The Origin of Species by Charles Darwin.

Not forgetting a book, a two volume work written by a prisoner that became a bestseller in Germany in the 1930's, influencing the belief systems and subsequent behaviour of all Germans, going on to become a catalyst for the complicity of a nation in the worst mass murder in human history, that book being Mein Kamf by Adolf Hitler.

Further to these and from a religious or spiritual perspective we have The Qur'an or Koran, The Torah, The Tibetan Book of the Dead, The Analects by Confucius, and naturally the Bible, probably regarded as the most influential book of all time in terms of its influence on societal belief systems. With regards to its publication over the centuries, the Bible has had a colourful history. The primary biblical publication for early Christians was known as the Septuagint, which contained a Greek translation of the original Hebrew Old Testament, presumably made for the Jewish community in Egypt when Greek was the common language throughout the region.

The canon of the New Testament however was developed over time. The first translation of the New Testament was into Latin in the year 175, and by the year 600 the Gospels had been translated into eight languages. However over time with all this copying and translating occurring, we began to witness a confusing variety of scriptures circulating throughout the early church. For this reason the Pope commissioned the scholar Eusebius Sophronius Hieronymus, now commonly known as Saint Jerome, to make a definitive translation into Latin, which was completed in the year 405, and for nearly a thousand years this translation, known as the Vulgate, reigned supreme. However anyone who was not a priest was forbidden by the Catholic Church to own one of these Vulgate Bibles, as they became known.

As mentioned at the end of the previous chapter it was due to the desire and urgings of the Roman Emperor Constantine for a special book able to unify the masses and thus dismantle any potential for social unrest, that the compilation of religious writings that came to be known as the Bible came into being. To put it in modern language, Constantine wanted everybody to be reading from the same social behaviour handbook, from the same page, for being an astute politician he realised that he needed to have a greater measure of social order and cohesion in his Empire if he was ever to maintain control of his position as Emperor. There were a lot of highly ambitious military men in the Roman forces who knew how to garner societal unrest and use it for their own personal benefit in their desire to further their careers. Constantine had seen many emperors before him deposed in similar circumstances.

History tells us that Constantine had experienced a major conversion to Christianity in the year 312, reputedly seeing the sign of the cross in the heavens. You could describe it as an experience not unlike the one of that renowned persecutor of Christians Saul of Tarsus, who after his conversion later became known as the Apostle Paul. Paul had a similar experience on the road to Damascus. Eusebius the scholar tells the story that in the years following his conversion Constantine declared an amnesty for Christians, who up until this time were being severely persecuted, and Constantine himself became their imperial patron. He proclaimed recognition of what he called "the lawful and most holy Catholic Church", and ordered that anyone who had confiscated property of the church during the decades long persecution of Christians, were to return the property immediately with adequate compensation.

In this new era of government attitudinal change, bishops of the church constantly received personal letters, honours and financial gifts from Constantine, and he exempted all Christian clergy from financial obligations, taxes and other governmental charges that were incumbent on all citizens. Was all this simply a matter of a changed heart one could fairly ask, remembering that the ego of man does not simply disappear upon one's conversion to Christianity, or was there something more devious at play here? For historical records tell us that Constantine lived most of his life as a pagan, and that he only "officially" joined the Christian faith being baptised by Eusebius on his deathbed. Since Constantine's priority at the time of his 'miraculous conversion' to Christianity was in settling social unrest, was he simply greasing the palms of the Bishops so to speak, to obtain their co-operation with regards to anything that might be included in the Bible concerning obedience to lawful authorities? For interestingly we see in the New Testament quite a few specific references to a Christian's responsibility for unquestioning obedience to the governing authorities, such as in Romans 13 and Titus 3 and elsewhere.

In saying that however Constantine was not the first to see the necessity for a holy book, but for this other person, the desire was not based on a high level of worldly self-interest, and not based on the quelling of social unrest, but more so it was a desire centred around the unification of the faithful through one set of spiritual beliefs. This man, one of the early non-political pioneers of the idea to create an official collection of religious writings for church use, was not well known in the annals of history as a senior church leader, nor as an astute politician, but rather he was a little known businessman, one Marcion of Sinope. Marcion was in the shipping industry, very rich, and a generous contributor financially to the church. But he was different from most businessmen of the day in that he was extremely theological in his thinking and outlook on life. His brand of theology rejected the deity described in the Hebrew Scriptures, the God of fire, wrath and vengeance, the hurtful God you could call him, but embraced writings similar to those we see in the New Testament today, the teachings of Jesus, which depicted God as a God of love and mercy.

Without permission from the church authorities of the day, around the mid second century, Marcion set about creating his own version of a Bible, rejecting the use of the Hebrew writings that are still represented today in the Old Testament. Amongst the writings that he did include in his Bible, that also subsequently appeared some centuries later in the official church sanctioned New Testament, were most of the Epistles of the Apostle Paul and the Gospel of Luke. However it was Luke's Gospel with all its references to the Hebrew Scriptures erased. Conflicts over this emerged within the Roman Catholic Church, who disagreed with his selection, and the church excommunicated Marcion. Excommunication was a type of spiritual "go to your room and don't come out" method that the Catholic Church used to remove anyone who disagreed with them on any Catholic belief or process, whether on the teaching aspect of the church or in their creeds and doctrines. He subsequently returned to Asia Minor, a geographic region in the south-western part of Asia comprising most of what is present day Turkey, where he continued to lead and oversee many church congregations and teach from his Bible, aptly named the Gospel of Marcion.

Marcionism, the church denomination named after him, which you could describe as one of the original Christian denominations, and its adherents the Marcionites, believed that Jesus was the Saviour sent by God and they also accepted Paul to be his first Apostle. But, and this was the major point of difference with the Roman Catholic Church, they totally rejected the wrathful God of Israel as witnessed in the books of the Old Testament, in favour of the all-forgiving God, the God of love, preached by Jesus and Paul. In what you could describe as a pretty sensible argument for truth, they believed that God couldn't be both a God of love as in the New Testament, and a God of hate as in the Old Testament. That God could not be both a God of blessing and forgiveness as in the New Testament and a God of cursing and retribution as in the Old Testament. God could not be dualistic in nature and character.

In spite of his notoriety as a rebel amongst the early church leaders and their sometime derogatory description of him as the firstborn of Satan, mainly to discredit him to any who would be considering joining his church, Marcion's attempt to take charge of the production of a Bible to be used by all and not just the Catholic priesthood, became the catalyst that spurred the Catholic church leaders on, along with the urgings of Constantine, in their creation of an official, church sanctioned collection of writings, a Catholic Bible. This would be a Bible not available to all believers but only to be used by the priestly hierarchy to support their own firmly entrenched and institutionalised set of theological doctrines and creeds.

And so the will of Emperor Constantine prevailed. Around 300 years after the crucifixion of Jesus, Constantine summoned all the Catholic Bishops to his palace in Nicaea in what is today modern Turkey, at which time agreement was hammered out on which of the ancient texts were to be included in the Bible and which were absolutely forbidden. Following this around 331 A.D. Emperor Constantine wrote a letter to Eusebius the Catholic Bishop of Caesarea in Palestine that I believe may have read something like this:

"My Dear Eusebius,

It happens through the favouring providence of God that great numbers have united themselves to the most holy church in the city, which is called by my name. It seems therefore highly requisite, since that city is rapidly advancing in prosperity in all other respects, that the number of churches should also be increased. Do you therefore receive with all readiness my determination on this behalf. I have also thought it expedient to instruct your Prudence to prepare fifty copies of the sacred scriptures to be written on parchment in a legible manner and in a convenient portable form by professional transcribers thoroughly practiced in their art. Grace be with you. Sincerely, His Excellency Victor Constantinus Maximus Augustus.

Eusebius was a man who held a deep fascination for the historical past of Christianity, and by the time that the Council of Bishops met in Nicaea he had done at lot of research into church history and had himself already decided on eighteen books that should make up this holy book that Constantine was wanting to produce. In his collection he was careful not to include any of the historical records coming out of local Christian communities, particularly the peoples own personal recollections of the Jesus they knew. The primary barometer that Eusebius used in his selection was, "do these writings fit in with the emerging dogmas and creeds of the Roman Catholic church?" Of course Constantine was in full agreement with this process since the Roman Catholic Church had become Constantine's own personal vehicle for controlling the masses and thus securing his determined ambition to remain Emperor of Rome and beyond for as long as possible.

For Eusebius, if the potential books to be included did not fit in with the creeds and dogmas of the Catholic Church they were banned, and in some cases branded heretical, said branding then being written into and secured in Canon Law, so that anyone who dared to try and read or teach these texts and accept them as truth would be at the minimum excommunicated from the church, and at the maximum burned alive at the stake as a heretic. A list was also created called the Index Librorum Prohibitorum, meaning the Index of Forbidden Books. It was a list of books collated by the Catholic bishops that were forbidden to be read by any Catholic Church leaders or congregation members. It was supposedly continued until the 1960's, but is believed to still exist today. Thousands of books were reviewed over the centuries by a group of Vatican censors. In the construction of Eusebius's Bible many of the popular scriptures of the day were excluded by order of the Bishops, a lot of which were more popular in the Christian communities than some of those that were approved by Eusebius.

Books were banned that were in conflict with the Catholic Church belief that they were the only true church, as were books that promoted a scientific perspective on things, like the works of Galileo. In more recent times books such as Victor Hugo's Les Miserables has been included believing it calls into question the need to respect God ordained lawful authorities which the church sees itself as. The Catholic Church in fact sees itself as above all authority save God. And whilst in modern society the Vatican no longer has the right to execute people for going to see the stage production of Les Miserables, one could almost believe that if some of the current diehard Bishops, religious descendants of the early Catholic church fathers, still had the right to execute people for going against the will of the Vatican, then they certainly would. That arrogance of so called religious privilege still exists in the inner circle of the Vatican and in many cases flows down through the Cardinals, Bishops and Priests.

In noticeable contrast to Marcion's version of a Bible, the volume put together by Eusebius was heavily influenced by Hebrew Scriptures and was divided into an Old Testament and a New Testament. Yet it would be 40 years after Constantine's fifty beautifully rendered Bibles were delivered to the churches in Constantinople that the final number of New Testament books to be included, 27 in all, were officially canonised by the Roman Catholic Church. However these fifty Bibles commissioned by Constantine were eventually lost to time and no one really knows to a perfect degree of accuracy which books they contained. Those who say they do are merely speculating. So regardless of the fact that the Bible has come to be referred to as God's Holy Word and the infallible Word of God, we should understand that God did not write the Bible as so many Christians have been led to believe, neither did

God miraculously select the particular books that were to be included in the Old and New Testaments that compose the Bible that we have in our possession today. Nor did God decide which books were to be excluded from the Bible; all these matters were decided by the bishops at the Council of Nicaea.

For instance with regards to the Old Testament, a little known ancient text called The Life of Adam and Eve, which was a far more detailed story of creation than what we see in the Book of Genesis was excluded, but interestingly 600 years later that same more detailed version found its way into the Quran (Koran) the Holy Scripture for those of the Muslim faith. In fact Christianity, Islam and Judaism, all teach that Adam and Eve were the first humans created by God and that all humans have descended from them. Adam is also a prophet in Islam, and in the Quran, mankind is often referred to as the Tribe of Adam. So who said that Christianity and the religion of Islam have nothing in common.

Neither can we be sure of the authenticity of some of the authors of the Gospel books Matthew, Mark, Luke and John that were included in Eusebius's Bible, even though all four gospels are named after men who supposedly lived during Jesus' time on earth. Whilst tradition does consider that these men are the authors, scholars question the veracity of this for many reasons and maintain that the only book giving some reference to authorship is the Gospel of John, where at the very end of the book the author implies that the book was "written by the disciple who Jesus loved." Another point to note regarding the authorship of the New Testament books is this. The Apostle Paul was considered by many of the Roman Catholic clergy to be more influential to the masses than Jesus, and since coercive influence was in the DNA of the early church fathers, for some bishops and priests the words of Paul held an authority unlike any other theological writings at that time; so for certain bishops on the Council Of Nicaea if they were able to successfully convince Eusebius and his team of Vatican censors that a particularly authoritarian type of writing had more than likely come from Paul's hand, it increased the probability that it would be included by Eusebius in the finished Bible, the final and formal Canon of Scripture.

The word Canon in Canon of Scriptures is derived from the Greek Kanon, meaning a measuring rod or rule. The Canon of Scripture is the list of books recognized by the church to constitute the Holy Scriptures. Canons are the written rules that provide a code of laws, which includes a code of conduct, for the governance of the church and control of the faithful. So in essence the Bible, apart from its historical content, was put together with books solely selected on the basis of their suitability to be used as a type of measuring rod or rulebook for the church and subsequently a rulebook for measuring the expected behaviour of parishioners, which as well as suiting the Pope and his bishops also totally suited Emperor Constantine.

In its essence the Bible is an assembled library of documents put together after a major discussion by a group of bishops as to the eligibility of each document. A major discussion not wholly centred on the theological aspect of the individual writings, but on the political and social aspects of each one as well, meaning how they related to the social order that was needed by the Roman rulers of the day. Many books more popular than some of those included were rejected. The premise for the selection was always, "what are the right books for the people to read and what books should never be allowed to pass before the eyes of the faithful." Hundreds of writings of ancient wisdom, gnosis, knowledge of spiritual mysteries, and writings about the relationship between God and Man that existed long before the birth of Jesus were deliberately excluded from the final canon. A book titled the Infancy Gospel of Jesus by Thomas was a popular book of the day. It too was rejected, as were all the Gnostic texts discovered at Nag Hammadi in 1945.

You see the Council of Bishops were determined to create a Bible that as mentioned before would conform to the already hardening forms of Catholic creeds and doctrines, but more so in order that the church would have both a firm legal and spiritual basis for withstanding any opposing viewpoints that might emerge, not only from various other Christian groups or any non-Christian belief systems, but also from the Roman authorities themselves. Amongst the different Jewish and Christian groups at that time there were individuals writing and preaching different points of view as to what a true spiritual or Christian life is all about, but far more concerning for the church fathers was that some of these writings were teaching about what they saw was the true messianic message that Jesus came to bring, which differed to some degree from the Catholic Church version.

The attraction of these teachings was that it gave people the opportunity to experience what most human beings subconsciously desire more than anything else, freedom of thought, freedom of opinion, and freedom of expression, which in the minds of the Catholic Church and the Roman authorities was an enormous threat to their own survival. Any writings or teachings that did not conform in substance or thought to what became termed as 'orthodoxy', the beliefs and teachings and rules and regulations of the Catholic Church, or any free expression of thought that was seen as different or contrary to that of Judaism or orthodox religion could not be tolerated.

What is helpful to understand also is that when Christianity post Jesus was in its early growth stages as a movement, it was fully aware that to be seen to be doing its own thing so to speak, had the potential to raise ire amongst the ruling Roman authorities, who were spending a lot of their thinking time on alert almost in a paranoid state, for anyone who was seemingly gaining influence socially over the masses or had the potential to create some sort of alternate power base. Seeing the willingness of the Christian populace to embrace martyrdom rather than accept the tyrannical rule of the authorities tended to bother those in power. They were frightened that this attitude would catch on. Consequently when the Catholic Church component of the Christian populace realised that Rome indeed had the potential to be a threat to the church's existence and growth, the Pope and his Bishops sought to align themselves with those in power by establishing an institution, that through rules and regulations contained in their governing charter, could be seen to be supporting the authorities and encouraging others to do the same.

This they believed would ingratiate them to the Roman authorities and in doing so the Roman Catholic Church would become the only Christian group that was "legitimate" so to speak. They killed two birds with one stone you could say. They got in cosy with the ruling Roman authorities and in doing so got the government's support in dealing with any Christian groups that were teaching anything contrary to what they the Catholic Church were teaching; and because of this those Christians who sought a deeper and meaningful relationship and experience with God, drifted away from the established church into breakaway or splinter groups. Some of those of Gnostic or mystic disposition not only broke away due to the increasing pressure on them to conform, but also took with them the secret revelations and secret knowledge that they had received through the Holy Spirit, because in the face of such ongoing persecution they needed to stop these writings from falling into the hands of the Catholic Church or the Roman authorities, knowing full well that if that happened the writings would be labelled heretical and destroyed. Such is the reason many historians believe that the texts found at Nag Hammadi and the Dead Sea Scrolls had been hidden away, buried to preserve them for future generations.

You see the more the Catholic Church moved forward in its process of institutionalising itself the more political in its behaviours it became. The church felt in the beginning that it could sustain within itself and accommodate the contradictory elements of Gnostic practice, as long as the Gnostics remained within its institutional structure. However when hundreds of Catholic Christians who were seeking spiritual insights began isolating themselves in monasteries, explaining to the church hierarchy that they needed this kind of freedom to practice the contemplative meditation necessary for having visions and ecstatic experiences, the church felt that the time had come to rein them in. The terms monk and monastery coming from the Greek word monachos meaning solitude or single one. Rather than excommunicate them, which would probably have suited these monks because they liked isolation, the church in the fourth century chose to bring them into line with Episcopal authority, meaning the authoritative powers wielded by the bishops.

Some scholars have speculated that the Gnostic texts uncovered at Nag Hammadi by Muhammed Ali may have been hidden by the monks who lived in isolation at the Monastery of St. Pachomius, which is situated just a short distance from the place where the texts were unearthed. It is believed that when Bishop Athanasius, the influential Archbishop of Alexandria sent out orders for all books with any type of heretical overtones to be destroyed, the monks in that monastery who in all likelihood had in their possession writings such as those of the Gospel of Thomas, wanting to preserve them for future generations, may have hidden them in the jar that Muhammed discovered some 1600 years later.

Whilst the book purge was heralded by the church as being necessary to destroy heretical writings and protect the minds of all believers, in truth it was done solely to remove any teaching that differed from that of the church. It was a politically and religiously motivated strategic move. Hitler did something similar in order to protect his own ideological viewpoint and burned over 25, 000 books in Germany in 1933, to remove the Jewish influence from the German culture. During that book burning many irreplaceable books were destroyed including many written by Sigmund Freud, Albert Einstein and other renowned scholars and scientists.

If you look broadly at what is happening in the spiritual dynamic of people's lives in the world today, we can observe a growing return to a deeper philosophical and spiritual curiosity, since for a lot of people mainstream religion, with all its inherent hypocrisies becoming more and more visible, no longer cuts it. The dark cycle of religious control for some is over, it has run its course. Documents such as the Pistis Sophia a Gnostic text, which was discovered archeologically in 1773, and which I discuss in Chapter 10, now enables the modern seeker of truth to comprehend to some extent the nature and teachings about the Christ within as spoken of by the Apostle Paul. And not only this but also allows one to understand more clearly the hidden wisdom secreted away in parts of the Canonical Scriptures in particular the Book of John in the New Testament; the ancient wisdom that was not completely extinguished by the early Vatican censors.

As touched on previously a point to note is this. Prior to the construction of the Bible there were hundreds of other writings of note about religious and Christian matters circulating through the land, including the Epistle of Barnabas, the Preaching of Peter, the Revelation of Peter, the Gospel according to the Hebrews as well as many Gnostic texts. Those scriptures that were rejected and not included in the construction of the Bible came to be known as apocryphal, a term employed by the church fathers around the 5th century meaning they were rejected supposedly because of their doubtful authenticity, even though most of them were widely in circulation in Christian communities. So the communities thought they were authentic even if the bishops refused to accept them.

However the original word apocryphal was the Greek word *apokrupho,* describing works of literature that contained secret knowledge too excellent to be communicated to the ordinary person, and the egoistic nature of many of the bishops of the day demonstrated that they did not see themselves as ordinary people, but far superior. So one can see perhaps a more sinister motive at work in the establishment of the apocryphal collection. Maybe it was done to keep certain teachings away from non-clergy citizens. So a final question on this matter:

"Does the current Christian Bible contain all of those writings of the disciples of Jesus and of the ancient masters that were written and then passed down through the centuries?"

The simple answer: No it does not. By the year 150 A.D. hundreds of manuscripts were being written by emerging Christian leaders and would be theologians throughout the Roman Empire and beyond, purporting to tell the truth of the Christ and of God. Since then and to this day most Christians accept this small but incomplete library of ancient writings that were included in the official Word of God, the Bible. But hundreds of religious writings that early Christians considered to be true accounts of the message of Christ and of great importance to the faith were deliberately and systematically chosen to be excluded.

One such particular text that the Catholic bishops would have found disturbing if it made its way into the hands and minds of believers was The Revelation of Zostrianos, the main surviving copies of it now being stored in the Nag Hammadi Library in Cairo. It was a third century Sethian Gnostic text. The Sethians, whose name was derived from Seth the third son of Adam and Eve, were a Christian Gnostic sect. Their existence is dated back to before Christianity, and their influence was spread widely through the Mediterranean. Whilst there were many writings by early Christians giving an account of Jesus and his teachings, the nature of God, and the teachings of his Apostles and their lives, perhaps one of the things in The Revelation of Zostrianos that caused the Bishops great concern and saw them subsequently reject it, is a story centring on the human condition of doubt and fear and anxiety. The person spoken of in the story who was suffering from this condition had a direct encounter with God that did in fact set him free.

It speaks in the voice of a young male who was secretly planning to kill himself after struggling for a long time with what we would nowadays call depression and suicidal thoughts. He speaks of being determined to end his life by going out into the desert to give himself over to the wild animals for death. As he headed off he describes how he became suddenly aware of a luminous presence challenging him not to do so, and as he turned he found himself in a cloud of light, which rescued him from his state of despair. In the text he detailed the realisation he came to that the power in him was greater than the darkness without. The story is similar in terms of the involvement of an illuminating Light in it, as the stories of the conversions of Constantine and the Apostle Paul. This type of spiritual self-medication for what is in this day and age a very common ailment, depression, or this idea of God dealing directly with a person and not just through a priest was definitely not the way of church process, for only the priest was the dispenser of God's healing medication, and only the priest could communicate directly with God. So this particular writing as with many others similar to it had little chance of making its way into the construction of the Bible.

Over time the ongoing surfacing of new language translations of the Bible brought about many difficulties for the Catholic Church in its efforts to maintain a vice like grip on the Christian faith, particularly with the advent of the Bible translated into the French language in A.D. 1229, which was the catalyst for a significant event occurring. It was at a meeting of bishops at the Council of Toulouse where it was decreed that the common people, meaning those who were not priests, should not be able to read versions or copies or translations of the Bible that had not been authorised by the Vatican. The main reason for this move was this.

Around the 11th century some new beliefs had found their way into Manichaeism, a religion founded by Mani a Persian prophet and Iranian religious leader. Manichaeism taught an elaborate dualistic cosmology describing the struggle between a good spiritual world of light and an evil material world of darkness, very similar to the Apostle Paul's teaching in the Book of Ephesians. Teaching that the human person is the battleground for these powers, and that the soul, which defines the person, is under constant attack and continuously under the influence of both the powers of light and the powers of darkness. Which does align itself with the Apostle Paul's teaching that life is a spiritual warfare. Manichaeism contended that humanity after Adam and Eve was a flawed creation, the formation of which God did not take part in alone, but rather creation was formed as the outcome of a battle by the devil against God. The teaching did have overtones of Gnostic thought which no doubt upset the leaders of the Catholic Church. It thrived between the third and seventh centuries and at its height was one of the most widespread religions in the world and was briefly the main rival to Christianity before the spread of Islam joined in the competition to replace classical paganism. In the 11th century Manichaeism spread into some parts of France and Italy, into a community of believers known as the Albigensians.

The Albigensians considered themselves Christians but what made them different was their belief in the God of Light and the God of Darkness, and how this constant struggle between the two was manifest in the everyday life of all human beings. I have no problem with that as to me it is the same as the constant struggle people have between the ego mind and the Christ Mind within, as the Apostle Paul taught. A few other Albigensian beliefs that the Catholic Church disapproved of were the ban on eating meat, they were obviously vegetarians, their belief that men and women are equal, this could not be accepted in the male dominated attitude of the Catholic Church, and their refusal to submit to the unreasonable demands of the feudal lords.

As the number of Albigensian converts increased the Pope became alarmed at the spread of what he called these "heretical beliefs." The local bishops assembled at the Council of Toulouse and told the people to look for heretics in their own areas and gave the people permission that if any were found for their houses to be burned to the ground, and any bibles in their possession that were in the French language or any other non-Latin language to be taken and destroyed. One of the first incidents leading to what eventually became known as the Inquisition. So once again we see the dramatic steps that the Catholic Church continued to take to preserve their vision of Catholicism being the only true universal religion in Christianity.

However none of these things nor that which occurred in the centuries to follow could extinguish the fascination that the Bible has held for millions and millions of people since the writing of Constantine's letter to Bishop Eusebius. Of all the books ever published that have singularly influenced the course of history and changed the lives of individuals, societies and nations, none can compare to what the book known as the Bible has brought about since its original printing. It is still recognized that the Bible more than any other book ever produced has had the greatest continuing influence on world affairs ever, having done more to shape literature, history, entertainment, and culture than any other book ever written. Its impact on world history is unparalleled, and with estimated sales to date of over 5 billion copies, and continuing annual sales of around 100 million copies, it is widely considered to be the most influential and best selling book of all time.

But here is a point to note regarding our spiritual evolution. The Bible per sae as a material inanimate object has no power to either change our lives as individuals or bring us to an understanding of God's Cosmic plan for humanity. But certain writings within the Bible definitely do. The power to change our lives and give us an understanding of God's plan is hidden in a mystery within specific teachings in the Bible, particularly in the parables of Jesus and the teachings of the Apostle Paul and the Apostle John; teachings that the early church bishops in their lack of wisdom and ego driven agenda failed to detect, simply because in their selection of books they sought the advice of themselves and not the Spirit. They took on the task of constructing a book from the ego's point of view and not God's point of view.

Hidden in the words and parables of Jesus, and in the teachings of the Apostle Paul and the Apostle John, is revelatory knowledge, keys to hidden mysteries, and the cosmic nature of Christ's mission on earth, that when unlocked are meant to lead us to a deeper understanding of the true reality of not only Jesus' messianic mission and the true reality of who we are in Christ, but to also give us an understanding of the cosmic purpose of humanity that is waiting to emerge.

So regardless of which books were selected, and not only selected but for some their originality edited out and certain parts randomly overwritten to ensure that the words and teaching conformed with an already hardening Catholic Church system of creeds and dogmas, it was extremely hard for these historicising and literalising early church bishops to exclude those documents that not openly but subtly reveal that they could only have originated from the ancient wisdom writings of the pre-Christ era, the wisdom hidden in a mystery as the Apostle Paul described it; hard to totally remove all evidence pointing to the fact that many of the writings were derived from an ancient wisdom or Gnosis. Hard for these founding fathers of the biggest religious institution ever, whose successors would centuries later plunge the Western world into the profound darkness, ignorance, atrocities and superstition of the Middle Ages, to totally extinguish the Truth and Light that had always existed and that is calling all human beings to come home.

> "We must always remember that God's love and omnipresent nature is revealed not just in words in a Holy book, but witnessed more magnificently in the flowers in springtime, midst the stars on a cloudless summer night, in the early morning winter song of every song bird, all visible manifestations of the creative Mind of God."

“ “Two people have been living in you all your life. There is the ego, which is garrulous, demanding, and calculating, and there is the hidden spiritual being, whose still voice of Wisdom you have only rarely heard or attended to.

The Tibetan Book of Living and Dying by Sogyal Rinpoch

Transcendence of Thought from The Ego Mind to The Christ Mind

From the Author.

I mentioned this at the beginning of Chapter 1, but it bears repeating since at times during this chapter I will be using similar terminology as I used in Chapter 1.

When I talk about the Upper Mind and its workings I will refer to it in either of the following ways:

As the Upper Mind, as our Higher Nature or Higher Self, as the Mool Mind, as the Christ Mind, as our Intuitive Mind, as the Voice of the Holy Spirit emanating from the Christ mind or as Conscience.

When I talk about the Lower Mind and its workings I will refer to it in either of the following was:

As the Lower Mind, as the Lower Nature or Lower Self, as the Maya Mind, as the Ego Mind, as our Intellect or Rational Mind, or as the Voice of Ego at work in our minds.

FIVE

Siddhartha Gautama, also known as Gautama Buddha, also known as the Buddha, was a philosopher, spiritual teacher of meditation and a religious leader, who lived in ancient India around the 4th century B.C.E. Whilst the Buddha was born into an aristocratic family, he eventually gave up that type of lifestyle in favour of travelling throughout India, teaching that the goal of life should not be just to ascend to a state of extreme materialistic success, nor to just attain a state of extreme spiritual self-discipline, known as asceticism, but rather to achieve a state of balance between the two. He taught what was termed this middle way of obtaining happiness and peace, a way that would result in one achieving what is known in Buddhism as a state of Nirvana, a transcendent state of mind in which there is neither suffering nor desire, nor sense of the ego self. A state in which a person is released from the karmic cycle of birth, death and rebirth, and moves into a higher state of consciousness known as enlightenment.

In Buddhism Karma could be simply described as the debt we owe and have to pay back for any untoward actions we commit in life against our fellow human being, offences for which according to karmic law we must make restitution. In this religion, another opportunity to pay back our karmic debt if we die still owing it, is made possible through the process of reincarnation. Buddhism teaches that if we physically die having a karmic debt, whilst our physical body dies, our Soul which is imperishable does not die, and so returns in a new body to start a new life in order to make restitution, in order to make amends, in order to pay back our karmic debt. It may be a debt to an individual of the physical or psychological kind, or it may be a debt to society, but it is with certainty a debt flowing from some sort of attack or offense against a fellow human being.

Nirvana you could say is the final goal of Buddhism. It is the state that all Buddhists strive to attain to, and centres on achieving a new state of mind, where the thinking processes and resulting behaviours are no longer controlled by the Ego Mind, and we consequently no longer sin against our fellow man or against ourselves; which by implication means we no longer incur karmic debt. This spiritual principle of paying back a karmic debt is very similar to the principle of forgiveness as spoken of in the Bible, both designed to clear the slate of our mind, to remove all aspects of guilt from it, and to restore our spiritual standing with God. The only major difference is that Buddhism teaches that if you don't get it right in this lifetime you will have another lifetime to try again. Christianity teaches that you need to get it right in this lifetime or there are no second chances, however, and this is a big however, Jesus, while he was emphatic about the power and principle of forgiveness, neither confirmed nor denied in any way whether a second opportunity for our Soul is made available if we don't get it right in this lifetime.

There are parallels between this Buddhist process of enlightenment and the Atonement process in Christianity, in that the end result desired by both religions is that a person fully transcends out of a life lived through their ego nature and ego mind into a life lived through their God Nature and their God or Christ Mind. Whilst in Buddhism this is referred to as a life lived in Nirvana, in Christianity it is referred to as a life lived in the Spirit. Similar to Buddhism the final goal of Christianity's Atonement process, is a transcendent state of mind, a new state of mind, where through the technique of mind renewal, our thinking processes and resultant actions are no longer controlled by the Ego Mind, but aligned with the Mind of Christ. Consequently we no longer sin against our fellow man, because to sin against our fellow man would be as to sin against Christ, and to sin against Christ is to sin against ourselves.

The simple practicality of both journeys, the journey to Enlightenment in Buddhism and the Atonement journey in Christianity can be described as an individual's movement from a dualistic mental lifestyle to a non-dualistic one, from an ego driven existence to an intuitive way of life. In the dualistic mental lifestyle, which is an inherited state of being that everyone shares from the moment of birth, two spiritual forces, or you could say two cosmic energy forces jockey for supremacy, both desiring to govern and control a human being's thought processes, which in turn then influences and directs a person's behaviours and actions. These forces are referred to in spiritual writings as the lower nature and the higher nature, the lower nature being primarily the dominant and most active one in most human beings. Carl Jung referred to the operational aspects of this lower mind or lower nature as "the shadow attributes of one's personality," whilst Abraham Lincoln, a man who whilst not overtly religious nevertheless had a deep knowledge of the Bible, referred to our functioning upper mind or our active higher nature as "the better angels of our nature."

Since the beginning of time people have always had a subtle awareness of the existence of these two forces, our lower nature and our higher nature, albeit expressed more commonly by most as the struggle between good and evil, with many spiritual teachers also referring to these two opposing natures as a battle between the forces of light and the forces of darkness. The Apostle Paul when speaking to the people of Ephesus about this battle put it this way. "For we do not wrestle against flesh and blood, but against principalities, against powers, against the rulers of the darkness of this age, against spiritual hosts of wickedness in the heavenly places."

So to try and simplify our understanding of how these two natures work, let's look at them separately. Firstly we have the lower nature, or as it is called in some writings the ego or the lower mind, which is in simple terms that little voice in our head that speaks to us constantly. It is commonly known as our rational mind, the voice of supposed logic and reasoning, and spends all its time analysing and interpreting and deciphering every thought that comes before it. If the thought is just a vague mental wandering it is quickly discarded, but if it has relevance it goes through the analysing process and then is sifted through the rational mind's faculty of logic and reasoning to be dealt with accordingly. Sometimes all this can occur in a moment of time. Research confirms that a human being can have anywhere from 12,000 to 70,000 thoughts per day, and whilst a high percentage of these thoughts are repeats from the previous day, a cumulative effect, they are still an individual thought in their own right.

Included in this thinking process, dependant naturally on our level of spiritual awareness, we will see occasional input into our thought processes of the voice of our higher nature or the voice of intuition. In Gnostic Christianity this voice of our higher nature is known as the voice of the Holy Spirit, or the voice of the Christ Mind within. But for most people having limited understanding of the realm of the spirit, it is simply referred to as the voice of our conscience. Conscience is seen as that part of our thinking process that discerns right from wrong, that in fact points out how our higher nature would look at some situation against how our lower nature is attempting to get us to look at it or engage with it.

We hear people quite commonly in tricky situations use those words, "my conscience got the better of me," or "I decided to follow my heart and not my head," which basically means that even though the voice of my rational mind, my lower nature, was telling me to do this, another small voice within, being the voice of my higher nature, was whispering, "no don't do that, do this which is the right thing to do." The Bible in both the Old Testament and the New Testament describes this conscience thought phenomena as "the word of God written on our hearts being brought back to our remembrance by the Holy Spirit." This is referring to the fact that at the moment of our conception, God's laws of life, God's guidance principles, Universal Spiritual Laws you could call them, are written on our hearts, meaning embedded into our minds, into our thought processes. But unfortunately due to humankind's original psychological separation from God, recorded first in the Garden of Eden story, we have forgotten them. So the voice of conscience, that which represents our higher nature, in that moment is bringing one of God's righteous guidance principles, one of God's Universal Laws back to our conscious mind causing us to remember it.

Gnostics and Christian Mystics would see this activity of our higher nature as the voice of the Holy Spirit coming out of the Christ Mind within, guiding us and giving us God's answer in a particular situation we are facing. Jesus, in one of His final conversations with His disciples told them that when He departed He would give them the Holy Spirit, who would teach them all they needed to know, "and bring all things back to their remembrance." What did Jesus mean by all things? They are everything He Jesus had taught them, as well as the Universal Laws of God written on every human heart or mind.

In the process of Atonement or Enlightenment, we cross over or transcend to a non-dualistic thinking lifestyle, where our higher nature or higher consciousness or the Mind of Christ is active, and where our so-called rational thought based time bound existence is no longer the dominant part of our functioning life. We still use rational thinking naturally, but it is always subservient to the voice of the Holy Spirit within our upper nature, the voice of the Christ Mind within us. So in this process of transcendence we move from a state of personhood, which as explained in Chapter 1 is a life dominated by a rational thought based existence, into what is known as a life of Presence, or a Spirit led life; a life dominated by an intuitive thought based existence. We move from an ego-controlled life to a Spirit led life. The New Testament puts it this way, "and as many as are led by the Spirit of God, meaning the Holy Spirit, they shall be called the sons and daughters of God." There is no higher status in a family whether that be a physical family or God's spiritual family, than that of a son or a daughter. The immediate descendants in a family are always the first inheritors of the Father's promises and possessions.

This is what a life lived "in the Spirit" that the Bible speaks of is all about, but it is not a passive arrangement, it is an active arrangement with us deliberately involving the Holy Spirit in our lives, rather than just waiting and hoping for God to get involved. The Holy Spirit is not your tennis doubles partner sitting on the sidelines whilst you are on the court by yourself. Both of you are out on the court involved in the game of life together at all times for the whole match. This movement from a state of personhood to a state of presence is what happened to both Jesus and the Buddha in their transcendence experiences in the wilderness desert, which I speak of in Chapter 9. Both Jesus and the Buddha overcame the power and influence of their rational ego driven mind. Thought, and in particular the self-interested aspect of the thought controlled life, the lower or rational mind, became no longer the dominate driver in their lives. Sure the logic and reasoning aspect of the rational mind is necessary as an active component of our thinking process, but was never meant to be the dominant partner in our thought activity.

That is how Jesus was able to endure the physical and psychological agony and suffering He went through during His crucifixion, He had transcended the rational or lower mind. But it was not eliminated, rational thought was still functioning, but it was renewed to a state of subservience to the God Mind within Him, which was evidenced in Jesus' words, "not my will, but thy will be done." In other words, it's not about what I'm thinking, and it's not about what I'm feeling, and it's not about what I'm hoping, it's about what you God are thinking and about the Truth that you God know. Those words of Jesus were a perfect demonstration for us of an act of rational mind transcendence.

We must remember that all Christians and all Buddhists, well all people for that matter, are meant to live life in complete transcendence;

transcendence of the rational mind in our earthly life, leading to transcendence of time with regards to eternal life. This is what Jesus came to teach, this is what the Buddha came to teach. My life situation exists in time but my life exists in timelessness. My life situation is temporal, but my life purpose is eternal. The Bible says that the last thing to be conquered in our lives is the time-based event called death. Death is the ultimate act that is time based. Everything dies. As we read in the Book of Corinthians this conquering of death in his own life was celebrated by the Apostle Paul with the words, 'O death, where is your victory? Where death is your sting?" The resurrected life that Jesus ushered in after the crucifixion was a demonstration of transcendence from mortality to immortality. Time based physical death was conquered. The true message of the story of Jesus in the wilderness and his crucifixion are that first of all we must transcend the mind, as Jesus did in the wilderness and in His crucifixion, and then we can transcend the body, which Jesus demonstrated in His resurrection.

But unfortunately many Christians are not aware of this simply because the church in most cases has never really taught it. It has in fact skirted around the edges of the truth of this. The church will quote the scripture where the Apostle Paul says, "be ye transformed by the renewal of your mind, ' and where He says, "but you have the Mind of Christ", and then they will leave it at that, and the congregation is left wondering. So with nothing else to cling to they just accept that it must have happened at their confirmation or baptism, or when they got saved as the evangelicals express it. It must just automatically happen. No it doesn't. Why does the church skirt around the edges with this? I can think of two probable reasons. Either because they don't understand it themselves, or simply because to teach this is to give the individual power and a measure of self-control over their own spiritual evolution, and the church in particular the Catholic Church, is fearful of losing that control, because their whole institution, even sometimes in the most subtle ways, is based on control.

It is extremely important that as part of our individual spiritual evolution, we come to understand how life works, and not just the spiritual life, but life holistically. There are three key components that make up our humanness or state of being you could call it. They are our Body, our Mind or Intellect, and our Soul, and in using the word Soul I am referring to that inner space that houses the Mind of Christ or God's Spirit. Whilst they all have different operating mechanisms they are meant to function holistically as a three part whole, each playing their part. This is the miracle of God's creative power. To break this operational process down even further we can say that our body's operating system is Instinct, our mind's operating system is Intellect, and our Soul's operating system is Intuition. Here is how the Body's Instinct, the Mind's Intellect, and the Soul's Intuition operate, commencing with the body.

When we look closely at how our bodies operate to keep us alive and fully functioning at optimum performance, and the orderly state in which they work, it becomes increasingly difficult to hold to the theory that we are all that there is, or that our existence is the result of some big bang, and that there was no Supreme Being participating in our creation and continuously involved in every waking and sleeping moment of our lives. Years ago I did some study in the area of Naturopathic Medicine and Ayurvedic Medicine and in doing so not only learned some fascinating things about the human body, but also gained a far greater appreciation and respect, far more than I ever previously had, for this marvellous vehicle, this miracle of flesh and blood that transports us through life.

Our human bodies are spectacular complex machines composed of thousands and thousands of parts that individually play their specific role, but also work collectively with our mind and Soul, interacting holistically to maximise our potential for a positive successful and healthy life. The human body is composed of more than a hundred trillion cells, a cell being the smallest living unit of an organism, which are so small that they can only be viewed under a microscope. Cells are the basic building blocks of all living things, each cell measuring approximately 1/1000 of an inch in diameter and containing enough information within its DNA to fill 600,000 pages of a book. Cells are not all the same, but differ from each other so as to enable them to perform specific functions in different areas of our body, and operate in separate groups or clusters, which are known as tissue. There are four types of these specific groups of tissue. The *epithelial group* which provides a protective outer layer, called the skin, to protect our organs, the *nerve tissue group* which transports messages from our brain to the rest of our body by electrical impulses affecting everything from the beat of our heart to movement, the *muscle tissue group* whose muscle cells contract and relax because they receive electrical impulses from nerve tissue, and lastly the *connective tissue group* which hold the body together, for example our bones, tendons, and ligaments.

As well as this we have *organ systems* that perform specific tasks individually and collectively, such as our circulatory, digestive, immune, respiratory, urinary, and reproductive systems and others that all interact with each other every second, of every day of our lives, and it all happens with no prompting or reminder or focus from us, the whole process happens "*instinctively*". How amazing is our circulatory system, which is responsible for transporting materials throughout our entire body. It transports nutrients, water, and oxygen to the billions of body cells and carries away wastes such as carbon dioxide that body cells produce. Our body is an amazing machine that "acts instinctively" in all that it does, no matter if we are awake or asleep. Our body's instinctive behaviour cannot be questioned. It just continues to operate day in day out every year of our life, instinctively.

This is why people can survive in a coma for years and years and still stay alive. They don't have to think about what is happening it just happens *instinctively*. Our heart keeps on beating, our breath keeps on breathing, our circulatory system keeps on circulating, our digestive system keeps on digesting and our intellect is not needed in any way to give instructions to ensure all this happens. Our intellect does not have a timer set ready to announce on the hour, "hey body don't forget to breathe in and out". Our body just carries on *instinctively*, which for the average person is around 80 years or more, and the instinctive operating power stays on from when it was originally switched on at conception until our appointed time when we release our final breath.

The human body is a beautiful self-operating spiritually charged miracle, and the recognition and appreciation of the holistic operation of it has always been acknowledged by spiritual leaders. In the Book of Psalms King David continually praises his Creator for the wonderful Divine way in which he was created, and does it with a sense of awe and wonderment. The Buddha also knew the respect and appreciation we must maintain for our bodies teaching on the importance of maintaining a healthy body in order to have a strong functioning mind. Everything in our beautiful body, this Divine gift to us, goes to plan according to the 600,000 pages of coded information and instruction stored within each of its cells, and we don't even have to turn the page of the manual, it turns itself.

The next aspect of our holistic self after the body is the mind or intellect. *Intellect* is the term used to describe the operating component of our mind with the ability to reason, critically analyse and come to a conclusion about whatever is placed before it. Intelligence is supposedly the end result of the intellect in action, the conclusion or answer that comes forth. However if the answer we are seeking comes out of a flawed belief system, an illusionary belief, or in fact out of lack of knowledge, then the intelligence level of that conclusion could be regarded as not very substantial. The ancient prophet Hosea said, "my people perish for lack of knowledge."

The major difference between the operating system of the body, which is instinct, and the operating component of the mind, which is the intellect, is this. There are no performance levels with regard to instinct it will always get it right according to its blueprint as long as we in caretaking our body co-operate with Universal Law in how we treat and respect it. However our intellect working from an ego driven mind base, when given carte blanche to direct our lives, gives absolutely no guarantee of a successful life filled with love, joy, and peace. It cannot be 100 percent relied on for anything, which is really why we have instinct in charge of our bodily functions. If our intellect was in charge of our body most of us would be dead pretty quickly, because our intellect does not operate from a Divinely ordained blueprint, unless we through the process of mind renewal get it to that point. But in the meantime it is we who have created the blueprint for our intellect totally centred on our own brand of logic and reasoning.

Our intellect operates continually from a point of reference that includes every piece of human knowledge, and every human experience we have fed into it in the course of our lifetime, whether truth or illusion, those things forming our belief system which I spoke of in Chapter 3. The uncontrolled intellect is a continual disturbance to a peace filled existence, whereas the controlled intellect when used as a bridge from our intuitive thought processes, becomes a positive contributor to our lives. This is what our rational ego driven mind with its intellectual faculty was designed for, subservience not dominance, to be the servant of our life and not the master, but unfortunately for most it isn't. It wants to be king.

The main thing to understand about the intellect is this:

> "Our intellect's operational platform is fed by our past learning, our past experiences, our philosophical beliefs, our ingrained ideologies and archetypal hereditary influences, all of which form our subconscious belief system."

I will talk more about these archetypal hereditary influences further in Chapter 8.

The third component of our complete person is Intuition, the operational aspect of our Soul. To understand the intuitive nature of our Soul is the most important part of the holistic journey that we shall ever undertake. Whilst in our unenlightened state we might think that our study, our work, our career, our external success evidenced with intellectual, material and financial achievements and our relationships are the priorities in our journey of life, we must remember that all these things are temporal, they pass when our body passes, whereas the journey of our Soul is eternal in nature. Jesus spoke of this when he lovingly chastised the people asking what was it going to profit them by having all this visible external success and material excess if in the process they should lose their own Soul. Unfortunately much of humankind has over the centuries chosen to use this time, our lifetime Divinely given, not to focus on the Soul and the development of the faculty of intuition, but rather devote most of life focusing instead on the mind and it's faculty of intellect and what in return the intellect can do for them.

Intuition, in definitional terms, has been described commonly as the ability to acquire knowledge without the use of the intellect, or without the use of logic or reasoning. In most writings intuition is conceived as an inner invisible awareness of thought. The secular meaning of intuition is, "the ability to understand something without the need for conscious reasoning," with synonyms of intuition in our everyday language being words like hunch, gut feel, impression, a feeling in one's bones, co-incidence, and conscience. The English word intuition comes from the Latin word *intueor* meaning 'to see', or 'to look inside and contemplate.'

As our instinct is programmed to always get it right all the time in a normal environment likewise it is with intuition. Even if at this stage we haven't developed our capacity to use it fully, when we do use it, we will come to see that the wisdom coming forth from our faculty of intuition is always ultimate wisdom, ultimate truth, and it is unchangeable. As our body will never make a mistake and half breathe for us, and our circulatory system will never only process half our blood, nor our digestive system only digest half a meal, so too there is no such thing as God the author of our intuition getting it half-right. This is totally different from the intellect in that an uncontrolled intellect in the role of master during moments of logic and reasoning, is not concerned with ultimate truth or what is in your own best interest. The uncontrolled intellect is only concerned with the facts given it, and the conclusions that can be drawn from those facts when it moves into its rational and self-interested influenced mode of operation.

In Biblical teaching the Apostle Paul in his letter to the Romans, gives insight into the necessity for us to relegate our intellect to its rightful place as that of a servant, when he teaches the people that they should not place prominence on existing worldly knowledge in their journey of life, but rather transform themselves through renewing their mind and placing it in subjection to the Spirit. Now he doesn't say discard your rational mind and its faculty of intellect, he is indicating that the way of using it has to be revisited by us. He goes on to teach that once you renew or recreate your mind to its rightful role or function, you will then open yourself up to the Divine's perfect will and right truth for your life, which can be then maintained continuously through the voice of intuition or the inner voice emanating from our Soul.

According to renowned neuropsychologist and neurobiologist Roger Wolcott Sperry, intuition is a right-brain activity whilst the intellect, factual analysis, is a left-brain activity. From his scientific point of view he sees them as two separately functioning mind activities. In Biblical teaching reference is made to these two functioning mind activities. With the intuitive mind we see in the New Testament the Apostle Paul telling the people of Corinth, "you have been given the Mind of Christ," and when speaking to the Romans he said, "be transformed by the renewing of your mind." The Romans were obviously examples of a corrupted thinking process. Paul speaks of two minds. The intuitive mind or the Mind of Christ coming from our higher nature and the rational mind or intellect coming from our lower nature that has to be renewed to a Christ way of thinking and thus align our will with God's will. That saying, "*I'm of two minds about this*," a saying commonly used, usually indicates a situation of our intuitive mind being in disagreement with our rational mind, or our rational mind being in conflict with our intuitive mind, in a type of attack mode, as part of the spiritual warfare we are involved in.

Your rational mind was created to be the lower power working in a support function to the higher power, the intuitive mind, residing in your Soul, where the filter system, that separates truth from falsity, is the Christ Mind within you. Your rational mind was designed to be the servant and not the master. The key to living a successful life is in understanding this hierarchy of functioning, and in putting the operating process of each of them back into their rightful place. When Albert Einstein described the intuitive mind as a sacred gift, and the role of the rational mind to be that of a faithful servant to that gift, he was speaking out of his own personal experience as a scientist. Our Soul, with its faculty of intuitive thought, the inner voice of the Holy Spirit, is designed to be the final arbiter in ensuring that all the choices we make in life come from a platform of Divine Love and Divine Wisdom. The rational mind then becomes the servant of the Soul, and the practical implementer of that we need to do to turn the Soul's choice into a successful and blessed reality.

Life can be legitimately classed as a psychological warfare, a warfare between the Ego Mind of our Lower Nature and the Christ Mind of our Higher Nature. Our Ego Mind whilst carrying out an association with ourselves in terms of logic and reasoning, is in fact working with an agenda of its own, which is separate and distinct from the agenda of the Christ Mind within. It is working with an agenda that focuses on dominating and attempting to suppress the workings of our Higher Nature. By definition the ego is regarded as a person's sense of self-importance, however in psychoanalysis it is referenced as that part of the mind that mediates between the conscious and the unconscious and is responsible for reality testing. In my observation and experience the functioning of the ego has never been quite as succinct as that. In other writings this entity within an entity, our ego entity within our mind entity, has been described as one of the most self-destructive facets of a person's character that exists, and I personally believe that this is closer to the truth than the definitive psychoanalyst's understanding of what the ego is. I would define the ego as this:

> "The ego is an entity within the thinking faculty known as the rational or lower mind. It manipulates, exaggerates, antagonizes, controls, directs and exploits people and situations for its own selfish ends. Its actions can destroy the connectedness of a relationship, a family, a community, and a country, and are always prejudiced towards and in defence of its own survival."

The ego in a human being is the living personification of the principalities and powers that we wrestle with in our daily life as spoken of in the Bible. There is no such thing as a healthy ego, even though that expression is used at times to describe a person who comes across as overconfident in his or her own opinion of themselves. Our ego is an invisible entity constantly bent on self-gratification, and will adopt any mode of operation to achieve this. The ego is anti-connectedness, anti-God, and totally self-interested, having no interest in or concern about the universal interconnectedness of all things and is one hundred percent absolutely Luciferian in nature, seeking its own glory at all times. Its relationship with the working of our rational mind is based solely on it having secured the rational mind as an operational vehicle for its mission of self-interest, and this is the position it continuously operates from. It is basically always interpreting everything that happens to us through the prism of, "but how is this going to affect my position and level of control in the universe." How will this affect me? It is always alert to anything that is a threat to its own identity.

People say you are what you eat; I say you are what you think, for as Jesus is recorded saying in the Book of Luke, out of the abundance of the heart, meaning the mind, the mouth speaks. If we speak from the ego's point of view we will begin to reproduce the ego's thinking patterns in our own life situation. For instance if we continually think bitter thoughts towards a person we will become a bitter person. If we allow worry or anxious thoughts to cloud our thinking continually, we will become an anxious and fearful person. It's a simple matter; it's one of God's Universal laws, the law of cause and effect. I speak more about these Universal Laws in Chapter 11.

Ego driven thoughts, which are purely thoughts of self-interest, become both the cause and the effect and always bounce back and impact us. They don't impact the person we have bitterness towards one iota. When Jesus on the cross looked down at His tormentors and saw the anger and hatred coming forth and said Father forgive them for they know not what they do He was not just being kind. What He was saying was Father forgive them for they know not what they do to themselves.

We must remember that the ego thinks it is God as we see referenced in the Bible in the Book of Isaiah. The ego has its own counterfeit plan of salvation for the individual however it results in death not life. Your body, the source of all the ego's attention dies alienated from God and the ego wins. At the cross the ego driven crowd was focused on and driven by the concept of the guilt of Jesus whilst Jesus Himself was focused on humanity's guiltlessness in God's eyes. People indulge the body and in doing so indulge the guilt aspect of their minds. You hear people say perhaps after purchasing something expensive, "I feel so guilty about it." It is called buyers remorse. We feed guilt by holding secrets we don't want anyone to find out about. We consider it is natural to use the guilt of past experiences as a filter or reference point from which we judge the present. The use of guilt as a motivating factor for salvation is in many ways where evangelical Christianity got it wrong. They tell people to confess that they are guilty rather than guiltless and this can nullify the ongoing

Atonement process because guilt shackles us in our Atonement journey. It becomes one ongoing guilt trip as the saying goes.

One of the chief characteristics of the Ego Mind is judgement and when a human being aligns their rational mind with the judgemental thought processes of the ego, by being judgemental, it is in fact making an unholy alliance with the ego and disengaging from the holiness of the Christ Mind within. To judge someone is to consider that person unworthy, but in God's eyes every human being has been found worthy through Christ. So when a person criticises someone they are in fact judging that person to be unworthy, unworthy of being accepted and unworthy of having an opinion, which is part of the process of alienation, a characteristic of the principle of separation. When a person steals from another person they are judging that person to be unworthy of owning that thing taken. When a person kills someone they are judging that person to be unworthy of physical life. When a person gets angry with another person because of what they said, they are judging that person as being unworthy of respect or of having an opinion. The ego mind loves the antagonistic and combative method of human interaction because it reinforces the principle of separation.

A tremendous peace will come into a person's life when they set their intention to be non-judgmental and in a practical way cease to criticise or condemn. Criticism and condemnation are the active components of a judgmental attitude. A tremendous joy will come into a person's life when they set their intention to show mercy and compassion and follow through in their actions, because these two attitudes in action are a demonstration that the Christ Mind within you is in ascendancy, you are functioning from your higher nature. When we allow our lower nature our ego influenced lower mind to be the author and creator of our life we will insist on holding onto our judgemental attitude, rationalising its behaviour.

This was the message that Christ was bringing when in that moment of complete physical agony and mental anguish on the cross He chose not to be offended by what those around Him were doing to Him, but rather chose an attitude of mercy by saying "Father forgive them for they know not what they do." What Jesus was saying was that even though my body is agonising I will not allow my rational mind to dominate my thought process, rather I will align my will with that of my Father. When He said, "Father forgive them," He was advocating mercy, when he followed this the words, "for they know not what they do," He was offering no judgement.

Eckhart Tolle in his powerful book The Power Of Now said, "the ego mode of mind is dysfunctional, it is always concerned with keeping the past alive and projecting itself into the future to ensure its survival." Let me add to that and say this. Our ego is a supernatural disturbance to both instinctive and intuitive behaviour. It will, in an attempt to preserve its control base, do everything within its power to discredit the instinctive behaviour of our body and the intuitive behaviour of our Soul, to keep us as far away as possible from a successful connected spiritual relationship with the Christ Mind, at the same time doing its best to discredit and disrupt our human connections by invoking argument and disagreement, desperately trying to create a disconnect. The Bible tells us that Jesus alerted people to this truth, that the death of the ego is a pre-requisite to enable connection to the Divine within, teaching that to touch God's Kingdom we must become like little children. A little child is in a sense egoless, having not had the life experiences to cultivate and embrace this faculty to any dysfunctional degree.

Venturing into the subject of our intuitive mind and its operational process of intuition can be daunting for many people, because there is so much seemingly not known about this subject, so much mystery. The reason for this is of course due to the fact that most human beings are primarily driven by and base their lives around what we describe as the "known and the unknown". The "known" being that which can be experienced by our five senses and known and understood by our intellect, and the unknown being that which we can't experience with our senses and don't understand, but believe that some day in the future if we keep searching we will.

However the Gnostic or Christian Mystic, or someone else who pursues spiritual truth beyond the normal human experience, would say intuition would fall into the category of "the unknowable." Not the known, not the unknown, but the unknowable. To the Christian Mystic intuition happens without us knowing how and with no possibility of knowing how, it just happens. A gut feel happens and a coincidences happens, and whilst the causality of how they happen is at times a puzzle to us, if we were able to explain it intellectually we would then be bringing the intuitive process back to the same functioning level of the intellect, and it would therefore not be intuition at all.

Given the right ingredients and right measure of participation by ourselves intuitive thought will rise within us and bring the Divine's amazing grace into our lives. We don't really know how it works and we don't really have to know how it works, we just accept that it does. But if we look at what we do know, we know that if we Google the meaning of intuition it will probably describe intuition as the ability to acquire knowledge without interference or the use of reasoning. If we then looked up the meaning of reasoning, we would find that it means the ability of the mind to think and understand things in a logical way. So in combining these definitions in an attempt to bring the subject of intuition into a slightly more understood mode we could simplify things a little by saying that:

> "Intuition is the process of acquiring knowledge from somewhere else other than the mind, and does not include the use of any of the mind's mental processes including reasoning and logic."

That 'somewhere else' that it comes from is Divinity, the world of God's Spirit. The source of intuition is the Mind of God the creative life force known as universal consciousness. Intuitive thought is delivered by the Holy Spirit straight from the Mind of God." Albert Einstein, a man whose achievements made the name Einstein synonymous with the word genius, a man who possessed an unbelievable intellectual capacity and used the faculty of his rational mind to the absolute limit, was the same man who believed that no single problem he encountered could ever be solved from the same level of awareness occurring when he discovered it, meaning the level of intellectual awareness. He believed that the truly valuable faculty influencing his successful achievements and the true measure of intelligence was in using his imagination facilitated by the power of intuition.

Developing and cultivating your faculty of intuition as the master in your life can become for you the most liberating and empowering project that you have ever involved yourself in. As well as this it will bring into your life a beautiful sense of calmness and confidence that will be far superior to any self-help practice you have ever adopted in your life so far, and in addition it will take you to a higher level of self-honesty in your life. Remember all you have to do is set your intent, as the connection is already there, it is just a matter of turning the switch on. And that is as simple as making the Holy Spirit a co-conspirator so to speak in your life, talking and listening to and remembering the Holy Spirit every day of the week and not just on Sundays.

We are reminded that the intuitive aspect of our being is nothing like the intellect in that the intellect is always hell bent on driving us forward towards something. Whereas intuition, the inner voice of the Holy Spirit gently coaxes us towards God. The intuitive side of our nature, which is our upper nature, has been with us from the moment of our birth and is with us throughout our life, all we have to do is recognize its existence and release it to function. Our willingness and acknowledgement is all it needs. The intuitive side of our nature is our inherited consciousness, the intellectual side of our being is not inherited but self-created. And whilst intuition unlike the intellect does not have the capacity to grow exponentially, it does have the capacity to expand its state of awareness, but that is proportionate to the amount of co-operation and pre-eminence it is given in the everyday life of a human being.

"Intuition expanded and developed gives a person increasing levels of Wisdom, God's Wisdom, Universal Law, which can then be released into the realm of the intellect and subsequently get expressed in a human beings life through their intent and actions."

Whilst intuition and the intellect can function in a co-operative manner this liaison can only be effective if the intuitive side of our being takes the pre-eminent role. The ego controlled intellect however at times will not go quietly for its central ambition is to set its throne above that of God. The ego has one primary aim and one aim only, and that is to protect and maintain the sense of psychological separation from God that exists in all humanity. It will protect this aim by monopolising your thinking process, thus leading you further and further away from a state of oneness with God through a barrage of insane thoughts. That's how an insane person protects their thought system by adding more and more insane thoughts in an attempt to justify the preceding insane thought. That is how a clinically diagnosed insane person protects and defends their insane state, their false sense of reality, by continually thinking more insane thoughts, reinforcing that insane reality that is their life and which to them is true reality.

Christians must always be alert to the potential for a psychological blending to occur, a blending of the Christ Mind and the Ego Mind. If the ego can't get you all to itself in the first instance it will be quite happy with a blend. The Book of First Peter in the New Testament and the Book of James speak of this. It is referred to as being in a state of double mindedness, being in a state of two minds. When we become locked into this blended way of thinking our thoughts can become a mixture of opposites. We love and hate depending on which person we have in our sights, and we entertain a mixture of peace and anxiety depending on what circumstances we find ourselves in.

Then we find solace in attempting to, as an act of our will, tip the balance in our favour between these two blended opposites, towards more of that which makes us feel better. Since in terms of peace and anxiety it is peace that makes us feel better, so to tip the balance we take a holiday. To tip the balance between loneliness and emotional fulfilment we find someone to partner up with. To tip the balance between joy and melancholy we seek out fun. The problem is that tipping the balance is just another ineffective ploy of the ego mind. It doesn't last. It is just a temporary redirection of a thought pattern; it is not a renewal of a thought process.

Remember the whole mission of the Ego Mind is to help you maintain your illusionary idea of your separation from God and of course by us being that way, being psychologically separated from God, the ego sees us as providing subtle allegiance to it. That's the war tactics the entity of ego uses in its fight against God and God's representative the Holy Spirit. When we defer to the ego by allowing it to dominate our thinking process, that is all the ego really wants of us. To keep our thought processes as far away as possible from the knowledge of God and the attainment of God's Wisdom.

> "Our ego is a supernatural disturbance to both instinctive and intuitive behaviour. It will in an attempt to preserve its control base do everything within its power to discredit the instinctive behaviour of our body, and the intuitive behaviour of our Soul, to keep us as far away as possible from a successful connected spiritual relationship with God, and to discredit and disrupt our human relationships."

In his masterful book The Tibetan Book Of Living and Dying, Sogyal Rinpoche says the following: "Two people have been living in you all your life. There is the ego, which is garrulous, demanding, and calculating, and there is the hidden spiritual being, whose still voice of wisdom you have only rarely heard or attended to."

Let me assure you that as you continue to develop your communicative relationship with the Holy Spirit, as you expand and increase your present moment intuitive awareness and begin to observe the continuous chatter and clatter of your rational thought processes and quietly reject them, as you allow the Holy Spirit to actively participate in your thought life and your decision making, you will progressively hear and recognize those messages and words of encouragement that come from the Holy Spirit, more clearly and more often and receive more and more answers to all of the practical problems that you face in life; and the peace of God that passes all human understanding will be increasingly felt physically and psychologically guarding your heart and your mind.

It only requires a degree of patience, persistence and application, and you will come to know and experience what a life truly lived in the Spirit and a life truly being led by the Spirit really is, as opposed to a life lived in the flesh. You will discover that life it is not just a chaotic blend of bad things and good things occurring on a daily basis, but rather primarily a psychological warfare between the forces of Light and the Forces of darkness that bring these things to the surface of our lives occurring on a moment by moment basis. When you have discovered that you have discovered the Truth that sets you free.

"The intuitive mind is a sacred gift and the rational mind is a faithful servant. We have created a society that honours the servant but has forgotten the gift."

Albert Eenstein

“No matter how much evil tries, no matter how many people embrace its perverted logic, it can still never match up to the power and might of goodness. For whilst evil may appear to be successfully destructive in its mission for a time, it eventually becomes destructive of itself and implodes within the mind of the perpetrator, its host, as the powers of rightness raise up a standard to oppose its wrongness.”

The Origins and Nature of Goodness and Evil

SIX

Oscar Fingal O'Flahertie Wills Wilde, was born in October 1854 and died in November 1900. More commonly known as Oscar Wilde, he was an Irish poet and playwright, who after spending many years involved in different forms of writing, in the early 1890's he eventually became one of the most popular playwrights in London. Oscar is most remembered in his style of writing for the inclusion of what is known as epigrams, which are sayings or remarks or ideas that are expressed in a clever or amusing way. Some would call them witticisms. Known for his biting wit, flamboyant dress and glittering conversational skills, Wilde became one of the best-known personalities of his day. He is perhaps best remembered, apart from his notorious lifestyle, for his novel The Picture of Dorian Gray, eventually made into a movie, which centred on the circumstances of Dorian Gray's criminal arrest for gross indecency, his trial and conviction on that charge, his subsequent imprisonment, and his untimely early death at 46 years of age. Which co-incidentally was the same age as Oscar was when he passed.

In 2017 I published a 467-page work titled Lila, The Shepherd and The Wolf, which whilst being deemed fictional, did contain elements of philosophical, historical and spiritual truth. The storyline was set in the late 60's during the heyday of the hippie and new age movement, a time when the world was still witnessing the horrors of the Vietnam War. The theme of the book centred on that age old question, "is it possible to recognize evil in another person before they activate their wickedness, or is it a fact of life that those in society who have intrinsically evil natures just look and talk like everyone else, right up until their heart's intent reveals itself as their actions explode into the lives of others?" Oscar Wilde was of a similar thinking I believe in that at one time during his playwriting career after musing on the ongoing existence of wickedness and evil in society for some time he wrote, "I believe that I have never really met a wicked person, but then again perhaps I have but didn't recognize them as being wicked, because they walked and talked just like everyone else."

Someone, I can't remember who, once said when speaking of evil, that it is something that lurks like a silent entity in the hearts of men. They didn't say that evil could be seen on the faces of men, they spoke of it as an invisible force hiding in the shadowy thoughts of the mind. What is an entity? An entity is something that exists in itself but need not be of material substance. In many spiritual writings the word entity has been used to describe the two opposing spiritual forces of Angels and Demons or Goodness and Evil. In my book Lila The Shepherd and The Wolf, in a chapter titled The Two Entities, I wrote a monologue in conversational tone that might occur if the Entity of Evil was asked the simple question, "who are you, really?" As well as a separate monologue showing the contrary answer given if the Entity of Goodness its opposite was asked the same question. As a precursor to a deeper spiritual explanation of Goodness and Evil in this chapter, I share these imaginary monologues now, believing that they may give you insight into the concept of spiritual warfare and the potential practicalities of its operation, commencing first with the monologue given by the Entity of Evil.

"Hello, let me introduce myself, for I may be a stranger to you. You may not have spent a lot of time with me thus far in your life, but then again perhaps you have, unknowingly. We may have crossed each other's path in a major way or even as is more common, in a seemingly minor way. It is conceivable that you have just had some momentary connection with me, unwittingly or even perhaps deliberately; courtesy of those people you have conversed and interacted with in your journey through life thus far. Perhaps you may have been a participant in one of my well-planned and precisely orchestrated life events and given to me, even unintentionally, unwavering support and assistance in my mission. This being the case you could conclude that in achieving a successful outcome in each mission I undertake, whilst I operate through human beings, I also operate independently of them, and certainly not with their best interests in mind. It really is only all about me."

"My chronicled history of interventions and interference in the affairs of humankind as they universally unfold are extensive and expansive. They are high numerically and wide geographically. My singular goal, the end design of all my endeavours, is always to create a separation of some kind. It may be a separation physically, a separation emotionally, a separation spiritually or a separation culturally. It can happen between one human being and another, between one family member and another, between a community and another, or between a nation and another nation. But rest assured, when I go to work it will happen. For me it really doesn't matter who it involves or indeed how many, as long as separation happens, since separating human beings, either physically, psychologically or spiritually is the primary purpose of every mission I undertake. I am a destroyer of connected human emotional and spiritual relationships. Oneness and unity is not part of my agenda."

"I am sure there would have been many times in your life when you noticed my masterful work at play, evolving, influencing and impacting on the lives of individuals or groups, and you probably didn't even realize it was me. You see you only observed what was visible. You observed hurtful or tragic things happening, you gave an inner sigh, but just couldn't quite figure out the causal agent, and so any capacity or desire to care further was quickly cast aside by you, which really means you probably became overcome by the influence of one of my cohorts, the Entity of Indifference. These observations may have occurred as you read about my exploits in your local newspaper, or sat quietly following stories about me on your television or radio news programme, or on the internet, perhaps even eagerly anticipating the next instalment with a macabre sense of curiosity. Yet even though what you were reading, watching or listening to, in a way brought a certain amount of revulsion to you, some details of my work subconsciously intrigued you, causing you to raise the same subject matter again later in conversation with family or friends. You know, the conversation that always starts with, "did you hear about?" or "did you see that...?"

"Over the centuries I have been described differently by various writers and commentators, particularly those of the religious or spiritual persuasion, with many saying that I evil am pure entity. You see an entity is something that exists in itself as a separate being, but does not have a material visible appearance, it has no discernible form: you know like a spirit, or a ghost as you call them. I understand that when you human beings of a spiritual persuasion and an understanding of the cosmic nature of the world use the word entity, you are referring to an invisible energy force operating alone and separately from all other things. So yes, this is true about me, for I am not visibly obvious to those I work through or work on, but the results of my activities and handiwork are very real and very noticeable and highly visible."

"I am an isolationist by nature and love creating a feeling of isolation in my victim. That's an intrinsic part of my work. In fact the art of separating people, communities and cultures from each other whilst inflicting as much emotional and physical discomfort and distress as I can is what I am best at. So yes, being a pure entity is in fact necessary to enable me to spread my reach as far and as effectively as possible."

"Perhaps to give you a clearer picture about myself, you could liken me to a specific animal in the animal kingdom: can you guess what it is? Of course you can, it's the wolf. You see the wolf is regarded by most ethologists, those who study animal behaviour in their natural habitat, as one of the earth's most cowardly and fearful animals. Not much of a compliment for me I suppose. What is that line in the children's nursery rhyme? Oh yes. "Who's afraid of the big bad wolf, the big bad wolf, the big bad wolf," always sung in a slightly contemptuous tone by young children. Well according to the intonation in that rhyme, nobody is afraid of the big bad wolf, nobody. So why would I be likened to a wolf, or indeed be proud enough to liken myself to a wolf, if no one is really afraid of me?"

"I will tell you why. It is because of my wolf like character qualities, generally not known about and certainly not very obvious to anyone who is not a trained ethologist. Sure a wolf might be cowardly and fearful, but it is also sly and cunning, and as it is well documented, a wolf is one of the most vicious and bloodthirsty of all animals. It takes no prisoners. It is known to be the only animal that destroys as much prey as possible regardless of hunger and appetite. It is smart; it likes to manoeuvre its prey to a situation of helplessness and a feeling of hopelessness with nowhere to go and no one to turn to, trapped, with no obvious way out. Like a wolf I love to be in control. I enjoy it when my prey has seemingly nowhere to turn. Then they are completely under my control and become an ongoing participant in my persistent prosecution of a particular event I have ensnared them in. Yes think of me as a wolf, and if you like, sometimes a wolf in sheep's clothing, for deception is one of my other powerful character qualities. However enough about my comparative animal characteristics, you wanted to know who I really am, let's look more closely at me the pure entity."

"You know people do talk about me a lot, more than you think. Over the centuries I have become a popular topic of discussion with teachers and authors from a wide variety of philosophical genres, all attempting to come to an understanding of me, evil, and what motivates me to do what I do. However more often than not, whilst they have been able to touch on a few of the obvious components of my nature and activity, they have never really come to a complete understanding of the real me, of what inspires me to do what I do, or even how I became active in this role in the first place. Today scholars of social behaviour continue to describe me in many different ways: an interventionist, wicked, immoral, without conscience, and readily acknowledge the varying degrees of intensity I possess as I involve myself in the practical lives of specific people both individually and in collective society. Yes, collective society, I must say that I do like the collective approach to my work. The more people I can involve in one intervention the more satisfied I am. You could call it getting more bang for my buck."

"Some would also say that I am not gender or individual specific, but choose whichever human being I see promise in, as a vehicle for the distribution of my venom, and embrace any ego dominated candidate, someone who has the right qualifications for the job you might say, and this is true. Others say that I lie in stillness, lurking in the hearts of all men and women, watching and waiting for the ones that show great potential to fulfil my separation agenda. Yes, once again all true. But no matter what these scholars espouse when discussing my origin and intent, there are really only two beings in this universe who in total truth know why I do what I do, and how I go about selectively choosing my vehicle of operation and area of participation. Those two beings are the Divine Life Force commonly referred to by you humans as God, and of course myself."

"So you ask, what am I? Am I pure entity? Are there any others like me? How did I come to be? What is my history? Let me try and help you understand as simply as I can."

"Yes look I am an entity, a pure entity, and there are others like me but I am the first amongst equals. We are actually a group of entities working as a team; I guess you could call it a family business. We have what you might call a wolf pack mentality with all of us my siblings and myself each having a role to play in the affairs of men and women, a specific area of expertise you could call it. And yes I am an interventionist in my calling; consequently I never sit still for too long. I like to keep busy. I am always looking for a victim, and always searching for an opening to fulfil my mission of separation. Our family is very patriarchal in type, with me as its head, and also very organized with all members being given set tasks according to what I determine is the individual intensity and the level of impact needed in any singular event. The better they are at their job the more work they get."

"So who are we? What is our family name?"

"Well even though I and my fellow siblings are known, particularly in some religious organizations by our individual names based on the role each one has, our family name is universal and recognized by all humans no matter what their spiritual persuasion. It is the name used to describe us when the everyday news of singular events that we are involved in are broadcast into the living rooms of the world. Love the media. They give me so much publicity, much more than my polar opposite. It is the name people use to detail not only our activities but also to describe the character of the people we work through, those who are chosen to host our schemes and fulfil our plan. It is the name that was given to us when long ago we were birthed on our mission into this world to separate the inhabitants of this world religiously, culturally, physically and emotionally."

"Who are we? We are in fact evil, entities of evil, pure evil. I myself am the head, the first amongst equals and leading agent of this our family of evil, and I am named Lucifer. Some of you know me as Satan or the Devil, names I find slightly common to be quite honest. I am known as Lucifer in the world of spirit, and my deputy, the contact agent within each human being that I work through, is named the Entity of Ego. Ego when not on duty lies dormant within the rational mind of every human being ready to be activated. You ask who are my spirit siblings, my fellow agents of evil, those I choose most frequently to use when I make entry into the affairs of humankind, and how many of them are there? Well past scholars of my handiwork would say that they number in the area of seven. But I say seven thousand times seven. Nevertheless these academics over the centuries have mistakenly settled on seven and have named their own chosen seven as these: The Entity of Greed, the Entity of Envy, the Entity of Gluttony, the Entity of Laziness, the Entity of Anger, the Entity of Lust and the Entity of Pride. They have even given them a cute group title, the Seven Deadly Sins."

"Quaint, but in terms of the numbers and their belief that there are only seven, not quite correct. Sure each one in this group work hard at what they do. Look around at how effective the Spirit of Gluttony has been in influencing today's society. But who is best to judge the effectiveness of each individual on my team? Yes, me of course, and if asked to name my top most effective life separating and life destroying agents I would offer up these. The Entity of Discord or Disunity, the Entity of Fear, the Entity of Control, the Entity of Lies and Deceit, the Entity of Guilt and yes I agree with past writers on the other three, the Entity of Lust, the Entity of Pride and Arrogance, and the Entity of Greed and Selfishness. However I must reiterate, there are thousands more than these whose name badges are hanging on our Luciferian family tree just waiting to be summoned to their mission."

"Now as with all our interventions, once initiated, they automatically bring entry into our arena of activity of my nemesis, an entity of the Angelic kind, which like myself has also existed since the beginning of time. I am sure you would have come across it at times, the Spirit of Goodness. This interfering opposing force is in most cases not recognized as a spiritual entity and sometimes referred to by the spiritually bereft component of society as retributive justice, or karma, since it possesses the character qualities of righteous retribution and the power that comes with it. But it is in fact actually the opposing force brought into play as part of a Divine Game to prevent my family from being totally victorious in the final wash up no matter how much headway we make. Matter of fact it is the reason the phrase "goodness will always triumph over evil' was coined."

"Now whilst I personally really do not have any time for this Angelic spiritual force, my family called Evil does recognize the power of our nemesis. We continually witness these retributive justice entities, these Angelic warriors as they like to call themselves, running interference in our missions, turning our intrusions into a giant Goodness versus Evil battle for supremacy. I mean it can become a type of David and Goliath situation: a seemingly gladiatorial type of emotional and physical event involving my Goliath, my vehicle of expression, usually a self-interested, self-centred ego driven individual and my nemesis's vehicle of opposition to my work, their David, a righteous type of selfless personality with the well being of others being their foremost priority."

"But look, it's not for me to promote the existence or powerfulness of my nemesis, let them explain that for themselves."

This might be how the Spirit of Goodness explains the purpose of its existence.

"Hi, I am confident that most of you would have crossed paths with me or one of my spiritual siblings at one stage or another in your lifetime thus far. You may have witnessed us at work on one of our missions, carrying out some random act, and in doing so I am sure you would have acknowledged that what we did was nice and you may even have commented about the positive effect that we had on the life of someone be it materially, emotionally, or perhaps even psychologically. You perhaps may have even been one of those human beings used to carry out one of our missions as we sought to connect in some way with an individual or a group of people. You see we specialize in bringing happiness, peace, comfort and a feeling of safeness into a person's life or a group situation."

"Unlike our spiritual opposite, whose sole mission is to destroy, to disconnect and separate human beings from each other, our sole goal in this game of life is to maintain existing connections between individuals in society and fix those relationships that are broken. We work to prevent disconnections between people, to foster the reconnection of human beings who are separated from each other emotionally or culturally, and to propagate compassion between individual and individual, between community and community and between nation and nation. It's just what we do."

"We were spoken of in ancient times as those who bring tidings of comfort and joy, and peace on earth with goodwill to all. This was actually the proclamation given announcing the birth of our master. We are what you might call infiltrators but are interventionist by nature, which sees us as a type of spiritual warrior or as some people have more aptly described us, Angelic warriors or Angels. People also see us as a type of retributive justice, avenging Angels in the game of life you could call us, running interference for those people or groups impacted by the activities of the family of evil."

"In some cultures our work and our visitations have been given the interesting name of Karma. Our method of operation is always in all ways aligned with integrity and rightness and with what is in the best interest of those we are representing, whether that be an individual's life circumstance or a common collective cause. Sadly however, whilst our catalogue of activities in the affairs of humankind are far greater in number and more wide spread geographically than those of our opposing entities, many of our deeds go unnoticed and are unfortunately not reported or publicised with as much fervour as theirs are. Only in rare situations do we receive attention in big bold print on the front of a newspaper or as the lead story on the nightly television news. Occasionally our deeds do get a mention at the end of the news broadcast, which I suppose is better than nothing. But not being ego driven we are prepared to live with that knowing that sensationalism is just a part of the media reporting criteria."

"This may be because our work doesn't have any intriguing or unknown aspects to it. It is not open for analysis or interpretation, doesn't encourage ongoing titillating conversation, and rarely would produce divided opinions and judgments. Our missions, when accomplished and occasionally publicised, do not provoke the lingering question…why? They are just accepted as being good and right, and are usually more times than not greeted by genuine agreement from a singular observer or with positive concurrence by communities. Yes, they will say, I expected that would happen, or well I am pleased that happened, or what goes round comes around."

"So who am I? Who are we? What are we?"

"We are in fact all Angelic Beings commonly known Angels and I am the leader. I have many siblings that work hard at achieving successful outcomes on the chosen mission. I as the lead Angel am named the Angel of Goodness, and I work closely with my second lieutenant the Angel of Mercy. But my spiritual name is Michael the Archangel, and as the defender of all things pure and right my actions are the epitome of strength and courage. My agents and I intervene in the affairs of humankind protecting people from unjust attacks on their belongings and their reputations. I guard against all the effects of fear and fear based entities, and against all the negative energy forces that are behind everything that is unsavoury and evil in the world human beings inhabit."

"And yes similar to my opposite our family is all pure entity. We are Spirits, the Angelic agents of a Supreme Being following human beings wherever they go, watching over them, guarding them, and assisting them in their struggles in life. Because of this some people even refer to us as Guardian Angels. In ancient civilisations as recorded in mythological stories and in modern times in psychological circles we are seen as archetypes with our direct opposite being a shadow archetype."

"My fellow Angels and I work by receiving direction from the Holy Spirit who receives direction from the Christ Mind locked deep within the Soul of all human beings. Sometimes the Holy Spirit just works directly with the person needing assistance, through what is known as their conscience, but at times when bigger firepower is needed, we Angelic Warriors get called in to interfere with the work of the adversary and to support the victim. Our method of communicating differs completely from my polar opposite the Entity of Evil who works by directly influencing the rational mind. We are more guardians that direct influencers. It is recorded in writings known as The Psalms that a King named David, in one of his works Psalm 23 to be exact, acknowledged that myself Goodness and my lieutenant the Angel of Mercy followed him all the days of his life, guarding him, even when the dark shadow of Evil was closely lurking."

"I Michael the Archangel and my team of Angelic Warriors have been overseeing the Supreme Being's mission on earth ever since the rising up of the Luciferian family. I am both a record keeper and a manager helping human beings to discover the purpose for their lives and guiding and guarding them through life. You see time is of no consequence to me. I'll hang around as long as is necessary. The Angel of Goodness will always triumph over the Entity of Evil no matter how long it takes, so please don't be frustrated if you have cried out for our assistance."

"People may well ask how many of these Angels are there watching over humankind? I would answer thousands and thousands and tens of thousands. But the ones that seem to be most called upon are the Angels of Unity, the Angel of Courage, the Angel of Service, the Angel of Love, the Angel of Truth, the Angel of Compassion and the Angel of Kindness. The Angel of Unity to oppose the Entity of Discord, the Angel of Courage to oppose the Entity of Fear, the Angel of Service to oppose the Entity of Control, the Angel of Love to oppose the Entity of Hatred, the Angel of Truth to oppose the Lying Entity and the Entity of Deception, the Angel of Compassion to oppose the Entity of Indifference and the Angel of Kindness to oppose the Entity of Ill Will and the Entity of Selfishness."

"What is my role in the game? I choose which of my warriors I send into battle and direct them to the human they are to work through. An ancient prophet named Isaiah wrote of me saying that when the enemy, meaning Evil, shall come in like a flood, the Spirit meaning myself and my Angelic Warriors shall rise up a standard against him. You see a standard is a symbol like a flag in battle raised at a rallying point to lead a charge. Every standard has a bearer, one who raises the flag for the charge. I Michael the Archangel, the Angel of Goodness, am that standard bearer. I am he who raises the flag to lead my host of Angels into battle. I am the warrior who leads the charge into warfare against the enemy. I hope I have explained myself clearly."

Now I shared those two dialogues with you for s specific purpose. I believe that the dialogues explaining the role of these two entities probably would be totally different from what much of society has conceptualised about the role of Angels and Demons in our lives. I believe that the basic understanding of society is just that, very basic, probably simply that Angels help us and Demons hurt us. Now whether or not you believe that this dialogue is correct, whether or not you believe that Angels and Demons exist at all, does not really matter. But if we believe that the teachings of the Apostle Paul are deliberate, are true and are important, then we must believe some type of opposing entity forces exist, and that they are engaged in some sort of combative spiritual warfare as Paul expressed in the Book of Ephesians, and that the struggle is primarily for the control of the human Soul. It's all there in the Book of Ephesians so it can't be clearer than that.

However the Apostle Paul was not the only New Testament author who spoke about the existence of opposing entities involved in a cosmic spiritual warfare. The author of the Gospel of Mark did so too, totally deviating from normal Jewish tradition by not only bringing the devil into the opening part of his gospel, but by then going on to highlight the spiritual warfare component of Jesus' ministry, describing it as a struggle between God's Spirit and Satan's kingdom. However perhaps even more so than the Gospel of Mark we have the Gospel of John, which leans to a more cosmic belief in the world of the spirit, depicting life as we know it as being an ongoing battle between the forces of darkness and the forces of light.

If you look at the starting point of all four gospels Matthew, Mark, Luke and John, the Gospels of Matthew and Luke start at Jesus' conception and birth, Mark starts a bit further on in Jesus' life at his baptism, but John does the total opposite of them all. John perhaps in trying to emphasise the cosmic significance of the life of Jesus commences his gospel with words that go right back to the very beginning of the universe as recorded in the Book of Genesis, the very first book in the Old Testament. Referencing the fact that the Spirit of God was hovering over the darkness that pervaded the earth, and that in an instant the Spirit separated the light from the darkness.

Using similar terminology the Apostle John under Divine inspiration spoke of Jesus as the Light that would come into the world, to shine into the darkness that was in the world, and that the darkness would not overcome it. What was he getting at? John was taking the primordial elements separated in the original creation of the universe, the separation of the light from the darkness, and putting them into an earthly drama. He was speaking of Jesus as a similar light, a similar spiritual force, God in human form, who would take away the psychological darkness in the world, speaking of the evil potential in the rational mind of all human beings, and replace it with psychological Light, the Mind of Christ. John's words were in fact of cosmic significance. According to the Gospel of John the creative Divine Light, God's Spirit, took on form, that form being Jesus, and as God's Spirit in the beginning of time removed the environmental darkness from the atmosphere of the world, similarly God the Spirit in the form of Jesus would dissolve the darkness in the human soul or the human mind.

As we see in the Gospel of John, the Light meaning the Spirit of God in the form of Jesus came into the world to confront the darkness in the human soul, and you could substitute that with the phrase "to confront the darkness in the human mind." Jesus came not to confront the person, but rather the spirit that is influencing the person. You see this is where a lot of church teaching has got it wrong in an attempt to convince people to embrace the Christian faith. They confront the person and not the thing or entity that is influencing or possessing the person, the controlling ego that has taken over a person's life. And the tactics the church uses to do this are fear and guilt, guilt for the person's behaviour and fear of eternal punishment. When God looks on a person God does not see an evil person, God sees one of His creations that needs to come to an understanding of eternal truth. Ancient Christians of Gnostic and Mystic disposition understood this and thus had one aim and one aim only. Not to convert people and get them to join a church, but to enable or equip them to gain a greater understanding of the cosmic nature of our existence.

Terrible things do happen, and as history has evidenced over the last couple of centuries yes evil and horror does seem to exist and suffering is universal. Some individuals obviously of evil intent and often in positions of power do torment and kill others on a daily basis. Moreover terrible things also happen that are not caused by human beings such as earthquakes, fires, floods and famine. So whilst the perversities of human nature are responsible for some of the suffering in this world not all suffering is the result of evil human behaviour contrary to what some ideologically driven people will propagate to fulfil their own personal agenda or to accommodate their own personal sense of aggrievement. And whilst these propagators get a personal sense of fulfilment in espousing these claims as they use collective guilt as a weapon for their cause, for example making out human beings to be the sole destroyers of the environment, the cultivation of guilt is no remedy for evil. This merely drives people into defence or opposition mode and prolongs the evolution of a right course of action.

Carl Jung the well known Swiss psychiatrist and psychoanalyst, a man known to be a Gnostic sympathiser, spent his whole life totally devoted to analysing this darkness within the minds of his patients, in the hope that by doing so he would find a way to lead them out of their prison of darkness into the freedom of light; that he would find a way to remove the darkness from their mind and so bring them peace and happiness. He saw himself as a healer, a healer of the Soul as he expressed it. However during that period of time that Jung was looking at finding psychological freedom for his patients, once again as in centuries past, the institutionalised church raised its condemnatory head to oppose him. As Jung progressively published papers on his discoveries, he was met with much opposition from the theologians of the day who differed from his views.

Church leaders emerging from their heresy chasing hibernation began attempting to refute Jung's findings saying that he was of the devil and that the darkness in a person's Soul could only be removed from a person's mind through the blood of Christ, a theory that Jung found quite fanciful. Jung in speaking of Jesus went on to say, "On the level of the Son there is no answer to the question of good and evil; there is only an incurable separation of the opposites. It seems to me the Holy Spirit's task and charge is to reconcile and reunite those opposites in the human individual through a special development of the human soul." Who was right? Was Jung right, were the theologians right, were the church leaders right, or did they all possess a certain measure of truth in what they believed and espoused. I share my thoughts on this and other aspects of Jung's life quest in the following chapter.

Gnostics have always believed that human beings are in truth spirits temporarily inhabiting a physical body in a physical world, and that owing to the indwelling spirit, pneuma, deeply imbedded in our physical and psychic selves, we are capable of responding solely to the Divine Wisdom and love that comes to us in moments of significant physical emotional upheaval, you could call them evil moments or moments of momentary madness, rather than responding to the activity occurring in the flawed moment that we find ourselves physically in. That we are able to, by our own choice, transcend the evil urgings and transition to a higher level of righteousness or right-mindedness. When we transcend the evil moment we thus transcend the world, which is what Jesus was encouraging us to do when He said, "be in the world, but not of the world."

So in relation to this matter of the existence of evil in the world and how we in our own way might understand it, if we look at it from a cosmological and psychological point of view, the existence of evil in the world and its ongoing operation can only be contained by the application of human self-will. In other words in order for someone to "not carry out" an evil act they must as an act of their will choose not to participate in the evil act. That being case the only point at which a potential evil act can be deterred from coming to fruition is at that point in which the thought of committing that act enters into the thinking process. This rubbish that the courts are increasingly entertaining in defence of deliberate perpetrators of an evil deed that the offence was committed whilst the person was under the influence of alcohol or a drug is just that, rubbish. Evil is the base intent in the person's mind and takes up its position regardless of whether a person is drunk or sober. The ability of evil to influence a person's thought process and bring about harm to a fellow member of the human race can only be due to the fact that the root cause of evil is of a cosmological nature which influences humankind's psychological nature and then through willing co-operation of an individual or a collective an evil act comes to fruition.

The Gnostic's opinion of the origin and nature of evil was just that, pure and simple, that the foundation of evil is supernatural and spiritual rather than naturalistic, sociological or economic. That the origin of evil is in fact, in the words of Paul the Apostle, " spiritual wickedness in high places," and that evil intent is about unholy psychological influences that can either be embraced or rejected by us as an act of our Holy Spirit supported will; meaning only spiritual means which include higher levels of collective consciousness can contain it. Which pretty much aligns with Carl Jung's thoughts on the matter.

> "Much of the evil in the world is due to the fact that man in general is hopelessly unconscious."
>
> Carl Jung

“In times of collective turmoil and crisis a powerful force will always arrive at the right time to help. A force of the Universal Consciousness that powers everyone, sometimes through suffering, into a positive unknown, transitioning them to a new and higher level of psychological existence, a higher state of consciousness. It is a cosmic force that as the saying goes “brings out the best in people.” Opposing this we will always witness a cosmic force of an opposite and antagonistic nature, a force that as the saying goes “brings out the worst in people.”

Jung and the Collective Unconscious Archetypes, Myths and Mysteries

SEVEN

Carl Gustav Jung was a Swiss psychiatrist and psychoanalyst, recognized as the founder of what is known as analytical psychology. He was born in July 1875 and passed away on 6th June 1961, aged 86 years. Analytical psychology is the theory of psychoanalysis that focuses on the concept of the existence of a collective unconscious, and the importance of balancing opposing forces within the personality that emanate from this collective unconscious. The concept of the collective unconscious sometimes called the objective psyche refers to the idea that a segment of the deepest unconscious mind is genetically inherited, and is not shaped by personal experience as so many aspects of our personalities are. According to Jung's teachings the collective unconscious is common to all human beings, and is responsible for a number of deep-seated beliefs and instincts including spirituality, sexual behaviour and life or death instincts, which in turn are drives that lead to specific patterns of behaviour in life.

Carl Jung brought to the world what you could say was an almost mystical approach to analytical psychology. For a while he was a close associate of Sigmund Freud the notable Austrian neurologist of his day, but over time with disagreements arising on a lot of Freud's theories on the functioning of the personality, Jung chose not to remain with Freudianism but rather carve a separate path for himself. He subsequently developed his own set of theories, a blending of the natural laws of physics with psychological functioning. He also introduced concepts surrounding the different personality types in society, some of his most notable work being done regarding the role of archetypal influences in the psychological constructs of a human being's mind. Having always been controversial as seen in the papers he published, he further alienated himself from the rest of his psychiatry brethren with his leaning towards a blend of religion and psychology, contrary to his fellow psychiatrists who preferred to pursue the subject of personality or mental illness purely from a scientific point of view.

Of all the beliefs that Carl Jung held, perhaps more than any other, that motivated him and drove him forward in his quest to come to a greater understanding of how the human mind works, so that he could become more effective in what he saw as his calling to be a healer of the human soul, was his belief that there is a common deep substratum of the totality of all human minds known as the collective unconscious, which every individual is connected to, and which all individuals draw from continuously as each person's life unfolds. For Jung the collective unconscious was seen as a grouping of minds, a collective group of minds comprising all the minds and their content that have ever existed, a group mind the contents of which we all share, something we are born with, that contain what you could describe as humanity's shared concepts or what I would describe as "humanity's shared personality profile."

Jung believed that this collective unconscious or collective mind is the part of the mind containing everybody's ancestral memories and experiences, some perhaps in the form of specific archetypes and myths, that whilst having shaped a particular society are also common to all of humankind. He believed that within the collective unconscious lies a force of instinctive nature that stays mostly dormant in functioning societies, but at certain times comes alive, usually during a time of personal suffering, or as societal revolutions or crises appear; a state of aliveness that brings us to a higher spiritual, moral and ethical level of being. Whilst Jung seemingly saw this as purely a psychological process, and never really publicly acknowledged it as perhaps being a transitionary spiritual occurrence as well, I see it as being exactly that, as a primary component of God's cosmic plan for all humanity. I put it this way:

"In times of personal or collective turmoil, suffering or crisis, a powerful force, perhaps of the archangel Gabriel type you could say, will always arrive at the right time to help. A force of the collective unconscious that powers a person, sometimes through suffering, into a positive unknown, transitioning them to a new and higher level of psychological existence. It is a force that as the saying goes "brings out the best in a person or collectively brings out the best in people." In opposition to this we will always witness a cosmic force arising of a confrontational and antagonistic nature, a force that as the saying goes, "brings out the worst in people."

This psychological transitionary event to me is the first pre-destined and pre-determined state of mind transition that occurs in every individual at some stage in his or her life. If a person misses the boat so to speak because they choose to reject the opportunity to transition in their thinking process, they will at a future date and time be given another opportunity to do so, even if it is in another lifetime. Our own will is in charge from a chronological time aspect of how soon we transition or how much later we move forward in this part of God's Atonement process. After this first transition the collective unconscious, still functioning but at a much lower level of influence and intensity, will be replaced by a collective consciousness, which strives to take an individual or society to a greater level of societal connection, and to a higher level of spiritual endeavour, seeing those involved embracing a deeper social conscience. One tends to start thinking more of the needs of others than they do of their own needs. They become more selfless in attitude and deed.

The Bible references this as being in a behavioural state of good works or righteous deeds. This 'state of mind', the state of collective consciousness, is purposed by God as part of His cosmic plan to be the launching pad that takes people with their next transition completely out of the collective conscious state into a state of complete immersion in the Universal Consciousness. The Universal Consciousness could be described as God's own personal collective unconscious, God's Nature, the totality of God's Mind and God's thought processes. When a person moves into a state of Universal Consciousness they move into what is spoken of in Biblical terminology as "a life lived in the Spirit, a life of being led by the Spirit," and is described in Eastern Religion as "the state of Enlightenment."

Now I said above that after this first transition, from a state of collective unconsciousness to a state of collective consciousness, the collective unconscious, will still be functioning but at a much lower level of influence and intensity, and unfortunately this is where a lot of Christians come to a dead stop in their spiritual journey through the Atonement process. Because the Atonement process has not yet been completed, they stop developing spiritually at the point of good works so to speak. They believe that the Christian life is solely about good works and acts of service to their fellow man. Consequently with their thinking process still being partially influenced by the collective unconscious of humanity, or as I call it, "humanity's shared personality profile", they live in a continuous state of double mindedness with one foot in Christ's camp and one foot, if not firmly in the Ego's camp, then wanting to be in the ego's camp, wanting to get involved in the non-Godly aspects of the world.

Thus the Christian is still drawn into the ways of the world and the things of self-interest, and that is what can lead to spiritual regression in the life of a believer, or to what is commonly known in Christian circles as backsliding, a state of sliding back into the ways of the world as the Bible describes it; which is really a sliding back into the wiles and way of the ego mind. Jesus recognized the potential for this to happen which is why He taught that we should be in the world but not of the world. Being in both leads to a life lived in what the Bible describes as a state of double-mindedness, two minds pulling in different directions. This spiritual regression can occur in many ways including sexual sin, which in itself is an act of betrayal of ones holiness and the inner sacredness of another person.

It can also be witnessed in a person displaying combative attitudes in their relationships with others, always having to be right or always wanting to have the last word. The sexual sin aspect is one of the biggest weapons in the arsenal of the adversary, particularly in its attempt to separate members of the clergy from their transitionary spiritual journey, or stall them in it, and unfortunately many members of the clergy willingly co-operate with the ego mind in this. In this spiritual warfare in which we are all involved, the ego will always direct its mode of attack towards something involving one of the three basic drives of humanity, greed, power or sex, and with many clergy seeing themselves in positions of power to influence people the sexual control drive sometimes links up with the power drive to bring them undone.

Now if we look in more detail at this theory of the existence of a collective unconscious at work in the minds of all human beings that was the central pillar to all of Jung's work, we find the following. Human beings from the moment of their very first thought become connected to the collective unconsciousness, because all thought is creative energy that is sent out into the universe. So we all become participators through the play of personhood that I spoke of in Chapter 1 from our moment of birth. Now whilst the Greek philosopher Plato is credited with originating the concept of archetypes, in his research and writings it was Jung who coined the name archetypes for these shared mind concepts lying in the collective unconscious, these shared personality profiles.

Scholars would say the word archetype comes from the Latin noun archetypum, which means "the original pattern from which copies are made." However the term archetype like so many words in the English language had its origins in ancient Greece, in the word archein, which means original, and typos, which means pattern or type. Combine these two and you get the meaning of archetype to be the original pattern from which all other persons, objects, theories or concepts are derived, copied, modelled, emulated or imitated. In Jung's world of psychotherapy he used the term archetypes to refer to "personality patterns" that have existed since the beginning of time, patterns that influence the behaviour of people in a particular direction, theorising that as active components of the collective unconscious archetypes serve to organize, direct, inform and influence human thought and behaviour.

People living out of similar archetype influences sometimes unknowingly refer to someone with the same personality behaviours as their own as being "like minded." Meaning the other person's mind behaviour, the way they think is the same as theirs. In Jungian psychology archetypes are seen as collectively inherited conscious ideas, images or patterns of thought present in every person's psyche or mind. And here is the important point. The food source for these individual established personality patterns are in fact our behaviours, and the more repetitive a behaviour is, the deeper the personality pattern that first induced it becomes embedded in our psyche. It becomes what is commonly known as a compulsive habit or behaviour, and in the extreme a psychosis. People then get labelled accordingly. "Oh she's a worry wart," labelling a person who appears to worry about everything, to have worry thoughts continuously, or "he's a hypochondriac" labelling someone who continually thinks about and professes to having some sort of sickness.

Our behaviours emanating out of our thought life or personality patterns energise and sustain these patterns, which then reinforce and maintain the same behaviour. So it can be a never-ending cycle of either bad behaviour or good behaviour depending on the pattern resident in our personality. If we choose as an act of our will to no longer engage in a particular type of behaviour that weakens the pattern and progressively disables it. And the point of disablement is the mind or our thought process, because it was a mind thought that created this pattern in the first place. Which is why the Apostle Paul taught, "be transformed by the renewing of your mind." To give you a practical example of how these archetypes or personality patterns work in life, here are a few that are common in society, both the positive and negative aspects remembering that every archetype can have both positive and negative aspects, the negative ones sometimes being referred to as shadow archetypes.

Firstly the negative "gossip" archetypal influence or personality pattern. Its negative manifestations are rumour spreading, backbiting, and thriving on the power generated by passing on secret or private news and misleading information, creating even more damaging rumours. Then we have the negative "victim" personality pattern. Its negative manifestations see the personality moving into the role commonly known as "playing the victim," because of the positive feedback it gets in terms of sympathy and pity, which reinforces a feeling of self-worth, a feeling of wow I am important, someone is listening to me and feeling for me. On the positive side we have the "teacher" archetypal influence or personality pattern. The positive personality attributes of this archetype are in that it freely communicates knowledge, experience, skills and wisdom to those around them. Then finally we have the positive "rescuer" personality pattern. We see it manifesting in someone who always provides strength and support to others in a crisis. One who acts out of love or kindness with no expectation of reward.

Now the following is important in understanding the spiritual connotations behind much of Jung's work. There is a correlation between Jung's psycho-secular theory of specific archetypes being present and active in a person's personality, working through a person's mind or thinking process, and Christianity's teaching about demonic and angelic influencers being present in a person's personality or visiting a person's mind; Angels being the positive representatives of God or Goodness, and demons being the negative representatives of Satan or evil. This is where the term archangel came from as in the archangel Gabriel and the archangel Michael, they are "archetypal Angels," and we see them mentioned in various places in the Bible including in the Old Testament Book of Enoch and in the New Testament Books of Luke and Jude. These are Angels of a type, which I spoke of in the imaginary monologue in the previous chapter.

In some ways more than others the Pentecostal religion was one of the few organizations in Christianity who got it right, in that they recognized the presence of demons as supernatural influencers of a person's thoughts or behaviours, but where they got it wrong was that they believed these influencers could be simply cast out in a moment as witnessed in the stories of Jesus. They did not consider the possibility of their return. However as we see in the Book of Matthew this is not correct. For it speaks of the fact that if the house, meaning the mind is not thoroughly cleaned then, these demonic influencers will return and the second state of the person will be worse than the first. What does that mean? It means that if the mind has not been renewed, if the thinking process has not changed, then nothing is gained by casting the demon or personality influencer out. It means that these personality influencers will simply return in greater numbers at a time of their own choosing as a person re-establishes specific patterns of behaviour.

Jung was also very interested in the way societies and different cultures for hundreds of centuries have used archetypes in myths, attaching a specific archetype to a mythological story to enable a culture or tradition to be easily passed down, almost in storybook mode, from generation to generation. We often see this in various types of religious writings including the Bible, but whilst in Eastern Religion they are readily embraced, not so in Western Religion. Some over superstitious elements of Christianity are very reluctant to entertain the possibility that some stories in the Bible may in fact be of a mythological nature so as to teach some moral or spiritual lesson; stories such as the serpent appearing to Eve in the Garden of Eden or the story of Jonah and the whale in the Old Testament. The definitive meaning of a myth is that it is a traditional story mostly centred on the early history of a people or society, explaining a natural or social phenomenon typically involving supernatural beings or events.

Jung also spent some time investigating and studying the similarities in the symbolism used in different myths and in religious and magic systems, symbols that have continuously occurred in many different cultures during the course of history, cultures with absolutely no historical connection. To account for this similarity of symbols used throughout different ages in different religious myths, he suggested that there were two layers in this collective unconscious, two layers in this group mind that we are all involved with. Firstly there is a personal layer coming out of individual personality patterns of behaviour that we have acquired throughout our life mainly through all our interpersonal relationships and experiences, and then a second layer that contains memory traces of experiences that are common to all of humankind. These second layer personality patterns when formed are what he referred to as archetypes, and archetypes when embedded into a storyline become what are known as a myth.

George Walton Lucas Jr., the Filmmaker, Philanthropist and creator of the Star Wars and Indiana Jones franchises once rightly said, "I've come to the conclusion that mythology is really a form of archaeological psychology. Mythology gives you a sense of what a society believes, and what they fear."

Archetypes are in fact pre-conscious psychic dispositions or in simple language subconscious attitudes of thinking that form the substrate, the underlying layer, from which the basic themes of life occur. Archetypes that we see present to a greater or lesser degree in most religious writings and in certain religious brands, particularly in Eastern Religions such as Hinduism, and in specific cultures such as the Australian Aborigine and the American Indian, are with their inclusion into what is called a myth, used to explain the original pattern or model from which that particular society, tradition or religion first sprang. The problem for a lot of people though in light of this is as the saying goes "separating truth from fiction,' discerning what actually or literally happened and what is merely myth designed to share a truth principle or theory, but this really does not have to be a problem.

For instance with Christians this happens a lot with regards to some Biblical stories such as Noah and the flood, the serpent speaking to Adam and Eve in the Garden of Eden, and the trials of Job, which some use as a point of debate. Are they true stories or is there some form of life lesson buried in them that the universe wants to teach us? I think, well does that really matter, if there is a life lesson in it take it, if not move on. Jung believed that the same archetypal images that reside in certain stories in the Bible also reside in the human soul, and manifest in the lives of people causing them to do psychologically inspired things such as love and hate, and in certain circumstances causing them to do things which they would not ordinarily do as a matter of conscious will. We have all heard people use the expression, "Honestly I don't know what made me do it." Nothing made them do it, but something of a cosmic nature may certainly have influenced them to do it.

Archetypal myths in literature can be described as an action, event or situation, that with the involvement usually of a specific character or characters represent a universal pattern of human nature and subsequent human behaviour. Sometimes called universal symbols, in certain myths different archetypes arise representing opposite character qualities, positive and negative you could say. For example an archetype representing a hero and one representing a villain, both these characters then are blended into a singular story to create a theme of behaviour for certain individuals or indeed societies who oppose each other. This relates closely to Descartes principle of dualism, which I spoke of in Chapter 1, which sees two opposite life forces such as good and evil existing in a combative environment opposing each other. The storyline in myths and also in most fairy tales, which are equally a form of myth, is usually centred on the character of a person or thing exhibiting a quality of goodness or righteousness, referred to as the hero or heroine, going up against a person who predominantly exhibits evil, referred to as the villain, in order to restore harmony and justice to society.

I had the privilege some years ago of attending the opening of the musical stage production called The Wizard of Oz with a friend in St. Louis Missouri, which was an adaptation of L. Frank Baum's children's novel The Wonderful Wizard of Oz. Amongst the characters representing both sides of the coin, goodness and evil, we have Glinda the good witch of the south and then the opposite archetypal character, the wicked witch of the north. More modern day perhaps is what we are seeing in the Marvel series of films, with heroic figures such as Batman going up against enemies of goodness such as the Joker, similarly Superman going up against the arch villain Lex Luther. Even board games can emerge out of the world of myth. If one looks at the history behind the much-loved Snakes and Ladders board game, one will discover the mythological overtones behind its creation.

When Carl Jung used the concept of the archetype in his theorising on the workings of the soul, he was mostly referencing what he saw as timeless, ageless, universal mythical characters that reside within this invisible collective unconscious of people and societies all over the world. In their functional role you could say they manifest in our personalities and subsequent behaviour as motivating factors, and are specific recognizable types. Aspects of our personality that cause us in our thinking, communicating and behavioural processes, to be as we are, say what we say, and do what we do, and with regards to the emotional side of our nature to feel how we feel. Archetypes have been recognized as being present in humankind since the time of Plato, who probably went a bit further than Jung believing that these pre-existing personality influencers were present in all manner of visible things, whether that be of the human kind or material objects such as sunrises and sunsets; the archetype or character quality in that instance being "beauty."

Archetypes are said to provide the foundation of a person's personality and can explain why some people are seen as being quote, "such a kind and generous person," whilst another person can be typed as "a mean selfish ole bastard." People unknowingly use the phrase when talking about a particular person's attitude or behaviour and perhaps semi-excusing it, "oh well he's just that "type" (archetype) of person." When understood, archetypes can be universally used to help us understand why different people think like they think and behave like they behave, at the same time not justifying bad behaviour. We must understand that archetypes are only mind influencers in terms of thought patterns, they do not force us to behave in certain ways as we do, such as being kind or being unkind, that still comes back to free will, our choice. Free will always has the power to overcome mind influences. Which is why I do not accept the increasing attitude of today's legal system to promote mental issues as an excuse for criminal behaviour.

In relation to spirituality myths with their archetypal lead characters are stories of an imaginative type that are eternal and mysterious, and that seem to fulfil in various cultures a need to find a deeper meaning and understanding of life as we know it. Many spiritual myths give clues as to the spiritual potential of human life and are sometimes used as an excuse for what does or doesn't happen in one's spiritual life. In many ways you could say that myths are stories that link together the outer with the inner, the experience of life on the physical plane with the human mind's need for an explanation of the spiritual or inner life of a person. Since to the Gnostic one of the main areas used to tap into more knowledge was in the realm of visions and dreams, the storytelling aspect of myth was for them easier to understand and certainly more desired than the dogmatic and literal teaching of orthodox Christianity. Gnostics saw myths as being able to help us understand those "life things" which we are capable of not only knowing inwardly, but also experiencing outwardly.

This Gnostic attitude to myth was one of the biggest fears that the Catholic Church fathers had in relation to the rise of Gnostic thought, similar to the fear Jewish religious leaders had with those belonging to the Jewish religious group known as the Essenes, a Gnostic type of group which many theological historians believe Jesus and His parents were members of. The Catholic fathers fear being the tendency of Gnostic thought and teaching to lean towards the inner person, that which was of a metaphysical, mythological or mystic nature. The Gnostics use of archetypal symbolism to represent these myths deepened the fear of the fathers, since the presence of occult practices which they believed mythology was a part of, was alive and well in society in those days in the form of magic and sorcery, attracting quite a following. One of the well-known magicians of the day was Simon Magnus, also known as Simon the Sorcerer or Simon the Magician, who is mentioned in the Book of Acts in the Bible.

As mentioned before, whilst Jung in his role as a psychiatrist was continually interested in anything that pertained to why people think what they think, why people believe what they believe, and why people behave as they behave, when Jung sought out information of a spiritual nature, rather than it being a search for something to believe in and something that he could put into practice and experience, as it was with the Gnostics, his was more a search to find spiritual verification or confirmation on something that he already pretty much believed in from a psychological point of view; he was mainly seeking verification of something he himself or one of his patients had experienced. You could say that in terms of the spiritual, Jung had an investigative passion and deep desire to align the experience of the psyche with the world of the spirit. When he turned his interest towards the Gnostic text or teachings it was seemingly to support and confirm his own understanding of the psyche or soul, including those manifestations with mythological overtones that some of his patients were experiencing.

I spoke in Chapter 2 of the archaeological discovery in 1945 in Egypt of an earthenware vessel full of ancient scrolls, containing writings pertaining to the ancient Christian religion of Gnosticism, a group of scrolls which eventually became known as the Nag Hammadi Codex. The discovery of these texts of course generated extreme scholarly interest from around the world, including from some high profile parties desiring access to them. Due to their interest in the Gnostic aspect of early Christianity, two central figures caught up in the saga of the finds were in fact Carl G. Jung and Gilles Quispel, a Dutch theologian and historian of Christianity and Gnosticism, and a professor of early Christian History at Utrecht University in the Netherlands. Quispel subsequently became involved in the first editing of the Nag Hammadi Codex, and also, being acutely aware of Jung's interest in all things Gnostic, purchased part of it in 1951. The purchased single codex was subsequently renamed the Jung Codex and found a home in the C.J. Jung Institute in Zurich.

You see Jung understood that the only Christian philosophy that regarded the mind as the receptacle for the fulfilment of humankind's search for oneness with God was that of Gnosticism. Consequently throughout his life he always advocated that there should be a renewed interest and appreciation for this ancient Christian teaching that pointed towards a knowledge driven understanding of God's presence within the human mind. A presence directing and guiding a person in their daily life, and, as a fundamental component of the Christian experience ensuring the maximum potential for said Christian to fulfil their spiritual destiny. Perhaps partly from having witnessed the horrors of World War 2, Jung believed that society was crying out for balance, rather than the mental imbalance that seemed to be present in the ideologically inspired insanity of the war, particularly in Nazism. He also suggested that even though some religious organizations were aware of this mental imbalance in society, by them establishing their own philosophical outlook they were in fact still contributing to the imbalance in their teaching rather than trying to lessen it.

However when it was widely reported in psychological circles of Jung's interest or leaning towards Gnostic text or teaching, he was heard once again to reiterate that his interest was purely to support and confirm from a spiritual aspect his own scientific understanding of experiences of the psyche, though others would still say it seemed more than this. Thus for all his apparent interest in all things Gnostic he stopped short of openly identifying himself as a Gnostic, rather still seeing himself in his role of a psychiatrist purely being that of a healer of the soul, the functional part of a person that most would describe as their personality. However he did in a television interview when asked the question, "do you believe in God?" interestingly answer, "I don't need to believe, I know." A reply that caused some controversy but a reply that would have bode well with any Christian of a Mystic or Gnostic disposition.

From a non-religious or secular perspective as surgery can be described as a physical process designed to restore a body to its original state of functioning, so psychotherapy could be described as a therapeutic process for the restoration of the mind to its original state. So in this regard the psychiatrist is seen in medical circles as a healer of the mind, similarly as a surgeon is seen as a healer of the body. The original proponents of depth psychotherapy, like Jung, would describe it as a means to an end, the means being to question the validity of what an individual has for so long seen as their reality, and the end resulting in the patient being guided into an understanding of the illusionary nature of their thought processes. This then frees them to choose a new true reality.

The patients discover the so called cause or reasons behind their insane way of thinking, the blockages to sanity are revealed, which in turn allows the mind to be introduced to a sane way of thinking. It's simply a process of mind correction or mind renewal as the Apostle Paul described it, but coming from a psychological position only, not including the Holy Spirit in the process. The patient being helped by the psychiatrist to "change their mind" as to what is reality and what is simply an illusion, what is merely a figment of their imagination.

Similarly from a religious perspective, the process of enlightenment in Eastern Religion and the Atonement process in Christianity, involves seeing and understanding what is true reality. It involves the removal of blockages to God's Truth that are affecting a person's perception of who they really are, of who God knows they are, blockages which are detrimental to a person's eternal spiritual wellbeing. There is a link between the psychotherapy process and the Atonement process but with one major difference. Whilst both psychotherapy and the Atonement process have one singular objective, that being the renewing of the mind or the renewal of the thought processes, or giving a person understanding of what is reality and what isn't, the psychotherapeutic approach has only temporal or earthly implications and the Atonement process has eternal or heavenly implications.

The role of psychotherapy in a functioning society has over the centuries long been a source of much debate and differing opinion by theologians; mostly depending on which church they belong to. Extreme Pentecostalism would see any disturbance of the mind that a person might experience, which includes things like anxiety and depression, as being caused by the activity of a particular demonic spirit in the person, a spirit that can be simply cast out through the blood of Jesus. This point of view I feel is not only of the extreme, but does not pass the spiritual pub test, misrepresenting the scriptures that talk of Jesus casting out demons or Jesus saying greater works that I do shall you do.

I see it this way. Whilst the psychotherapeutic approach to the mind healing process has the potential to leave the patient with a renewed or healed mind it still leaves the patient with a rational mind based approach to life. However the Apostle Paul's mind renewal process, the Atonement process, God's way, whilst renewing the rational mind thought processes puts that rational mind in a position of subservience to the Christ Mind or the Holy Spirit within, and that's where the complete transformation becomes an ongoing thing. Minus the Jesus component, the psychotherapy process in its practical application is designed to reveal and remove blockages to truth and true reality in the psyche or mind, and thus in a psychological manner help a person abandon a false and delusional belief system that has ruled their lives, further assisting them by replacing that false reality with true reality.

So in the first instance there is nothing wrong with that for I see psychotherapy in fact as a God given intermediary process that will assist those in a mentally disturbed state to get to a point of freedom, not ultimate freedom but to a point of rational mind freedom even if only temporary. To a point where they can be enabled, having cleared the way to sanity so to speak, to be receptive to the reality of God, the teaching of the Holy Spirit and the complete appropriation of the Atonement, and that I believe was Carl Jung's true gift to the world and to a suffering section of society. Jung was opening the prison door of the mind to rational reality thus creating a type of pathway for a person to move forward into spiritual reality. So if a person is visiting a therapist for assistance I see nothing wrong with that, but the ultimate end game must always be to discover spiritual reality.

You see nothing in this world exists by accident, we are all emanations from the creative sea of Universal Consciousness, the Mind of God, and for that reason I believe that psychotherapy could be said to have been designed by God to be used by some as an interim means of establishing ephemeral reality of creating a measure of saneness enough to clear the pathway or remove ego mind blockages to spiritual reality. The cares of the world, cares that for many become mental tormentors, which obstruct a person in their spiritual evolution, are pushed aside but only for a moment in time, enabling one to push forward spiritually. It is in fact a type of renewal of the mind, but not the renewal of the mind that the Apostle Paul spoke of as the key component of the Atonement process. It has temporal implications and not eternal implications unless used as a springboard into the things of the Spirit.

The twentieth and twenty first centuries, more than the previous few centuries has witnessed a growing interest in the subject of mythology, influenced no doubt by the emergence of classic new works of literature such as Joanne Rowling's the Harry Potter series. This interest has in turn flowed over into an increased interest in mystical teachings such as Gnosticism. Certain areas of society are coming to realise that whilst philosophy in its essence is fundamentally a discipline that explains the phenomena of the visible life, mythology in its essence helps to explain the primordial reality that led to the creation of a particular way of philosophical thought.

In Jung's world of depth psychology philosophy was seen as being able to address the conscious part of the human mind, whilst mythology, inclusive of archetypal personality patterns, can give us not only greater understanding of the human mind, but also a greater understanding of the direct link it has to the functioning aspect of the unconscious mind. Which is probably why the Gnostics were drawn more to mythology and mysticism rather than to philosophical thought, seeing them use both mythological teachings and mystic ritual to in a sense turn their concept of an inner knowing into an outward practice, which in turn then strengthened their capacity to experience inner knowing. This differed from the orthodox church in the fact that as the church evolved into a more institutionalised state, it also evolved into a religion of pure form, ceremony and ritual only, to the exclusion of the quest for an inner knowing; it adopted a purely externalist approach to Christian worship and practice and ignored all aspects of the internal approach.

We see in the Gospel of Thomas, part of the Nag Hammadi finds, Jesus came to make the inner as the outer and the outer as the inner, to make the above as the below and the below as the above, that all the internal aspects of humanity and all the external ways may be as one. Jesus came to draw together the mind of humanity and the Mind of God. So Christianity, rather than being fearful of Jung's work owes him a debt of gratitude for his dedication in bringing both the theological world and the psychological world into a state of connectedness. Jung in his role as a healer of the soul saw himself as a healer of the mind and the emotions, guiding a person through a process of thinking correction, of understanding what was illusionary in their life particularly in the area of the emotions, things that that they had experienced in their interpersonal relationships that brought storms to their personal ocean of consciousness. However the process of psychotherapy cannot be creative, and whilst it can substitute in the mind one sane thought to replace one insane thought, it cannot in the creative aspect create a new person. Only the Christ Mind within can accomplish that kind of lasting psychological change.

> "Your vision will become clear only when you can look into your own heart. Who looks outside dreams; who looks inside awakes."
> Carl Jung

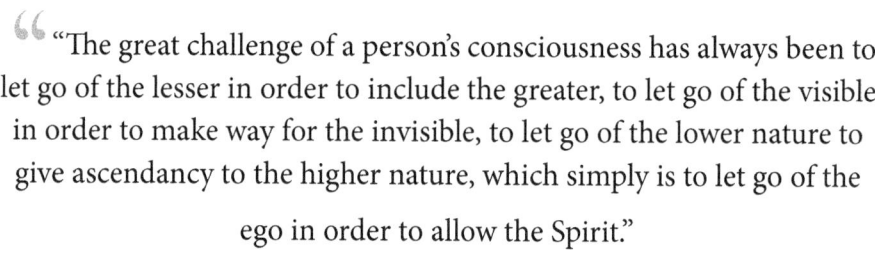

“The great challenge of a person’s consciousness has always been to let go of the lesser in order to include the greater, to let go of the visible in order to make way for the invisible, to let go of the lower nature to give ascendancy to the higher nature, which simply is to let go of the ego in order to allow the Spirit.”

The Evolutionary and Transitionary Nature of Humanity

EIGHT

Jiddu Krishnamurti was born May 12th 1895 and died February 17th 1986, at 91 years of age. Jiddhu was in his time in human form an Indian philosopher, speaker, writer, and teacher of contemporary alternative spirituality. His life focus was centred on the nature and function of the mind in the life of a human being, on meditation, and on human relationships, his primary intent always being that through his discoveries, a psychological revolution would occur as his impartation of wisdom was absorbed into people's lives. His sole aim in imparting this wisdom was to see each individual who received it go on to play their respective part in bringing about a radical change in the societal way of doing things, in society's manner of behaving and being, resulting in a permanent change in the spiritual and physical life practices of humanity.

Along the same lines as Carl Jung who also was at that time heavily involved in his studies of the human soul, Jiddhu emphasised society's need for an individualised revolution in the area of the psyche or soul, always believing and teaching that this revolution cannot and will not be brought about by any external entity of the religious, political or social kind. A viewpoint you could say that was the complete antithesis to that of those vociferous people of the day, who believed that the religious, political, social or philosophical ideology that one adheres to would do the job. He was one of the few teachers of his day who freely admitted that he held no allegiance to any culture, caste, religion or philosophy, and it was believed by many that he was also one of the few teachers of his day who possessed a wonderful aura, the name given to an energy field around a person, a type of presence, and that his aura contained not one ounce of selfishness in it. One of Jiddhu's notable beliefs was that truth is a land with no pathway to it, and consequently cannot be obtained by any pathway of the religious, political or ideological type. He believed that truth cannot be organized or formed or used to coerce people along a particular path, and that in the moment you follow someone who purports to be the bearer of sole truth, then that is the moment in which you cease to know and follow truth, rather you commence following a belief or an opinion.

In his small book titled At The Feet Of The Master, Jiddhu said the following, "in all the world there are only two kinds of people, those who know and those who do not know," in some ways aligning himself once again with a statement of Carl Jung who, when asked in a television interview "do you believe in God?" replied, "I don't need to believe in God, I know God." Although at times underestimated, Indian philosophers like Krishnamurti have a lot to add to the general philosophy of consciousness and mind, and whilst simplicity and elegance marked his work and writings, one needs to contemplate deeply his concepts in a meditative way to gain full benefit from them. Some would even say it is essential that those who are interested in the philosophy of the mind explore his life's work in order to gain insight into the truth of who we are as human beings, and that by exploring his work one can also gain much insight into consciousness and the evolutionary nature of the mind.

By now the more discerning of readers may have noticed that there is a reoccurring theme in this book, that I either keep returning to in some form or another in each new chapter, or just briefly make reference to it, and that subject or theme relates to "the functioning of the mind." In Chapter 1 I spoke about personhood and identity and the role "mind things" play in forming it. In Chapter 2 I discussed the complete healing of the body and mind as spoken of by the Apostle Paul in the Book of Romans when he said, "let God transform you into a new person by changing the way you think." (New Living Translation) In

Chapter 3 where I talk about belief being "a state of mind" that influences all our thoughts and behaviours. In Chapter 5 where I spoke of mind transcendence, from the Ego Mind way of thinking to the Christ Mind way of thinking. In Chapter 6 where I discussed the two natures of goodness and evil that wage a spiritual warfare for dominance in the human mind, and in Chapter 7 where I looked at one of the most well known secular pioneers of mind exploration and the restoration of a disturbed mind to its original functioning state, the psychoanalyst Carl C. Jung.

This chapter is an extension of our exploration into a greater understanding of the mind and how it works, the role it plays in the Atonement process, and subsequently the role it plays in our evolutionary spiritual journey. I do this because in this present day the singular most important part of the physiology of humankind that we must have a complete understanding of in order to manoeuvre our way physically and psychologically through this ever evolving society and through these ever changing times, to enable us to move confidently forward into our eternal spiritual destiny, is most certainly the subject matter of the mind and how it works.

Looking back in history one could safely say that society has always had some sort of inquisitive attitude or fascination with the workings of the mind particularly in relation to the societal behaviour of teenagers and adults, at times using phrases such as, "why would they behave like that," or "what were they thinking?" Whether it be from a secular or a spiritual perspective, society has always shown a high level of interest in the untapped potential that the mind seems to have to shape both an individual's life and the life of humanity as a whole, whether that be for better or worse. Works of literature are littered with terminology relating to both the welcome and the unwelcome aspects of the mind in both the psychological and physical behaviour of human beings from birth to death. From writers of both a secular mindset and writers of a spiritual mindset we have witnessed authors of a variety of genres extolling the virtues of the mind, the vanity of the mind, the variations in the mind, and the vices that lie dormant in the deep recesses of the mind waiting to emerge.

From preachers, to prophets, to poets, to purveyors of new age thought, the world has borne witness over the centuries of humankind's existence, to a variety of philosophical and to a lesser extent spiritual viewpoints and opinions on the power and purpose of the mind, expressed in all manner of phrase from all manner of people. From the mouth of Socrates the Greek philosopher of the ancient era who said, "strong minds discuss ideas, average minds discuss events, and weak minds discuss people." To lawyer and politician Mahatma Ghandi who said, "I will not let anyone walk through my mind with their dirty feet." To philosopher and poet Ralph Waldo Emerson who wrote, "nothing is as lastingly sacred but the integrity of your own mind." Not forgetting Eckhart Tolle spiritual teacher and author who said, "all things that truly matter, beauty, love, creativity, joy and inner peace arise from beyond the mind." And of course the Apostle Paul who said, "but you have been given the Mind of Christ," and Jesus Himself, who in Gnostic writings said, "Become a disciple of your mind, which is of the Father. I am come to give sight to those who seek after right-mindedness. Understanding is hidden from the heart and only revealed to the mind."

A survey done in Australia some three years ago showed that the number of Australian teenagers who are in severe psychological distress had increased dramatically over the previous five years. The statistics, in a report commissioned by an organization named Mission Australia, showed almost a quarter of teens surveyed met the criteria for probable serious mental illness, with girls twice as likely as boys to be affected. It was a report reflecting five years of annual surveys of thousands of teenagers across Australia. There are similar situations occurring with teenagers and adults in many other western cultures.

For instance recently in America, a report commissioned by the National Alliance on Mental Illness in 2018 revealed a disturbing trend.

The report revealed 19.1% of U.S. adults experienced mental illness during that year, around 47.6 million people, 4.6% of U.S. adults experienced "serious" mental illness, that's 11.4 million people, 16.55% of U.S. youth aged 6 to 17 years experienced a mental health disorder, that's around 7.7 million young people, and added to that the annual prevalence of adults experiencing "major depressive episodes" numbered 17.7 million, with 48 million people experiencing anxiety disorders, all of these psychological illnesses appearing as fear induced sometimes physically paralysing feelings. Anxiety is a feeling, a mental feeling of worry, nervousness or unease. Depression is a feeling, a mental feeling of dejection, despondency and isolation, and all feelings have their origin in thought. It is always first the thought and then the feeling or the emotion applicable to that feeling.

Now whilst most books written on the subject of Christianity place great emphasis on the spirit, perhaps because of the continuous reference we see to the word spirit in the Bible, and consequently leave the "mind stuff" to the new age writers or the writers on Eastern Religion, one of my primary intentions in writing this book was to shine a light on the extreme lack of understanding the Christian religion has concerning the role of the mind in the daily life of every human being. For some Christian faiths, even to show interest in the subject of the mind risks opening oneself up to satanic influence, which of course is absurd, but that's the way institutionalised ingrained belief works. If that were the case the Apostle Paul would have been the most demon-possessed person in the Bible since he makes continuous reference to the mind in his writings.

This chapter whilst proceeding along the same lines as previous chapters, in that its overarching purpose is once again to give one greater and deeper understanding of the role the mind plays in our very existence, digs a little deeper than the previous ones, looking more closely at the mind from a metaphysical aspect, from Eastern Religion's viewpoint and from Christian Mysticism's perspective, which are in fact very similar. Looking at it hopefully in a way that will not confuse, but rather quietly and progressively enlighten and expand your understanding of the cosmic nature of the mind. For I feel that for far too long society has separated the things of God to the spiritual side of our existence, at the same time relegating the things of the mind to the physical and mental side of our existence, when they are both in fact intrinsically linked. It follows on and gives greater detail on the various states of consciousness that I spoke of in the previous chapter; consciousness in simple terms being merely a state of mind or our state of awareness, how we perceive things that pass before our sense realms. It also looks a little deeper at how the three different states of consciousness, the collective unconscious, collective consciousness, and Universal Consciousness at various stages activate in a human being's life, and how in fact we are all intended to transition through these various stages of consciousness as part of our pre-destined spiritual evolution.

In both Jung's theories in analytical psychology and Jiddu's concepts regarding the workings of the mind we see a similar focus by both men on analysing the unconscious forces coming from the collective unconscious that motivate human behaviour, both good and bad, examining why people are as they are, why people think as they think, and why people behave as they behave, particularly when the behaviour is extremely outside of the acceptable social norms for societal behaviour. To understand these and other things relating to life practices and behaviours it helps if we understand the transitionary psychological nature of a human being. You hear people commonly use the phrase in a way of semi-justifying bad behaviour, "Oh he's only going through a stage," and in a way there is an element of truth in this. A human being's life is totally transitionary by nature. There are psycho-spiritual evolutionary stages to it.

We hear the term used quite often that life is a journey and in its essence that is true, for life is a holistic journey; it is a physical journey, it is a mental journey, and life is a spiritual or cosmic journey. I use the term cosmic journey because a true journey of spiritual awakening and inner transformation involves a coming together of all the invisible forces of the universe and blending them into a purpose filled agenda to accomplish the mission set before it. That mission being to guide a person to achieving an enlightened state of mind. From the physical aspect of our journey we are continuously moving forward or transitioning from one stage of physicality to a higher level of physicality, to an improved stage, a more developed stage. A baby does not commence walking as soon as it emerges from the womb. First it rolls over, then it sits up, then it crawls, then it walks, and then it starts running around at the same time transitioning in appearance through periods of regulated growth. This transition can't be paused or stopped because it is happening instinctively; we can't stop ourselves growing taller or stop our physical features from developing, it just happens. The body inside and out instinctively transitions to a more mature physical level of being.

Similarly life is a mental journey or a journey of the mind that, unlike the physical journey, is ignored by most people. People focus on physical health and appearance many in an obsessive way, and many of those same people have scant regard for their mental health. Why? Because the chief protagonist in the scenario of our mental evolution, the mind, is not visible like the body, and so its a case of out of sight, out of mind. Whilst people can't easily hide their physical appearance, their true thoughts and subsequent feelings can be hidden, and most people as the saying goes, "put on a brave face" to do this. From the mental transitionary aspect of our life journey encompassing the areas of intellect and intelligence, a child from the moment of leaving the womb is not able to perfectly articulate anything because its mind is in a sense in a type of vacuum, an empty void. It has not been around long enough to have absorbed enough information to make some conscious communication immediately it leaves the womb, such as, "Hi there glad to finally be here," or "you know I don't really think I can agree with Einstein on his theory of relativity, I see some basic floors in it."

No, long before your baby will ever speak or intellectually understand something and then begin to articulate it, baby's intent will be totally focused on only one thing. She or he will be only trying to let you know their "feelings." Baby will first smile at you at around 2 months of age. By 4 months, they will probably laugh. By six months of age, your baby should be able to turn and look at you when you are speaking to them. They may respond to their name having heard you say it repeatedly over the previous number of months, and they may be able to tell the difference between the happy and angry tones of your voice. Your baby will be able to express happiness by giggling or cooing, and unhappiness by crying, and they will continue to learn and evolve in body and mind, sometimes instinctively as with the physical body, but with the mind, because we are dealing with the intellect, more so through the guidance and teaching of their mum and dad.

Similarly from a spiritual perspective life is also a series of transitions, an evolutionary journey. The spiritual life has been set in place as a journey, a journey from the lower nature to the higher nature or a higher level of being. Whilst the physical life is all about physical growth and the mental or mind life is all about mental expansion, the gaining of knowledge and experience, all part of the visual side of existence, the spiritual life has nothing to do with the growth of those external aspects of our humanity or in fact with any one of our known sense realms, sight, hearing, touch, taste or smell. Rather it is totally centred on the internal aspects of our being, the invisible side of our existence. It is about internal growth not external growth. It is about cosmic experience not local physical experience.

No matter who you are every person at various stages of their life transition to a higher and deeper level of something. From the spiritual perspective a person does not simply step up from the level of their lower nature or lower mind to a state of fully functioning out of their higher nature or higher mind, we transition, and that is where the Christian Church has got it wrong. They teach that the transition simply occurs through a ritualised act. I spoke of the lower nature and the higher nature in Chapter 1 and if it helps please refer back to it in relation to this chapter. What we must understand is that in relation to the totality of a person's self, the body, mind and soul, it is the one in the middle, the mind, that is the biggest influencer on how the one before it, the body, and the one after it the soul, progresses and transitions successfully with minimal adverse or antagonistic cosmic interference.

You can have a magnificent body and movie star looks, you can have a deep religious leaning and an interesting philosophical outlook, but if you haven't got the mind right, if the mind is not in sync with the nature and laws of the universe, set in place by God and managed by the Holy Spirit, then no matter how pretty, handsome, healthy, gifted, religious or philosophical you are, life will always be a series of ongoing small to extreme psychological battles and consequently you will not transition through life in a balanced and peace filled way. You may have moments of short-term pleasure, but you will not have continuous extended periods of peace, the peace that the Apostle Paul spoke of in his address to the Philippian people, the peace that I like to call, "a supernatural rest in the midst of the enemy."

How does that peace come about? It happens through our understanding and embracing this truth.

> "Life is primarily a transitionary spiritual journey linked to a transitionary mind journey. It is not just a stop, start, and sometimes-stationary physical journey. We must come to understand the universality of our eternal existence and not just the particularity or peculiarity of our temporary existence. We must come to understand the cosmic nature of life and not just the carnal nature of it."

When the Apostle Paul spoke of us having received the Mind of Christ, that mind, the Mind of Christ he spoke of is in fact the Mind of

God. There is a single intelligent mind known as the Universal Mind or Universal Consciousness that pervades the whole universe. Now this is not just a religious idea or a philosophical thought bubble that has been passed down to us over the centuries, rather it is an exact scientific truth. The renowned scientist Albert Einstein told us that everything in existence is energy, a universal energy which human beings are all a part of. It is an omnipotent energy force, meaning it is all powerful, it is an omnificent force which means unlimited in its creative power, and it is an omnipresent force which means always present everywhere at the same time.

It is the energy force that was and still is present in the ongoing implementation and practicalities of the three mysteries, the Outgoing, the Evolution and the Return, that I spoke of at the beginning of this book. The Outgoing of God that created the universe was the same energy force that we are speaking about here now. It is the energy force that is known as the Universal Mind or the Mind of God. There are different terms of expression for it, simply because the understanding of the existence of this Universal Mind and its activity surfaced in different places at different times over the course of humankind's existence. It was given different names at various times by different cultures, different religions and different sciences and philosophical genres, but nevertheless names all still referring to the same creative energy force. In the scientific world it was referred to as the Unified Field, a term coined by Albert Einstein. In spiritual philosophy and in certain Eastern Religions it was referred to as The All or Universal Consciousness and in a different variety of religions it assumed various names such God, Jehovah, Allah, Braham and many others depending on what name the founder of the religion chose.

For the duration of this chapter I will refer to this creative energy force as Universal Consciousness or the Universal Mind, because I feel that those terms add to the relevance of the word God, rather than if I just keep saying the word God, an old Anglo Saxon word, which to many people has become a type of abstract religious term, a word the origin of which is really not known save that it is a relatively new European invention and was never used in any of the ancient Judaeo-Christian scriptures. Universal Consciousness is the source of all things and the creative aspect of God. It is the Mind of God and since Jesus was God in the flesh, it is the Mind of Christ, and since the Bible tells as that we have been given the Mind of Christ it means that this creative mind power has been built into us. Consequently an understanding of this Universal Mind, this Universal Consciousness within us, and its involvement in our evolutionary and transitionary journey through life, the second and third mysteries, is vitally important to enable us to move through the Atonement process. I give this explanation in the next few paragraphs in the simplest way I can, knowing that some readers will have to perhaps ruminate on it for a while to grasp it intuitively.

There are three terms that find a common home in some Eastern Religions, in Christian Mysticism, in Psychotherapy, and in Sociology. Sociology being the study of the development, structure and functioning of human society. These three terms are, **the collective unconscious, collective consciousness**, and **universal consciousness,** which I spoke of in the previous chapter. These **states of mind** you could call them are all participators and foremost players in the Atonement process in Western Religion and similarly in the journey to Enlightenment process in Eastern Religion. Now I touched a little on the **transitionary nature of humanity** collectively, and of human beings individually, but just want to detail this further.

There is a sequence of psychological transitions that occur in the minds of all individuals as they journey through life. It involves all three states of consciousness or awareness just mentioned, and the starting point is the state of mind known as **the collective unconscious**. What is the collective unconscious?

"The collective unconscious is that part of the unconscious mind that is shared by individuals and society as a whole and is composed of archetypal ancestral experiences and personal life relationship experiences. We are born with the ancestral ones and over time develop the personal ones."

From this point or state of mind we individually at a pre-destined time in our lives transition to the next state of mind, the state of **collective consciousness.**

"Collective consciousness is a state of mind in which a set of shared beliefs, ideas and moral attitudes operate as a unifying force within the minds of individuals and society."

This usually but not necessarily comes about as I spoke of in the previous chapter after the occurrence of some sort of significant event or crisis of the personal or collective kind, an event that has brought about some sort of suffering or psychological turmoil. It takes people to this higher level of consciousness, a greater awareness of our shared humanity.

Then from this point or state of mind, this state of collective consciousness, at a given time, differing according to the person involved, we individually, not collectively but individually, at a pre-destined time in our lives transition to a state of immersion in **Universal Consciousness, but it is not complete immersion.**

> "Universal Consciousness is the creative mind of the universe, or what many people including those writers in the Bible will simply refer to as the Spirit of God. This is the God Mind that we will be fully immersed in at the end of the Atonement process as it is termed in Western Religion or at the conclusion of the Enlightenment process as it is referred to in Eastern Religion."

However I said above that we would be immersed in the first instance, but that it would not be full immersion. It's like going for a wade in the waters of the God Mind, but not a full swim. There will still be aspects of the collective unconscious operating in our mind and lives, but gradually having less and less impact as full immersion progressively envelops us. Metaphorically it can be likened to walking into the ocean, but in this case it is the ocean of Universal Consciousness, we wade into the Mind of God. To follow on with this metaphor, when we have dived completely into the ocean, fully immersed ourselves, then we have completed the Atonement process as is the terminology in Western Religion or reached the state of Enlightenment as is the terminology in Eastern Religion and are ready to return to that from which we originally came out of, our source. That is the third mystery in the three mysteries known as the Return.

However until that moment, until we are fully immersed, even though we have transitioned from a state of collective unconsciousness through the state of collective consciousness into a state of Universal Consciousness, there will still be elements of the collective unconscious, waves on the surface, buffeting us, seeking to have an impact on us by influencing our minds and subsequent behaviour. So going back to expand more on these various states of consciousness or awareness that we transition through, this is how they work.

The life lived in the **collective unconscious** is the life of personhood, a life of psychological separation from God and Godly principles, that I spoke of in Chapter 1. It is a life influenced by past memories and future desires and impacted on "personality wise" by personality patterns of the individual personal kind or by personality patterns of the archetypal ancestral kind, all influencing in some way our patterns of thought and resultant behaviour, which can include particular types of emotional behaviour. We in many ways are living out of logic and reasoning and out of our feelings and emotions. Here is an example of an archetypal influence of the ancestral kind being excused and semi-justified by a person in conversation. "So I tend to get angry easily, it's not my fault it runs in the family. All the women in our family were quick to anger." Or an archetypal influence of the religious ancestral kind might be, "Sure I'm a Catholic. Our family has always been Catholic," or another example from a political perspective might be, "Labour, yes I vote labour, my family has always voted labour."

We are all born into a life lived in and being influenced constantly by the archetypal hereditary influences of the collective unconscious and then grow in life collecting personality patterns or influences of the personal relationship kind. Our lives are further formed and shaped by those who love us or those who have refused to love us. These things in particular have a significant effect in establishing personality patterns of behaviour. A point to note is that Jesus was not born into this state; Jesus being God in flesh was spotless and sinless and was born into the state of mind, one level higher than this, the state of collective consciousness. He was never influenced by the collective unconscious. Which is why from the get go He went about doing good works: a level just a little lower than the Angels so the Bible tells us, at the same time being driven to do good works which is evidence of a state of collective consciousness.

This is the mystery hidden in Hebrews 2 9. Jesus being God in flesh started at the point of Universal Consciousness and then descended to Collective Consciousness. Our mission or destiny is to go the opposite way, to ascend to a higher level, from collective consciousness to Universal Consciousness as Jesus set the example. Jesus descended to meet us and escort us to the higher level to bring us back home to where He came from. Jesus was the prototype of the Atonement process for us, sent to show us the way home.

The **first transition** from the **collective unconscious** life to a life lived in **collective consciousness** is in the journey from personhood to the cross, from the wilderness of personhood to the wisdom of the cross. We are saved from the self-life, from our state of personhood, from our state of self-will, and enter a new psychological state of God willingness. This state is one of having a less judgemental attitude towards our fellow man and sees those society connecting components of compassion and kindness and forgiveness emerge in our personality profile.

We become kinder, gentler, more compassionate people, we focus on others more than ourselves. We become doers of good works. These are the behavioural changes that occur when we psychologically transition from the collective unconscious state of mind to the collective conscious state of mind.

The **next transition** from a life of **collective consciousness** to a partial immersion in the **Universal Consciousness** or the Universal Mind that I likened to wading into the waters of Universal Consciousness, is the second part of the Atonement experience, the crucifixion of the ego or the death of self-will being the first part. This partial immersion experience in Eastern Religion is known as attaining a state of "Buddha Mindedness." In Christianity it is the state of being "led by the Spirit," or being in a state of "Christ Mindedness." It is a state of primary psychological alignment with the Christ Mind within rather than with our rational ego mind, which was previously the case. It is a state of progressive psychological oneness with the Mind of God. The psychological separation from God that we have lived with all our lives is progressively going, the gap of mind separation is being closed.

The Bible expresses it this way, "for as many as are led by the Spirit of the Lord, meaning the Holy Spirit, they shall be the Sons and Daughters of God." When we transition to the state of partial but progressive immersion in Universal Consciousness we become what the Bible describes as Sons and Daughters of God. We become part of God's family and heirs of God's blessings.

How does this process of immersion deepen and deepen. It happens through mind renewal, through the renewal of our thinking processes. It happens as we align our thoughts with God's thoughts. We continue to sink deeper into the ocean of Universal Consciousness through the process of mind renewal that the Apostle Paul spoke of and through the process of Budda Mindedness that the Buddha spoke of. When we have completed the process of mind renewal we have completed the Atonement process as in Christianity and reached Enlightenment as in

Eastern Religion. That's how it works. And it all centres on our state of mind. It is a psychological spiritual thing not a physical thing. It's not about works it's about willingness. It's the "not my will but thy will be done" attitude of Jesus on the cross.

Gershom Scholem, a highly regarded German born Israeli scholar, the first professor of Jewish Mysticism at the Hebrew University of Jerusalem, was greatly impressed by the Gnostics of the 2nd and 3rd centuries and their total dedication and focus on ascending through the various stages of consciousness, their unwavering commitment to transitioning through these psychological realms that were associated with the fullness of the Divine Light. The Apostle Paul described his renewed life after completing these two transitional processes in this way. "I have been crucified with Christ, (the transition from Collective Unconsciousness to Collect Consciousness), it is no longer I who live but Christ lives in me," (the transition from Collective Consciousness to Universal Consciousness).

This is the mystery hidden in the story of Jesus' baptism in the Jordan River by John the Apostle. He was fully immersed in the water, symbolic of God the water of life, He was immersed in the Universal Consciousness and a dove descended upon him symbolic of the Holy Spirit taking over His life completely. That is what this transitionary life we live in is all about and it only needs one thing from us to complete its evolutionary cycle, to take us out of the Outgoing, through the Involution and to the Return on the other side, and that one thing is our voluntary willingness. No one can force us to do this similarly as no one could force Jesus to stay on the cross. He did it as an act of His will.

For centuries and centuries philosophers have set about shaping our beliefs with their influence ever present in many of our existing practices, institutions, and basic assumptions about ourselves and the world we thought we knew. From the point of view of religion and more specifically from the Christian Mystic's point of view, the philosophical perspective is that there is only one consciousness, one mind, and one field of truth that is the source of the entire universe. This field is not a thing but rather a formless, unbounded, undivided Universal Consciousness. For the Christian Gnostic and Christian Mystic the eternal truth could be expressed as follows.

> "There is a cosmic energy which powers us, sustains us and motivates us, and it is a part of the Universal Supply which flows through the universe. It comes from the Creative Source of this universe, Universal Consciousness, the Mind of God. Its intensity of flow into our lives is proportionate to our depth of desire and sustainability of will."

"All the masters who have ever existed lived their faith in different forms, but the one thing that they all perfectly aligned on with each other was the belief that there is a Oneness of Reality, a Truth, a Way of God that exists beyond the veil of separation, which is the true reality of our existence that we are meant to find and destined to come home to."

The Transitionary Wilderness Experience of Jesus and The Buddha

NINE

Plato was an Athenian philosopher during what is known as the Classical Period in ancient Greece. The Classical Period in Greece occurred in the 5th and 4th centuries B.C. and was a memorable time in Greek culture, which saw the annexation of much of modern day Greece by the First Persian Empire or the Achaemenid Empire as it was also known. The Persian Empire was an ancient Iranian Kingdom based in Western Asia, founded by Cyrus the Great, which at the peak of its existence covered 5.5 million square kilometres and stretched from the Balkans and Eastern Europe proper in the west, to the Indus valley in the east. The empire itself incorporated various peoples of varying origins and religious faiths, and stands out in historical records as a progressive innovator through its building of different types of infrastructure such as road systems and a postal system, for its establishment of an official language across its territories, and for the development of civil services and a large professional army. The religions of the empire included Zoroastrianism, Mithraism and Babylonian.

During this period of time there existed a philosophical school of thought, a way of thinking known as Neo-Platonism. It flourished in the Greco-Roman world from around the middle of the third century to the middle of the seventh century, and became the dominant philosophical ideology of the period, offering a comprehensive understanding of this universe we live in, of how it operates, and what place or role the individual person is meant to have in that operation. Ancient history tells us that during the first few centuries of the Christian era, similarly as in the time of Neo-Platonism, schools of spirituality were established in order to transfer new philosophical outlooks to the ordinary person. Some of these Christian philosophical outlooks were in fact similar to those of Jung, for they taught of the majesty and revelatory nature of the active components of the soul, the psyche or mind, including the concepts of archetypes which Jung majored on in his lifelong work.

However after the initial emergence of these schools in the first few centuries of Christianity, whilst they flourished for a while, they did not last long, and the majesty of internal wisdom proceeding from the Soul as a part of Christian life and worship was replaced with an externalist attitude towards all things Christian, involving ritual, dogma, doctrine, pomp and ceremony; all things appealing to the external senses, all things outside of the internal realm of the Soul. Consequently the psychological aspect of Christianity, the internal approach to the things of God and the things of the spirit that the mystics had revered for centuries, were lost to a form of institutionalised Christianity. Those who wanted to continue with this internalised type of approach to Christianity, the Christ Within approach of the Apostle Paul, groups like the Christian Gnostics and other Christian Mystic groups, had to for the sake of self-preservation against an increased onslaught of Catholic persecution go to ground so to speak, with many fleeing to caves and to monasteries hidden in the hills, and thus the internalised approach to Christianity was lost to the formalistic externalised approach of the Catholic Church.

A new word became the religious catchcry of this institutionalised approach to the Christian life, it was the word "faith," hanging its hat on the scripture that speaks of it being impossible to please God without faith; once again bearing witness to the ongoing misinterpretation of scripture that the Catholic Church used to promote its institutionalised agenda. An institutionalised externalised approach that bore witness to the words of Jesus, "the people honour me with their lips but their hearts are far from me." This approach over time saw the church taking stories out of the Bible and turning them into some sort of ceremonial ritual. For example the story of the Last Supper of Jesus with his disciples was turned into a ritual that has duped people into thinking that all they have to do is take communion on a regular basis and all will be well with God.

The truth of the story was that Jesus, having what he probably thought was going to be His last meal with his friends, as was the custom at any meal according to Jewish tradition, broke bread. Bread was broken at every meal as a way to express thanks to God for providing food from the earth to eat, and the sharing of meals was and still is a very important thing to do for Jewish families. Jesus, believing He might be having His last meal was encouraging His disciples to continue gathering together as a family. This breaking of bread tradition is something that is only done in the context of a meal. The Catholic Church fathers took this Jewish family meal tradition, and turned it into a church ritual involving the breaking of a wafer, the sipping of red wine, accompanied with the words, "do this in remembrance of me." A Jewish family tradition thus became a sacrament or a communion process, to be administered only by a priest, so as to psychologically commit people to continue to return to the church regularly.

Within a short period of time ceremony and ritual had replaced the inner knowing or revelatory approach to the Christian faith of the mystic minded, and true communion with God was relegated to small pockets of monks and mystics hidden away in monasteries. The internal approach, which had opened the way for society to experience God you could say in a supernatural way, gave way to the external approach, a ritualistic attitude to the things of God, and the door had been fully opened to all manner of external intellectual influencers in the religious affairs of humankind, including the concept of rationalism, materialism and atheism.

There are five major milestones recorded in the Biblical narrative with regards to the earthly life of Jesus. They are his birth, his baptism, the transfiguration, his crucifixion and his ascension. The Gospel narrative of the transfiguration of Jesus was considered by Thomas Aquinas, an influential philosopher and theologian of the 13th century to be the greatest event ever amongst all the recorded experiences of the prophet, far greater than the story of His birth and that of His crucifixion. Thomas Aquinas believed the story of the transfiguration of Jesus was a demonstration of the perfection of life in heaven. That consideration however is slightly at odds with much of Christianity today, which tends to focus mostly in a celebratory manner on the virgin birth of Jesus at Christmas, and the cross of crucifixion at Easter, as being the two most pivotal moments in the earthly life of Jesus the Christ. Relating his ascension to heaven in the transfiguration purely as a picture of the reward that awaits all Christians when their earthly life ceases.

Whilst all these events, these five major milestones stand out in recorded history as significant stories, this chapter will focus primarily on what I have personally come to understand as the two primary experiences that occurred in the life of Jesus that shaped the fulfilment of His destiny, and that are meant to be seen as prototypes for us; experiences that I believe in earnest must become the cornerstones in the lives of not only those who seek to live a Christian life, but in fact for all those who desire to come to a realization of their true spiritual nature and destiny. Two experiences that are intended by Divinity to be a part of every human being's life regardless of race or religion as they journey through this mortal world into cosmic immortality.

Firstly we have the wilderness event, or what I call the tale of the transcendence of the ego, which occurred as Jesus sat alone in the desert, far from the crowds, focused in the moment on his present life, including I have no doubt on what was about to befall him in the immediate future; meditating on the now whilst contemplating his ongoing unfolding destiny. And secondly the importance of the event known as the transfiguration of Jesus, which is intrinsically linked to the underlying message of the wilderness experience and to the message given us in the crucifixion of Christ, as well as being a picture of the resultant end of the transitionary journey of all human beings that I spoke of in the previous chapter, a picture of the end game of the promise of the prophets of old regarding the messianic mission of Jesus. For those not familiar with the wilderness story I share it in paraphrased form now.

The story of Jesus in the wilderness of Judea according to the Bible occurred shortly after John the Baptist had baptised Him in the Jordan River. Jesus had travelled into the wilderness of Judea and had spent forty days in seclusion, during which time the Gospels record that He had a fascinating one on one encounter with the fallen angel Satan, who set about testing his allegiance to God by offering Him significant rewards if he would use His extraordinary powers in a demonstration of self interested ego driven behaviour. Over the centuries since Christianity's conception, most church teaching on the wilderness event has focused on the meaning of this story as being an example of the sinless nature of Christ, who could not be tempted, when that is not strictly the true message in it. Jesus' wilderness experience as it is known, was actually a pivotal moment in his cosmic journey, given as an example for us to follow in our journey into and through the Atonement process.

Unlike the story of Adam and Eve and the serpent in the Garden of Eden, which was for Lucifer seemingly a very successful strategy in which he brought about humankind's original psychological separation from God, this experience in the wilderness for Satan was not as successful. It was however the same strategy at work in that Lucifer attempted to cause a psychological separation between Jesus and God, a separation of the Mind of Christ from the Mind of God, attempting to break the oneness or unity of mind that existed between the two and to in fact cause Jesus who was God in flesh, to sin against His own Word. Similar to the Garden of Eden story it was the mind influencing principle of doubt that was used.

Why was this story given to us? To demonstrate to us that there will be a pivotal moment in our life journey when we are given opportunity to renounce the ego completely, and then by allowing the Christ Mind to control our responses, move forward in the Atonement process. Or alternately we can reject the opportunity, re-embrace the ego mind completely and thus alienate ourselves from our spiritual destiny. If Jesus had failed in this event there would in all likelihood not have been a crucifixion, however He could not fail because He was God in flesh. This Biblical event or the tale of transcendence of the ego, which occurred in the wilderness, similar to the Buddha's experience in the desert, is in its analogical and spiritual interpretation a picture of humankind's destiny to overcome the delusion of separateness from Divinity that we are born with. A separation continually reinforced throughout our lives by the contrived logic and reasoning of the dominating rational human mind, that has at the behest of the ego continuously orchestrated a thought based existence, which over time has become to us the true reality of our lives.

For both Jesus and the Buddha that moment of meditative stillness in their physical bodies, was also a moment of spiritual warfare in the mind, during which time after the ego mind's initial attack, the forces of goodness came to their aid, and a revelation came to them from the Spirit within them. It was an example for us of how, in this daily physical life we lead, whilst we may not be aware of it, there is an invisible force at work, prowling about seeking someone to mentally possess, an antagonistic aspect of our lower nature that is determined to uphold the subconscious sense of separateness from the Creator that all human beings feel from the moment of birth. The Apostle Peter in the New Testament put it this way, "be vigilant, because your adversary the devil (the ego mind) prowls around like a roaring lion seeking someone to devour."

For the Buddha that antagonistic entity was called Mara, the tempter, and for Jesus it was evidenced as Satan or the devil, with Mara pointing out to the Buddha that he should really be the king of the realm, and Satan offering Jesus the power to have dominion over all things. An offer appealing to the ego sense of the mind, not made in a gesture of generosity by this prince of darkness, but rather a subtle thought influence for both men to forsake their karmic destiny in favour of present and future moments of pleasure and happiness. So when Mara offered up his beautiful daughters and the Buddha refused the offer, and when the devil made mention to Jesus who was hungry that he would give him the power to change a rock into bread and Jesus replied, "man shall not live by bread alone," in both cases an ultimate transcendence of the lower nature or ego occurred, resulting in a complete collapse of the illusionary sense of their own separation from Divinity. This is a picture of the enlightenment process.

In truth the process of enlightenment is not as mystical and hard fought to attain as many would believe. To become enlightened one does not have to put on a loincloth and lock themselves away in a cave on top of a mountain for years and years, or in fact to go through a physical wilderness experience as did Jesus and the Buddha. Those who do so do as a matter of choice or as they are led by the Spirit, and that is fine too. Enlightenment is simply a complete conquering of the ego thought entity that controls our lives, and in many cases it has happened and can happen in a moment of time, as Eckhart Tolle in his book The Power of Now testified happened to him, but there is another way. I touched on this in Chapter 1, but to give you a little more detail whilst trying to explain it as simply as possible. Enlightenment is simply waking up from this dream we call life and recognizing the truth that has always been and always will be.

We need to understand that the Bible does have the truth of the process of enlightenment buried within the scriptures. The process of enlightenment does not solely lie within the domain of Eastern Religion. It is similarly referenced in Christianity but is referred to in the Bible as "being led by the Spirit of the Lord," or "a life lived in the Spirit," a life lived in the Light. But unfortunately most Christians have not appropriated the vital essence of this truth experientially, because the true meaning about this subject has over centuries of Christian teaching been obscured by the mind centric dogmas and creeds of a priestly hierarchy seeking complete religious dominance. This collapsing of the sense of separateness from Divinity, and entering into an enlightened state, is not a new teaching. It was being taught in the schools of the faithful long before the Bible ever came into existence.

Its pre-Christ existence is even verified in the Bible itself where it says, "Moses was educated in all the wisdom of the Egyptians." The whole basis of the Egyptian Book of The Dead is this conquest of the lower self or lower nature and union or reunion with our higher self or higher nature. It is known as Osirification, or identification with the Supreme God Osiris, and in the Old Testament it is seen as identification with the God Jehovah. Our God the Universal Consciousness is God no matter what name God has been given by different cultures throughout the centuries of humankind's existence. It is the fact of this truth that matters, not the form or words in which it is expressed. So in modern society, where does this imbedded sense of separateness from God and from every other person in the universe, a sense of alienation come from, and consequently subconsciously motivate our desire for enlightenment to break this psychological state? This is where it comes from.

This fundamental deception grew within us initially through our cultural conditioning, eventually being reinforced and embedded in us through our continual identification with form and our own individual sense of personhood as I discussed in Chapter 1. We have imagined our whole lives that there is us on one hand, our neighbour on the other, and God is way out there on the other side of us both, with a wide chasm in between. We have culturally and experientially influenced our psyche to believe that if we work hard and long enough, if we are good enough, if we pray earnestly enough, or simply if we believe fervently enough, that some day much later at the end of our earthly life in a kingdom called heaven we will get to be with God and will all live happily ever after.

We have believed as we have been taught or had passed down to us, that heaven is a habitation of love, joy, peace and contentment is some physical place far away in time and space, rather than the truth that heaven is a glorious or Glory filled mode of existence that God has intended for us to partake of right now in the present moment. We have failed to experientially appropriate this truth that Jesus, the Apostle Paul, and other great ancient spiritual masters of the pre-Christ era all espoused, that God's Presence or the Kingdom of God or Universal Consciousness is within us now. The truth is that the Divine Presence or the Christ within as the Apostle Paul described it, has been in us and with us all the time. We have simply allowed our dominating rational mind to draw a veil across the Holy of Holies within that contains all the mysteries of the Divine, and in doing so we have by choice separated ourselves in our outer being, our way of thinking, from that which our inner being already knows is true.

A sense of Divine separateness is the most toxic belief we can have. It causes us to sub-consciously believe that there is something wrong with our life, and that there is something in us or about us that needs continual changing or fixing. Consequently in every part of our life it becomes the driving energetic force that motivates us to want to change our present moment circumstances, to be someone else or to be somewhere else and to attach ourselves to an ever-increasing number of new experiences. And the only thing that can permanently change that illusionary understanding of life is a complete collapse of the sense of separation through transcendence of the ego mind. This is what happened to Jesus in the wilderness and the Buddha in the desert.

Now as well as the wilderness story, the story of the transfiguration of Jesus is also a most significant message. I share it in a very brief paraphrased version here for those readers who are not familiar with it.

It was about a week or so after Jesus had spoken to His disciples telling them that He would soon be crucified, killed and later raised to life, that He took Peter, James and John up a small mountain to pray. While He was praying His personal appearance was changed into a glorified form and His clothing glowed with a dazzling white. The Old Testament prophet leaders Moses and Elijah appeared and talked with Jesus about

His impending death and a voice from heaven called out, "Listen to Him", symbolic of the fact that the Law of the Old Testament delivered by men such as Abraham and Moses, must give way to the new universal law of the Spirit of Life in Christ Jesus. The disciples whilst finding it a little difficult to understand having only ever seen Jesus in human form and never in glorified form, were nevertheless able to gain greater understanding about the Divinity and Divine purpose of Christ.

This story is a picture showing the potential for all human beings, having transcended their old nature, having collapsed that sense of separateness, to discover the immortal nature of their true self, knowledge that in truth has been with them their whole life, but hidden in their inner mind. In other words a picture showing the potential for all human beings "to be transfigured or transformed" from mortality to immortality, thus conquering death. The transfiguration is the final meeting place of the ephemeral and temporal with the formless and eternal, the crossing over from the visible time bound existence into the invisible timeless one, from the ever changing to the changeless, a meeting of minds that bridges the gap between the earthly life and the heavenly life, between mortality and immortality. It is the final stage of a human being's evolutionary transitionary journey that I spoke of in the previous chapter.

The transfiguration of Jesus was also a demonstration by revelation of the Glory within and the transformative power made available to every human being in his or her earthly life who makes the shift from a dualistic rational mind dominated lifestyle to a non-dualistic existence; or you could say to every person who transcends from personhood to presence, who transitions from the collective unconscious and collective conscious state of mind to the universal consciousness state of mind.

This is the true message of the cross. Jesus transcended the mind in the wilderness experience and on the cross, and then as a final act of love on the cross He gave that transcended mind to us. We have the mind of Christ within, but in order for us to have a practical experience of that in our lives and the resultant transformation it can bring about, we must transcend our ego mind our old self, we must reject it, bury it daily, and then as we do this watch it resurrected and renewed in subservient form to the Mind of Christ within us, our True Self. Then as our old nature is progressively renewed to our new nature, after a while these ego thoughts will cease their attack, they will raise the flag and surrender.

What does it mean to transcend? It is going beyond, it is getting past it, and it is getting over it. When people perhaps unkindly but with good intent say, "you need to get over it," they should be saying, "you need to go beyond those current thoughts in your mind, those thoughts that are giving you some kind of grief or angst and transition to a higher level of thinking." You must get past the past, it's gone, bury it, and get over worrying about the future, let it take care of itself. And you must get over any egregious type thinking whatever form it takes, for example bitterness, dislike, animosity or hatred; any thinking that involves some sort of psychological attack on another human being. Forgive yourself for thinking the thought and forgive the person in a non-accusatory way whose actions may have introduced into your life that manner of thought.

That is how you transcend the ego mind. That is how Jesus did it on the cross with His tormentors. Jesus was not just being nice when He said "Father forgive them," He was putting into practice Universal Law, the new Law of the Spirit. And if the thought comes back again then forgive it again, until eventually you will find it no longer has any power to hurt you. Continue to resist it and eventually it will completely flee from you or at the minimum no longer have any power to impact on your behaviours.

The most important and common aspect of the spiritual life of Jesus, of the Buddha, and of all great past masters was the experience of transcendence, the collapsing of this illusionary sense of the separateness of our own self from God and our sense of separateness from the rest of humanity; an event which in itself is the catalyst for the final transitionary transfiguration. This is what our earthly life is all about. This is how we truly become witnesses for Him as the Bible describes it. A witness is one who gives evidence. The transforming power received by us in our moment of transcendence from our own personal wilderness, is the evidence that causes our earthly life to be a witness of the existence of the Christ within. People will say there's something different about you. Luke spoke of this in the Book of Acts. He was not saying that walking the neighbourhood knocking on doors, standing on a street corner handing out Jesus loves you pamphlets, trying to convert your neighbour or jumping in a boat and sailing across the world to "save" the heathen, were demonstrations of us being a witness, no matter how well intended those activities are. He was speaking of the life changing power in our earthly walk that witnesses to others the evidence of the Christ within.

The demonstration of an overcoming earthly life lived in power, non-attachment and in oneness with those around us, in love, peace, kindness calmness and contentment, no matter what our circumstance, is the true witness of the Christ within. It is the evidence of our transcendence from personhood to presence, from individuality to universality, from spiritual unconsciousness to Cosmic Consciousness. There exists within every human being a timeless place, one of endless spaciousness. Some will call it Cosmic Consciousness or Universal Consciousness, some an energetic force, some our true nature or our true self. In theological and spiritual writings it has been described in many ways, Absolute Truth, Awareness, the Christ within, the Holy Spirit, Atman, the Buddha within, the Light that lights every man, the Breath of Life and Presence to name a few. It matters not what you call it, it only matters that it does exist and that those who diligently seek to discover it, and do discover it through practical experience, will have a life-changing encounter, as did Jesus and the Buddha in the wilderness.

Cosmic Consciousness is not an imaginary place conjured up in our minds, but a subtle place, a place of absolute unchanging truth, the Divine orchard that houses all the good fruit necessary to enjoy a heavenly life on earth. It is the Christ within that the Apostle Paul spoke of in Rome and in the city of Corinth, urging the people to discover and know.

Human beings, regardless of race or creed are put on this planet for one primary reason and one reason only. We are here to find that common dimension within ourselves, that is deeper than thought, the thread that connects us to the fabric of the universal garment and subsequently links us in oneness and love to each other, the dimension of consciousness or the universal life force commonly referred to as God. Dr. Martin Luther King Jr., the great civil rights leader in America, spoke passionately about the desire of the universe to see humanity become aware of the cosmic nature of its own existence and the interconnectedness of all beings in Universal Consciousness, but to do it without all the effort attached to achieving that realisation. I was privileged some years ago, to with a friend, visit the Lorraine Motel in Memphis Tennessee where Dr. King was assassinated, the motel that was after his death permanently closed and turned into a small memorial museum. In researching his life some time later I came across some words that he spoke that have always stayed with me.

He said, "all of life is interrelated, we are all caught up in an inescapable network of mutuality, tied into a single garment of destiny." Dr. King understood that we don't need to acquire more worldly knowledge or take more courses or practice harder in order to come into a realisation of our oneness with the universe and with each other; we just have to accept that it exists. We just need to be still and know that God is God and is within us all; and that the core of our being, the Christ within is the ultimate reality, the root and ground of the universe and the source of all that exists; and to be immersed in His consciousness is all we need to do to play our part in His redemptive plan for the universe.

To try and put it in practical terms, to be immersed in Universal Consciousness is to live in the moment in a complete state of awareness of our true nature our true sense of self, to live in the Spirit, not distracted by the relentless murmurings of the mind. Rejecting them as they come and refocusing our thoughts on the Christ within until eventually their visitation becomes less often and finally ceases. Most of society functions within the time bound paradigm of the body mind. We celebrate the birth of our body; we celebrate time events of our functional life in the form of anniversaries of things like births, weddings and also death anniversaries such as in memorial services, and we give little regard to the timeless aspect of our existence, this indwelling and out dwelling Universal Consciousness. We spend most of our day every day interacting with a focus on the body mind aspect of our own personal existence; it's all at the body mind level.

The world has conceptualised God, mainly due to the activity of ego energy forces that insist on keeping people unaware of the true nature of their existence, to prevent humanity from discovering its true reality. And if we appear to at any stage be getting closer to a revelation of this inner consciousness, these ego forces will divert our attention away from impending Christ Consciousness to perhaps a religious experience, or some kind of spiritual experience, it too eventually being discarded as the ego mind begins its campaign of distraction and procrastination.

Since birth we have relied on engaging with new knowledge and new experiences to fulfil the yearning of the Voice of Consciousness within to bring its creative healing nature to our conscious level of awareness. This manifests in a constant state of varying degrees of uneasiness you might call it. This uneasiness is the yearning of God's Spirit within us, the Christ within saying I've had enough of these conceptual experiences; I want to return back to the beginning when all was well in the Garden metaphorically speaking, to my psychological connection with God. Since consciousness in the first instant is compelled to think of itself and express itself through the person, after you wake up to the truth of who you really are the persona, the personality patterns of your ego self will progressively be seen as less important and progressively more and more lessen their grip on your life, the grip that continuously pulls you towards ephemeral things, visible things you can attach yourself to.

To try to help them Jesus taught the conflicted and confused crowds with words such as, "the Kingdom of God is within you," and "seek ye first the Kingdom of God," and the Apostle Paul seemingly with less patience than Jesus in trying to explain this to the citizens of Corinth, said in what appeared to be an underlying tone of frustration, "don't you understand that your body is a temple and that the Spirit of God dwells in you?"

We are reminded in ancient texts that even before we were formed in the womb of our mother the Creator of all things *knew us* and from that point of *knowing* formed and fashioned our body-mind, our earthly vehicle. The original meaning of the word *knew* in this case means that the Supreme Being had a unified state with us; a merged state you could call it, a state of oneness with us. Yet many spiritually inclined people including Christians of all kinds in their search for spiritual truth fail to recognize the Cosmic or universal nature of life, merely settling for an intellectualised understanding of their chosen religion and you could say settling for a literalised interpretation of the wonderful truths in the Holy book, rather than a metaphysical interpretation of them. Preferring what is called the milk of the word rather than the meat. The mysteries of the indwelling are found in the meat and not in the milk.

Once we come to an understanding that our inner self, the Christ within is cosmically joined to our immortal nature, our higher self, and come to accept that our lower nature and its identification, fascination, and co-operation with visible form and all the material aspects of our life is just a passing phase, an illusion you could call it, and of such is inconsequential, the captivity to a life of personhood with its accompanying stresses ceases. This is the truth that Jesus spoke of when he said "you shall know the truth and the truth shall set you free." He meant this truth would set you psychologically free.

In the Book of Matthew we see the words of Jesus, "blessed are the poor in spirit." What was He meaning? He was talking about those who have made either a wrong investment spiritually or perhaps made no investment at all spiritually. Poverty of spirit is the result of someone having made an incorrect investment on behalf of his or her Soul. He was speaking of psychological poverty, poverty of the mind. If one is poor in terms of food sustenance there is a hunger for food. If one is poor in spirit there is a hunger for spiritual food, and if one shows a hunger for spiritual food God will bless them and give it to them. That is what Jesus meant when He said, "Blessed are the poor in spirit." The church can't satisfy this spiritual hunger, good works can't, and giving financially to the church can't. The only thing that can satisfy spiritual hunger is a relationship with the Holy Spirit.

Jesus, the egoless Jesus, through His wilderness experience and subsequent journey to the cross, overcame death and the grave, and went on through the resurrection process into the fullness of God. At the same time He ushered in the Teacher, the Comforter, the Holy Spirit to continue His role assisting us in fulfilling our side of the Atonement bargain. Yes there is a journey, but we are not left stranded in the desert. The Atonement process, the appropriation of all that the Atonement is meant to be is the key, bringing about in each individual a state of Christ likeness whilst we are still alive on earth; bringing us in fact back into the reconnected state, the state of oneness that was lost in humankind's original psychological separation from the Creator. The process of mind renewal, getting our thought life right, is the major component of that Atonement process and all this is accomplished in a partnership: a deliberate partnership between our will and the willingness of the Holy Spirit. It's as simple as that.

> "Become a disciple of your mind, which is of the Father. I am come to give sight to those who seek after right-mindedness. Understanding is hidden from the heart and only revealed to the mind."
>
> Words of Jesus from the Nag Hammadi texts.

“As the sea currents are the invisible arteries of the ocean supporting the myriads of life forms in their individual journey, so the Holy Spirit is the invisible artery in the ocean of consciousness that supports humanity’s life form in its evolutionary and transitionary journey through the realms of that consciousness into eternal oneness with God.”

The Holy Spirit...The God of Wisdom The Feminine Principle of God

TEN

Peter Seeger was born on May 3rd 1919 and died in January 2014. He was 94 years of age when he passed. Pete as he was known was an American folk singer and a colourful and controversial social activist. Regarded as one of the most creative songwriters of all time, he was responsible for writing such hit songs as On Top of Old Smoky, Kisses Sweeter Than Wine, Where Have All The Flowers Gone, If I had A Hammer, Turn, Turn, Turn, as well as many others, and for rearranging the lyrics of We Shall Overcome that saw it become the recognizable anthem of the Civil Rights Movement in America. Pete Seeger was always quick to acknowledge the reason for his being able to produce hit songs for entertainers like Peter, Paul and Mary, The Kingston Trio, Trini Lopez, The Byrds and many other artists, believing that he achieved his creative outcomes by tapping into his inner creative being as he described it. Kindness was an obvious component of his nature. Always generous of heart and ready to assist struggling musicians, he was the chief architect in obtaining a record contract for Bob Dylan after Dylan had experienced many rejections.

True to his inner and outer attitude to life, Seeger's banjo was emblazoned with the motto, "This Machine Surrounds Hate and Forces It To Surrender." In 2010, still active at 91 years of age, he wrote and performed the song God's Counting on Me, God's Counting on You. Always showing a keen interest in the spiritual dynamic of the universe, he was obviously a staunch believer in the non-dualistic nature of humankind, for when asked, "what are your religious or spiritual beliefs?" he was quick to reply, "I think God is in everything. Whenever I open my eyes

I'm looking at God, whenever I'm listening to something or someone I'm listening to God. I don't tell people God is an old white man with a long white beard. I think that God is in everything cause everything comes out of God; it can't come out of nothing. God has always been." It was obvious Pete Seeger saw the nature of God as being one of complete engagement with the whole universe and everything it contains.

Once having been asked the question, "how do you continue to write hit songs?" he was quick to reply, "I seek out much of my inspiration from spiritual writings." One can now understand his underlying thought process when he wrote the hit song recorded by The Byrds called "Turn, Turn, Turn." The lyrics of its main verse are, "to everything there is a season and a time for every purpose under heaven, a time to be born, a time to die, a time to plant, a time to reap," which came from the Old Testament Book of Ecclesiastes, from one of what are known as the five Books of Wisdom, it being the fourth book in the continuum. The lyrics "Turn, Turn, Turn" and those directly following, "I swear it's not too late," obviously an adaptation from the Book of Isaiah the Prophet which is the first book following the wisdom books. It says, "turn to the Lord before its too late."

At the beginning of this book I made the following statement. "Wisdom is not a transferable commodity between human beings. Wisdom is the one asset that can be neither bought nor taught. The Holy Spirit alone can birth true Wisdom into one's being. God is the only source of true Wisdom and the Holy Spirit is God's agent, gently delivering that Wisdom as it emanates from the Mind of Christ within us, in those moments in life that we choose as an act of our will, to be still, to be silent, and to listen."

The wisdom books in the Bible including the one Pete Seeger referenced for his song lyrics will not give you wisdom per se just by reading them, they are not an instructional manual that needs to be practised to get results, rather they are given to impart to us a greater understanding of the importance of Godly Wisdom itself, how it connects us with life and true reality, and how it is purposed by God to guide us through life confidently and safely. This chapter deals with exactly that, looking at the Holy Spirit's role in our lives as the Spirit of Wisdom, looking at God's purposed desire for us to have active engagement and relationship with Her, and looking at the correlation between the Holy Spirit's active involvement in our lives and our capacity to be positive expressions of Her Wisdom as we tap into our unlimited potential through wise decision making.

The key to one having the abundant life that Jesus continuously spoke of is engagement with the Holy Spirit; it's as simple as that. We read in the Book of John that Jesus said, "I am come that you might have life, and that you might have it more abundantly." The words "might have" are from the Greek tense that means "to have and to continually possess." The word "life" comes from the Greek "Zoë" a small word with a big meaning. It does not simply mean life as we use the word such as being alive, it means life lived as if we were God Himself, full of joy, peace, creativity, zest, vitality, good health and successful endeavour. That is what Jesus said He came to give us. That is what ongoing engagement with the Holy Spirit the Spirit of Wisdom who followed Jesus can bring into one's life. And that is why as we read in the Bible, towards the end of His earthly life, in one of His last conversations with His disciples, Jesus handed humanity over to the Holy Spirit, the Comforter. In doing this His desire was that as we transition through life, through the various levels of consciousness and physicality, we will do it abundantly and seamlessly, causing the minimum amount of psychological and physical damage to ourselves and to those around us in the process.

As I committed to previously, in this chapter we will also explore that age old question, "is the Holy Spirit of the male gender or of the female gender?" Whilst I have my own opinion on this I will after presenting certain facts and information leave it up to you personally to decide for yourself what the truth of the matter is. Is this earth shatteringly important in your spiritual evolution? Not necessarily, the engagement process with the Holy Spirit is what is most important, but it will give you greater understanding of the overall Godhead and how it functions and in the process perhaps bring correction to some long held beliefs that may have taken hold of you, and in doing so given institutionalised religion an opportunity to hijack your spiritual journey and hold it hostage to the realm of the ritual.

If I was asked to describe what God desires, not for us but rather of us, more than anything else, I would not fall back on all those old hackneyed terms and words that the church has promulgated to their congregations over the centuries; such as God desires obedience, or desires us worship Him, or that God desires us to love Jesus, or to gather together at church and to give tithes, I would turn to one word only and that word is "engagement," which is simply "to make a psychological connection." God wants us primarily in our Christian walk to engage with Him, because continuous engagement brings about long-term connection and relationship. Similarly as in a physical relationship the process of getting engaged is purposed as the entry pass into permanent relationship in the form of marriage.

The European origin of the engagement process as a pre-requisite to a physical marriage is found in the Jewish law the Torah, where marriage consists of two separate acts, "kiddushin" their word for sanctification, which means making something holy, and "chupah," the actual joining together process. So in accordance with original law, in order for there to be a complete union of two, there must first be engagement and that engagement opens the way for a relationship of a holy nature, which is followed by marriage, the result of which is the complete immersion of the two separate units into one functioning unit or family. Similarly in the world of the Spirit, in the first instance our engagement with the Holy Spirit is designed amongst other things to birth holiness into our life, the kiddushin, said engagement then progressively leading us into a spiritual marriage, chupah, a full immersion in Universal Consciousness, which is a point at which we become psychologically one with God.

However in most western societies save a few, thanks to the ego mind's ongoing manipulation and attempted influencing of any kind of law, whether it be secular or spiritual, we see the exact opposite. It is the complete reversal. In most western societies the union of bodies comes first, sometimes even on the first or second date, but certainly long before any thought of any potential engagement or marriage comes to mind, and the thought of having a holy relationship with someone in most cases never enters into the picture. Why does the ego mind see it as important to promote this complete reversal of the process, to promote promiscuity as we call it? Because promiscuity born out of an ego mind's desire for self-gratification disengages the potential for holiness to materialise through the engagement marriage process. It is the ego mind's way of attacking the holiness or sacredness of God's creation.

Thus in much of western society, if a relationship does make it to a point of marriage, the act of marriage does not become a holy union but an unholy union, even though the wedding vows have incorporated that type of phraseology symbolic of Jewish law into the actual church service. The everyday marriage ceremony has used the standard phraseology "united in holy matrimony" since time immemorial, whilst at the same time uniting in marriage some of the most unholy people ever. I am conscious of this because in my role as a minister, whilst I performed marriages that I believed were of a holy union, I also regrettably performed many marriages birthed out of an unholy relationship, evidenced by the fact that many of them later became either just a relationship of convenience or just another divorce statistic.

The same process, the engagement, marriage, joining together sequence of events occurs in the realm of the spirit in terms of us establishing a formal unified relationship between God and ourselves. But here's the thing. In the invisible world of God's Spirit it works in the exact reverse of the way it is supposed to work in the physical world according to Jewish law. In the world of the Spirit it commences firstly with us offering our bodies to God, we give our self, our complete person as we know and understand it to God. How do we do that? We take our complete person to the cross of Christ. Evangelical Christianity refers to this as "getting saved." We offer our body and mind, our complete self as we know it to Christ. It is a spiritual proposal. We are proposing to God that we want to spend our life with Him. In doing so we are saying I want a permanent relationship with you God. God then says "I accept your offer and here is your engagement ring, the Holy Spirit, who will lead you into all truth and guide you into a state of holiness and wholeness, who will prepare you for your spiritual marriage, and eventually lead you when you are ready into a complete union of minds with me, into a marriage of our minds. That's how it works in the spiritual realm.

Whilst the offering up of our complete self at the cross is the first step, the proposal, in doing this all our old ego driven mind attitudes and body behaviours and detrimental personality patterns don't just immediately and miraculously disappear, as many Christian churches teach, some do some don't; it requires of us our participation and co-operation during the engagement period for this to happen and for holiness to grow. Our engagement with the Holy Spirit is where we in a way learn all about God, similarly as happens in a physical engagement where a couple get to know each other in preparation for marriage, or at least that is what is meant to happen. Due to limited focus and lack of attention to detail this doesn't happen with many couples, sometimes leading to a deteriorating, unfruitful, sometimes disastrous ongoing relationship. Similarly with regards to the spiritual growth of their congregations this is where many Christian organizations get it wrong, at the point of engagement. They get "the cross" part right, evangelical Christianity is very good at this, but "the ongoing engagement process" wrong.

The Catholic Church with their dogmas, creeds and ritual tried in some ways to address this but due to the autocratic non-scriptural attitude they adopted they too got in wrong. The Pentecostal religion, which got it so right in bringing an awareness of certain aspects of the workings of the Spirit into the Christian life, got it totally wrong with the engagement process, pretty much teaching that once a person makes the journey to the cross then automatically, miraculously, God delivers a big beautiful gift wrapped box of fruit, the Fruit of the Spirit, to their doorstep. They completely neglected the engagement process, in particular the renewing of the mind process to the Christ Mind or God way of thinking, or to use a common expression neglected to get both parties involved on the same page, and left the door wide open to the ego mind's agenda.

The engagement process in the world of the Spirit involves a psychological reconnection rather than a strictly rational mind connection as it does in the physical world. It is through initial and subsequent ongoing engagement with the Holy Spirit, between our rational mind and the Christ Mind within, that we create a union of minds that will increase and grow our level of consciousness and holiness, eventually tipping the balance in the direction of the Christ Mind. The ultimate purpose for every human being in his or her journey through life, is to be totally immersed in the Universal Consciousness or the Universal Mind of God, and to reclaim completely that psychological connection with God that was lost in "the fall," to come out of exile and return psychologically home, and this is initiated and prosecuted through our willing engagement with the Holy Spirit the Spirit of Wisdom. We come out of spiritual exile and return to our God given inheritance.

The Gnostics of old that I spoke of in Chapter 2 were familiar with this state of psychological exile, a state of mental or mind separation from the Mind of God and all other cosmic aspects of the universe. They felt that the human Soul is in fact merely a stranger in a foreign land occupying itself with the trivial instead of the necessary. For the Gnostics however, rather than seeing this state of psychological alienation as something to be sorrowful about, as a physical refugee might see their own plight, they saw it as a place of opportunity to come forth and claim their spiritual land of promise through engagement and union with God, a spiritual land that was their God purposed inheritance. The

Gnostics believed that this darkness upon the mind that causes the subconscious psychological feeling of alienation or separation from God, could, if looked at from a positive point of view be the starting point, a turning point to take them onward into their journey out of the darkness of exile into the Light.

This concept of alienation or separation from ones source or home is also spoken of in a Gnostic archetypal myth called the story of Sophia. It is found in the Pistis Sophia, a Gnostic text discovered in 1773, believed to have been written around the 3rd or 4th century A.D. Before the discovery of the Nag Hammadi library the Pistis Sophia was the largest known source of ancient teachings in the Gnostic tradition. It was written in the Sahidic dialect of Upper Egypt and its title means Power and Wisdom. The manuscript was purchased by the British Museum in 1795 from a doctor who had obtained it from an unknown source. It tells in part the story of Sophia's fall from Grace, her ongoing alienation, and her subsequent restoration. The translated copy that I have is 600 pages long, so it is too long and detailed to discuss here, but in simple terms it is a type of mythological metaphor for the evolutionary or transitionary spiritual journey of humankind that I spoke of in Chapter 8.

Some readers may be familiar with a recent world news report in July 2020, centring on the controversy surrounding the Church of Hagia Sophia in Turkey, also called Church of the Holy Wisdom or Church of the Divine Wisdom. It is a magnificent building, which at one stage was the largest Roman Catholic Cathedral in the Eastern Roman Empire. It was built in Istanbul formerly Constantinople around the 6th century under the direction of the Byzantine emperor Justinian 1. I speak briefly of the Byzantine Christians, the Greek speaking Christian Romans of Late Antiquity and the Middle Ages in the next chapter, Chapter 11. The recent controversy surrounds a Turkish government decision to reconvert and change the former Catholic Cathedral from its existing museum status into the Hagia Sophia Grand Mosque of the Islamic faith.

The main protagonist in the Pistis Sophia text is a person named Sophia Archamoth, Archamoth coming from the Hebrew word chokmah, which means Wisdom. The Hebrew word chokmah then transitioned during the Hellenistic period into the Greek word Sophia. The Hellenistic period was that period of Mediterranean history between the death of Alexander the Great and the emergence of the Roman Empire, a time of immense Greek cultural development. In Gnosticism Sophia is the Spirit of Wisdom, the feminine aspect of God, and is in fact the Holy Spirit. The Pistis Sophia writings in part focus on Her separation from humankind and her struggle to be released back into humanity. It is as I said before, a type of mythical archetypal metaphor for humankind's psychological disconnection from God and its desperate need for a reconnection.

The primary text of the Pistis Sophia centres on the teachings of Jesus to His assembled disciples after His crucifixion and resurrection, a group that also included His mother Mary, Mary Magdalene and Martha. In this text the risen Jesus, having spent 11 years speaking with His disciples but always only sharing with them the lower mysteries of the cosmos, now, having received His robes of glory, reveals to them the higher mysteries of the cosmos that relate to the more complex cosmologies that are necessary for the Soul to attain, enabling it to reach the highest Divine realms, and enter into the eternal Light that has been beckoning humanity forward as God's cosmic plan for the redemption of humankind has evolved. The story of Sophia is in fact a picture of humankind's descent into ignorance and fear and its eventual ascent out of this state of mind through the intervention of Jesus and His Atonement principle. Sophia the person is in fact the feminine characterisation of Christ's Spirit, the Holy Spirit the Spirit of Wisdom, leading us out of the darkness of our ego mind into the Light of the Christ Mind.

The Books of Wisdom that I mention at the beginning of this chapter contain numerous references to the Wisdom of God as being of the feminine gender, and of Her existence before the creation of the world and also of Her participation in the first cosmic acts of creation. In the Old Testament books of Proverbs and Ecclesiastes She, Wisdom, addresses the reader in a type of revelatory monologue always speaking in the first person. If one wants to come to a greater and deeper understanding of why the Holy Spirit came into the world, more than the simple message that Jesus expressed to His disciples before His crucifixion which was that She came to teach us all things and to help us remember all the things of God, the Wisdom Books will encapsulate in a more lengthy and detailed way the profoundness of what Jesus was meaning, and give one a deeper understanding of what Jesus really meant with His specific terminology, "The Holy Spirit will teach you all things."

For instance if you look closely at the books of Proverbs and Ecclesiastes you will see Her talking about Herself where She says, "I was set up from everlasting, from the beginning, or ever the earth was, when there were no depths I was brought forth when He prepared the heavens I was there." She says, "I encompassed the circuit of the sea, walked in the bottom of the deep, in the waves of the sea and in all the earth and in every people and nation. He created me in the beginning before the world, and I shall never fail." She is talking about Herself, Universal Consciousness, the Mind of God. In terms of Her role as our comforter and teacher that Jesus promised She would undertake, then that is a pretty good resume of Her credentials.

There are two emanations of God that God has purposed for all human beings to engage with at some stage of their earthly life in order to complete the Atonement process and be successfully guided back to the bosom of God, the source from which they came. The first is the Logos, God's firstborn who we know as Jesus, and the second one is Sophia, the Spirit of Wisdom, who we know as the Holy Spirit. In order to transition to the fullness of God or Universal Consciousness we must as an act of our own choice engage with God the Son, and then with God the Mother or God the Holy Spirit, and then finally we transition into the bosom of God the Father; the first two both being

Divine emanations of the last, all being part of the one Trinity. Once we have initiated our transitionary proposal with the Son through the cross of crucifixion, we move on into the Atonement process through engagement with the feminine aspect of God, the Holy Spirit. When these two processes have been completed we become eligible for entry into Universal Consciousness, the bosom of God, to partake of the marriage supper of the Lamb as the Bible describes it; the proposal first, the engagement second, and the marriage third.

In its historical timeline the story of Sophia flourished to its fullest at the hands of the Gnostics for the first few centuries after the crucifixion of Jesus, but during the great suppression of Gnosticism by the Catholic Church in the 3rd and 4th centuries, the institutionalised church having got the Gnostics out of the way so to speak, then, through a campaign of deliberate neglect relegated the Wisdom Books of the Old Testament to the back of the line in their exegesis of the scriptures. If by chance at any stage in church teaching they were mentioned it was always done referring to wisdom as an abstract thing rather than Wisdom being an emanation of God seeking engagement and relationship with us. In order to appease those members of the church that still had a leaning towards the mystery of Sophia and Her role as the feminine emanation of God, the Catholic fathers substituted what remained of the myth of Sophia into the concept of the Virgin Mary to keep that proportion of the faithful happy.

There were still however practicing members of the Catholic priesthood who could not go along with this and whilst separating themselves from the Gnostic congregations as instructed by the Bishops, they still continued to embrace in a subtle and less obvious way many of the Gnostics revelatory beliefs. This included a priest known as Saint Bernhard of Clair Vaux, who at one stage, perhaps as a means of compensating for the loss of Sophia and her replacement with the imagery of the Virgin Mary, wrote a long mystical poetic treatise based on the Song of Songs wisdom book in the Old Testament which is also known as the Song of Solomon. But it was not only the mystics who showed some continuing affinity with the story of Sophia, certain secret brotherhoods such as the Rosicrucians and the Freemasons as well as some churches including the Greek Orthodox Church did so as well. I witnessed this when I visited a Greek Orthodox Church in Athens many years ago.

With regards to the gender of the Holy Spirit, for the inherently curious reader I share the following historical information also. Even though Christianity grew out of Judaism, one of the world's oldest father-mother spiritual belief systems, due to a decision made in Rome 400 years after Christ, western Christianity still remains today a *father, father-son, and father-spirit religion*, God the father, God the son, and God the Holy Spirit. However dating back more than 3,000 years, the image of God as Father and Mother is the cornerstone of the Judaeo-Christian belief system. The concept of a feminine Holy Spirit was vitally important to the ancient high priests. How do we know this? In the Old Testament Book of Genesis in referencing the pre-creation aspect of the universe we see "the Spirit of God hovers over the waters." The words used for Spirit of God were the feminine Rúache Elohim, which the Orthodox Jewish Bible still uses today. However before Christianity came to Rome, the Greek noun Pneuma, which carries no gender, replaced the feminine noun Rúach. Then, not surprisingly, in the first Latin Bible the Vulgate, the Roman Catholic Church being a male dominated order replaced the neuter gender Pneuma with the masculine gender Spiritus.

From a Biblical perspective there are numerous references to the Holy Spirit the Spirit of Wisdom all pointing in the direction of the feminine, including in the New Testament, similarly as there are in Gnostic texts. In the Book of Revelation where the Apostle John describes one of his prophetic visions he speaks of the sanctuary or temple of God in heaven being thrown open revealing a woman, which can only be a feminine emanation of God, dwelling there in the middle of the temple. The Apostle Paul aligns himself with this temple reference when he speaks of us being a temple of God with the Spirit dwelling in us, that same Holy Spirit that John is speaking of.

The Gnostic writings of old are littered with stories pertaining to the feminine component of the Trinity, but the Council of Bishops at Nicaea selected not one of them for inclusion in the canonical collection of writings that became known as the Bible. Every one of them was omitted and branded as heretical by those who called themselves orthodox Christians. By the time the sorting out of texts had concluded historians believe that all the visible feminine references, images and symbolism pertaining to the feminine principle of God were removed save for those ones that were invisible to the natural senses, ones that were hidden in a mystery, which went undetected by the bishops due to the lack of intuitive thought that went into their selections of which writings to include in the Bible and which to leave out.

Whilst most of these Bishops would not openly admit their ungodly prejudice against women, one particular bishop who I spoke of in Chapter 3 was quite open about it. He was Bishop Tertullian of Africa. Tertullian spent his whole life openly disparaging women seemingly with an underlying intense hatred for them. He once wrote, "women are audacious, they have no modesty, they are bold enough to think they can teach, they engage in argument wantonly desiring to participate in exorcisms, to undertake healing, and even to baptise." He once described a woman teacher of the Gospel who led a congregation in North Africa as a viper, and aligned himself totally with the Catholic precept of ecclesiastical discipline which says, "it is not permitted for a woman to speak in the church, nor is it permitted for her to teach, nor to baptize, nor to offer the Eucharist, nor to claim for herself a share in any masculine function, nor to maintain any priestly office." That's what this particular rule written into Catholic law says.

One of Tertullian's chief male targets with regards to these things was Marcion who I spoke of in Chapter 4 The Biblical Narrative, simply because Marcion in his church organizational structure was appointing women on an equal basis with men. And one wonders why for centuries and centuries both in the secular world and in the religious world women in society have had to fight so hard for basic rights, for equality with their male counterparts, when throughout history the two largest religious institutions in the world, Christianity and Islam, have so openly opposed any progressive move forward for some measure of feminine equality in religious affairs.

If you look closely at all of the religions practiced around the world, you see that there is a markedly noticeable difference between the three religions of Judaism, Islam and Christianity as against the rest of the world's religious organizations, in that these three religions are lacking in one fundamental aspect of the others, they lack any kind of Divine feminine symbolism or emphasis; and whilst they are all quick to emphasise in their exegesis of their respective holy books that God should not be considered as a gender biased deity, their teachings, ritual and ceremony are all laced with and directed towards the concept of a masculine God. Whilst the Catholic Church has venerated the Virgin Mary the Mother of Jesus into an elevated status of respect, in no way does it see her as being of the Divine Nature or on any sort of equal footing with God. Perhaps to placate some early Christian Catholics of Gnostic disposition and to prevent any potential for a mass exodus of believers to another religious organization, they may have started referring to her as Mary Mother of God meaning the mother of Jesus who was God in flesh, however they have never and will not ever refer to her as God the Mother.

This in its roots has been a major contributor to the lack of equality throughout society with regards to women in the workplace and in so many areas of normal life. Due to the culturally hereditary influences of gender bias favouring males in positions of authority in the religious world, we have witnessed for centuries and centuries the continuous denial of equality for women in the secular world. Things like the right to vote for elected government officials had to be vigorously fought for by women of so many generations before it was finally achieved, not forgetting the gender pay gap, the equal pay for equal work equation that continues to unjustly plague society.

The Jewish, Christian and Muslim religions are all basically male-oriented religions, thinking of the Deity they worship as a male god. In Christianity there is the Father, who is male, the Son, who is male, and the Holy Spirit, who is also male. In the Muslim religion there is just one God, who is male, and of course, in the Jewish religion God is also male. As a result of this, the ecclesiastical hierarchies of these religions are also male. The Jewish rabbis are male, the Muslim mullahs and church authorities are male, and the Christian priests are all male. The Anglican Church and most other denominational Protestant churches are an exception as they do allow female priests or female representatives of God such as ministers and pastors, but that wasn't the original idea of the Christian Church. So over time any thought that there might be a feminine power involved in the Deities of the Cosmos has been completely removed from the teachings of the largest religions in the world. In everything they do in their teachings and practice and organizational structure the emphasis and focus is always on the male.

In Eastern religion however, it is different, there is a greater emphasis on the balance between the male and female polarities, like Yin and Yang in the Chinese religions and the Gods and Goddesses in the Tibetan, Buddhist and Hindu religions, where it's quite normal for each God to have a corresponding Goddess. So the idea that you can worship a female deity in conjunction with a God, or go straight to a female deity for assistance, is quite normal in most Eastern religions. They believe that the female deity like the male has all kinds of powers, believing that if they so chose they can invoke a female deity for spiritual or material purpose.

To add to what I mentioned before, this is where the early Catholic Church got the idea of invoking Mary the Mother of Jesus, as Mary Mother of God, an idea that they encourage. The concept came from

Eastern Religion. But they do not encourage it as God the Mother, rather as Mary the Mother of God who became Jesus. And in its practical implementation into church teaching they left the "who became Jesus" out of it to make it more psychologically palatable. You see to accommodate this lack of feminine spiritual energy in the church teaching that the people were murmuring about, the early Church Fathers came up with what they thought was a brilliant idea. If Mary brought forth a Divine child let's make her Divine, like a type of Goddess but not in any way fully equal with God. Not part of the Deity, because that would intrude on the masculinity of the Deity, but let's make her a separate Divine being. Let's make her a sort of special emanation of God like an angel, but not strictly an angel, more so like a Queen of the Angels.

This worked well for a while but needed some tweaking to really settle Mary into her new role, so she eventually became Mary the Queen of the Heavens available to the masses if they would like to ask her for something. What was that supposed to achieve? It was to take people's minds off the ancient wisdom that believed in the feminine aspect of the Godhead itself. Would the ego mind have been happy with this? Yes and no. Yes because it took the people away from the Truth, which to the ego was good, but it still gave them some sort of feminine association with God, which was not so good to the ego mind. However it was an association and not a true equal footing, it was minus the true life-changing and transitionary power and purpose of the Holy Spirit, which to the ego, well that was okay. The congregations were given a wrong perception of what the Holy Spirit is, and a wrong conception of what the Feminine Principle of God is about.

Here's something to consider. If this purported Divine status the Catholic Church has given Mary was of God's doing and for a Godly purpose, why did Jesus encourage the believers to pray in His name only, and why did Jesus at the cross, as we read in the Book of John instruct the disciple John to look after His mother Mary when He was gone. One would have thought that if Mary were a Divine emissary by that time she would have shown it in some way or known it in some way. And she certainly wouldn't have needed a human to look after her. Mary was simply a mortal human chosen by God to be the birth mother of Jesus and it was not evidenced in any way that she was a worker of miracles. She was first a human mother and then later became a human disciple of her Son. She was not the Universal Creative feminine aspect of God that had been with God from the beginning, from which the whole Cosmos has come into being.

If you are a Roman Catholic, and influenced by Catholic hereditary beliefs, it is important to understand that this idea of worshipping Mary came about in a contorted and controversial way and that it is not a new idea at all. In actuality, the feminine aspect of the spiritual world was worshipped in all the ancient religions, and further to this there were women involved as leaders in most religious organizations. There were priestesses in Rome, in Egypt, in Greece, in India, in China, in Tibet and all over Asia. For the Catholic fathers it was all done for purely political religious expediency and to bring some sort of placatory offering to those in the church that were hungering for some feminine influence and feminine energy in their Christian lives.

There are numerous references to the feminine aspect of Divinity throughout the Old Testament, and in Gnostic texts. In the New Testament Book of Luke we catch a brief glimpse of Her through the son's eyes where Jesus proclaims Wisdom as His, as yours, and as our perfect Mother. In the Old Testament Book of Isaiah where the prophet is speaking of the coming of Jesus who shall have the Spirit of the Lord resting upon Him, the Hebrew word used for Spirit is the feminine Ruach Hakodesh. In the Gospel of Phillip, a Gnostic text discovered at Nag Hammadi in 1945, where Jesus says in relation to our Mother God, the Holy Spirit, "request of thy Mother and she will give to thee." Jesus was not referring to one's earthly mother Mary. In the Gnostic Gospel of Thomas Jesus makes a comparison between His earthly mother Mary and the Holy Spirit His heavenly Mother, the creative Spirit of God, where He says, "My mother bore my body but my true Mother gave me life," and in the Gospel of Phillip where Jesus speaking of the Holy Spirit as the Spirit of Wisdom and Truth says, "She alone is the truth, she makes the multitude, and concerning us she teaches this alone in a love through many."

It is vitally important that we all come to know this Spirit of Wisdom this Holy Spirit. The Holy Spirit is the spiritual emanation of the Mind of God. The Holy Spirit is the creative source or the creative agent for the Mind of God. Jesus was a walking talking demonstration of Her presence in a human being, and of Her creative power alive and functioning in a human life. If you desire to be more like Jesus you must get to know the Holy Spirit, that is the only way. If one truly wants to live an overcoming life we must tether our minds to the Mind of God through engagement with the Holy Spirit. One cannot live a true overcoming life whilst being tethered to the purported wisdom of the ego self. The Prophet Zechariah in the Old Testament put it this way, "it's not by might or by power but by my Spirit" says God. It's not by going to church or by doing good deeds as admirable as these things may be, that we are changed into the likeness of Christ the overcomer, we can only become more like Jesus through engagement with the Holy Spirit.

Remember the Holy Spirit's communication process is not confined to a location called the church or available only to members of the clergy, to ministers and priests. The Holy Spirit's Wisdom and assistance is available to all and works for all. The Holy Spirit, the Voice for Jesus, is our God given guide on earth from the moment of our physical birth to the moment of our physical death; we are never alone; Her role being to give us wisdom, understanding, knowledge and insight about all things temporal and eternal, about all earthly things and all heavenly things. However until we get to a state of readiness to hear with our inner ear, or you could say in order for God to bring us to a state of knowing, a state of mind where we recognize that it is the Spirit speaking to us, we are not left as orphans and uncared for. For the Holy Spirit will use all manner of interim measures to assist us, including specific people, books, circumstance, situations, and what we sometimes mistakenly call coincidences, to guide us gently into God's Truth.

Jesus the Son was sent to acclimatise us to the existence of God and God's love and redemptive plan for us, and having accomplished His part in the process to then hand the holy baton so to speak over to the Holy Spirit, God the Mother to finish the Atonement process's spiritual practicalities, to help us finish the race and obtain the prize. Jesus ushered in the Holy Spirit to finish the job of guiding us through the transitionary stages of our evolutionary journey. In this process the Holy Spirit will communicate to us those areas in our life that may need some sort of psychological or visible adjustment, as in detrimental thoughts or unhealthy behaviours to take us to a higher level of social consciousness and onward through to a full immersion in God Consciousness.

The Holy Spirit, but only with our co-operation and our willingness, will remove existing mind stains that are blots on our mental copybook, as in unhelpful memories and disruptive mind influences, progressively freeing us from their influence and replacing the psychological space created with the personality patterns of the Christ Mind within, described in the Book of Galatians in the New Testament as the Fruit of the Spirit. The Fruit of the Spirit are simply the new Christlike personality patterns and resultant behaviours that emerge or manifest as the end result of our leading a Spirit led life, a life of co-operation and mental co-existence with the Holy Spirit.

To be quite honest the Holy Spirit is really not bothered whether you think She is male or female, that to Her is inconsequential, and She is equally unperturbed that for a long time you may have been praying to Mary the mother of Jesus thinking this was the way to address your needs, particularly if your heart has always been of good intent. All the Holy Spirit wants is engagement with you. However it is helpful for us to grasp this. Jesus did not tell his disciples when His crucifixion was imminent that he would send His mother Mary in Divine form to look after them. He said, "I will send you the Comforter who will teach you all things." This Comforter, God the Mother, will hasten our spiritual evolution as we begin an engagement process with Her. Once you engage with Her you will begin to see that great cosmic transitionary plan unfold in your life, or as Jesus put it, "you shall know the truth and that Truth, will set you free."

> "Then is Jesus' final act of love He gave humanity the Holy Spirit to continue the Atonement process, to bring all things to the remembrance of humanity, including the cosmic mysteries of God that humanity forgot or lost sight of in the original separation incident; and to guide, instruct and teach all human beings everything necessary to restore their sense of holiness and wholeness."

“The Mind of Christ sits within the temple of emptiness and stillness within us, unperturbed by the chaos outside. The mental murmurings that are the most destructive in our temporal life and most constrictive to our spiritual life can be crowded out by willingness and desire, our willingness to discard everything that hinders our eternal destiny, and our earnest desire to enter into that place of stillness.”

The Holy Spirit the Spirit of Grace Guiding and Leading Us Home

ELEVEN

John Newton was born in August 1725 and passed in December 1807, aged 82 years. He was an English Anglican clergyman and an abolitionist. Abolitionism was a historic activist type of movement seeking to end the Atlantic slave trade and set all existing slaves free. Born in London, John was the son of a seaman, a shipmaster. His mother died of tuberculosis when he was around seven years of age, and he was sent off to boarding school. When he returned at 11 years of age he spent some time at sea with his father, before being conscripted into the Royal British Navy. He worked hard and was promoted to the rank of midshipman, but finally tired of the relentlessness of sea life, tried to desert, was caught, flogged with eight dozen lashes, and was demoted to the rank of seaman. Due to the disgrace and humiliation of this he suffered physically and mentally. He confessed later to having suicidal thoughts, at one time even contemplating throwing himself overboard into the turbulent seas. However he eventually recovered and was transferred to Pegasus, a slave ship bound for West Africa.

Pegasus was a trading ship, one that carried goods to Africa and traded them for slaves to be taken to the British colonies in the Caribbean and in North America. The descendants of these slaves in this modern day are the Afro-Americans. Still troubled by extended times at sea whilst having ongoing difficulties getting along with his fellow crew members due to his anti-slavery stance, resulted in the ship's captain making what he saw as a necessary decision to deliberately leave John behind when the ship set off on its return journey from Africa. He was subsequently handed over by authorities to a slave dealer whose wife Princess Peye an African Royal became his slave master. She treated him vilely as she did all her other slaves, continuously abusing him and mistreating him, but he was eventually rescued by a sea captain who had been asked by Newton's father to find him, and he was returned to England. During his return trip on that ship, when caught in a wild storm with the ship about to sink, he cried out in fear to God and the storm began to settle down. This incident had a remarkable spiritual impact on his life.

Upon his return to England he began reading the Bible and other spiritual literature and eventually converted to Christianity. He continued working in the slave trade, but after suffering a severe stroke at the age of 29 years he gave up seafaring, studied, became an evangelical lay minister and was eventually ordained as a priest of the Church of England. In 1788, some 34 years after he had retired from the slave trade, he broke the long silence he had maintained about his previous employment on slave ships, describing the horrific conditions he had experienced and he later published a written apology, a type of confession. It was a confession that he said came too late, but nevertheless one that had to be made, saying that his time in the slave trade was a time that he would always look back on as a humiliating reflection of his own character.

Newton sent copies of his apology to every member of the British Parliament and eventually became an ally of Wilbur Wilberforce, a politician, philanthropist and leader of a movement set on legally abolishing slavery. It was this movement that saw the eventual passage through parliament of a government bill titled the Slave Trade Act of 1807, a bill that officially abolished the slave trade making it illegal.

In 1767 William Cowper, the poet, moved to Olney and worshipped in Newton's church, collaborating with him on the publication of some of the Christian hymns that Newton had written. One of these hymns would later become immortalised in history, regarded as the greatest hymn ever. It was called "Faith's Review and Expectation", but became more commonly known around the world by its opening two words,

"Amazing Grace." At 82 years of age when he passed, his self-penned epitaph on his tomb simply read, "Once an infidel and libertine, a servant of slaves in Africa, was by the rich mercy and Grace of our Lord and Saviour Jesus Christ, preserved, restored, pardoned and appointed to preach the faith he had for so long laboured to destroy." In 1982 he was recognized for this influential hymn Amazing Grace and inducted into the Gospel Music's Hall of Fame in Nashville Tennessee.

The word itself, Grace, comes from the Greek word *Charis* and is of the feminine gender. It is a given name for women in Greece meaning kindness and life, and is related in Greek mythology to another Greek word Charites; in Greek mythology the Charites were goddesses of charm, beauty, nature, human creativity and fertility; they were feminine spiritual beings. Both Greek and Hebrew Biblical terminology added further to the meaning of Grace in the interpretation of Christian writings included in the Bible, saying that Charis also meant goodwill, loving-kindness, favour and God's mercy. So we see that long before Grace became an institutionalised sacrament in the Christian Church, it was a word commonly used in society and in early Christianity. This is witnessed in the writings of the Old Testament prophets and the New Testament Apostles, its use always centred on humankind's co-operative relationship with its creator God.

The word Grace appears in the Bible around 150 times depending on which version or translation you are reading. Of the 150 times that it appears around two thirds of them occur in the writings of the Apostle Paul. The most common consensual theological interpretation of what the word Grace actually means is that Grace is the spontaneous unmerited gift of Divine favour given to humanity, the church relating it directly to both the salvation experience and the ongoing sanctification process. Slightly different in meaning in Eastern Religion, we see that to experience Grace is considered to be the partaking of the Divine Nature, a type of imbibing of God Consciousness. The Byzantine Christians, the Greek speaking Christian Romans of Late Antiquity and the Middle Ages defined Grace as the uncreated energies of God, likening it to cosmic creations just waiting to manifest in the life of a believer, like gifts waiting to be handed out by the Holy Spirit.

That I believe is as close as you can get to a true description of what Grace is. Grace is not just a kind favour; the institutionalised church has however dumbed it down to just being this. Grace is in fact an energetic creative force working in accordance with God's Universal Laws, silently and patiently waiting to manifest as a person activates one of God's Universal Laws in their life.

Much different is the common interpretation of Grace in Western Christian theology where Grace is not seen as a creative force, an active agent of God, but rather simply seen as the ongoing love and mercy given by God to humanity, Divine favour and mercy given by God regardless of how a person has conducted their lives and regardless of how deserving or undeserving of it they are; and in particular the church places great emphasis on the cross of crucifixion as being the first evidence of the initial outpouring of that Grace, that kindness and that mercy. John Newton's opening words in his song, unintentionally I believe due to his theological training, merely reinforced that theological interpretation of the true meaning of Grace, relating it back to the kind favour alone of God where he says, "amazing grace that saved a wretch like me." You may be asking yourself well why is it important to know all this? Here is why.

When Western Religion adopted that stance regarding Grace, that Grace is just God's kind favour, the simple definition of how we receive God's Grace thus became that if Grace was reflected first in the giving of God's Son as a sacrifice, then to continually receive God's Grace we must continually remind ourselves over and over again of that sacrifice, the crucifixion. How was this proposition in particular implemented into church routine? It was done in the form of the sacrament of the Eucharist. That interpretation of Grace was about as close as any individual religious organization got to any kind of consensus on the concept of Grace, and even though the ceremony itself differed slightly in some churches, for example the Baptists refer to it as a communion service, and it is not compulsory in Protestant Churches as in the Catholic Church, it still became cemented in the minds of most believers that this was what Grace was all about, and that if we want God's favour in our lives, then this is the way we get it; not through intuitive engagement with the Holy Spirit, but rather through our repeated involvement in a particular sacramental ceremony or ritual.

Of all the Biblical subjects that have been used as a topic of debate amongst theologians in the centuries following the establishment of the Christian Church, faith and Grace are those two most often discussed and most often written about in Christian literature, and the Orthodox Church theologians in their attempt to convey some meaning into the concept of Grace and bring some consensus into that debate, made what I see as a spiritually retrograde decision, they chose to institutionalise it into church routine. They brought a specific ritual into their interpretation of how Grace works. The Christian Church has complicated and once again institutionalised the whole meaning of Grace and turned it into a transactional process, a "now if you will do this then God will do this" process.

The church turned Grace into a sacramental ritual. They turned it into an act of law, justifying it as a commemoration of the last supper that Jesus had with His disciples, teaching that if you partake of the Eucharist as it is called, then all the Grace, the kindness and mercy and help you need, will flow into your life. A type of spiritual arrangement whereby "if you will do this, if you will eat the wafer and drink the wine, then God in return will do this for you, God will bless you." The Catholic Church teaches that if a person partakes of the Eucharist, or the Mass, it is the most powerful way they will encounter the presence of Jesus Christ and thus become holy, and by inference that if you don't "go to Mass" you will not encounter the presence of Jesus in your life or attain a deeper level of holiness.

The cover of this book describes its content as straight talk about religion, so I say this. If partaking of the Mass brings the presence of Jesus into one's life why has it not worked for numerous Catholic priests who are continually being exposed as sexual predators, many having committed indecent acts on choir boys immediately after performing Mass. For those with an ingrained Catholic ideology who continue to deny that these things occur I would suggest you might read a recently published book written by an investigative journalist in Australia named Suzanne Smith; the book's title is The Altar Boys. Righteousness and holiness does not come from ritual, it comes from relationship with the Holy Spirit.

So we see church theology subtly prescribing that it is in accordance with the measure of ritual obedience given by us to the church institution or church law that God's measure of favour will be given back to us or poured out on us. That is simply Old Testament law, the Law of Abraham, the sacrifice, the shedding of blood being revisited over and over again under the guise of New Testament theology. When Jesus in His last moments on the cross cried out the words "it is finished," He was not saying I am finished, He was not talking about the fact that He was about to physically die, that would imply that He died defeated and exhausted, which He didn't. He cried out tetelestai, which is a Greek word meaning, "it is completed, it is accomplished;" tetelestai coming from the Greek verb teleo, which means to bring to an end. Jesus was saying "I have completed my part in my Father's cosmic redemptive plan for the universe, the Law of Abraham is gone, it has come to an end, and the Law of the Spirit has arrived. He was saying Abraham's Law has gone, Universal Law, the Law of the Spirit has arrived, it is a new beginning, and a new covenant has been invoked.

Jesus was saying I have fulfilled my part in that which the prophets of old spoke, that I was to become the final blood sacrifice. No longer would humankind need to petition God with animal sacrifice the ritualised practice of the Law of Abraham to enable God to meet its every need. No more law, no more ritual, no more ceremony, humankind shall receive all things by the Spirit, God's unmerited favour being poured out on all through the energetic creative force of the Holy Spirit. The crucifixion signified the end of ritualised obedience and ritualised petitioning and the introduction of a new era of being led by the Spirit of God, the Holy Spirit. Jesus cried out tetelestai meaning it is finished, no more sacrifice, don't keep coming back to a ritualised practice of sacrifice, this Old Covenant practice is finished. Jesus was saying God is bringing in a new Cosmic Covenant or Testament, one involving continuous engagement with the Spirit and being guided, directed and led by the Spirit.

But you may say, didn't Jesus at His last supper as He broke bread and drank wine with his disciples say, "do this in remembrance of me?" That's what my priest recites when he hands the wafer and bread out. Yes the Bible says that these are the words Jesus spoke, but Jesus had not yet had His body broken or His blood shed at that stage. As touched on previously, the church has taken the daily Jewish custom of breaking bread at the family dinnertime, taken Jesus having a final fellowship supper with His Jewish friends, who He saw as family, whilst encouraging them to continue to get together as family after He was gone, and turned it into a compulsory ritual.

Catholic, Eastern Orthodox and many Protestant churches have tethered Grace the energetic creative force of God, God's Spirit, to the sacraments, teaching that only if you partake of the sacraments will God's favour be given you. In other words only if you are obedient to the church law. There are numerous examples in institutionalised Christianity of the church honouring God with ritual whilst the hearts of many believers participating in the ritual are far away from Him, as Jesus so beautifully articulated in His day saying, "these people honour Me with their lips but their hearts are far from Me." Now in truth, participating in some of these things is not harmful if that's what one wants to do, but there is also certainly nothing to feel guilty about if a Christian doesn't participate in the ritual. The problem with any institutionalised ritual however is that it gives a person a false sense of spiritual and eternal security. It can make one psychologically spiritually complacent through ritual dependence, rather than psychologically confident from Holy Spirit reliance.

God's blessing is not freed to flow through ritual for it is not nor has it ever been tethered to a ritual, nor does it abide within the bread and wine used in the ritual as some churches will emphasise. There is a story in the Book of Matthew that some readers may be familiar with of Jesus in the temple overturning the tables of the merchants and money-lenders. It is interpreted by many theologians or you could say loosely interpreted as Jesus getting annoyed and angry at the merchants for supposedly using the church premises for business or material gain, and it has often become a source of debate amongst theologians as whether or not at times it is appropriate to get angry. Their interpretation is simply not correct. The story is really a type of analogy emphasising that the religious people of His day had turned the workings of God within us, within our inner temple, into a transactional type of experience, an experience of well if we do certain things we will gain certain things or God will give us certain things.

So sadly with regards to the true meaning of what Grace is, not only has the church turned Grace into a transactional experience, a ritual of the sacraments, but also as one noted religious historian said, and I quote his words, "the sacraments and their meaning are the watershed that divides Catholicism from Protestantism." They have turned it into a divisive issue, which the ego loves. Institutionalised religion involving ritual and penitent practices cannot and never will bring life-changing sanctifying favour into the life of a person. Only relationship with the Holy Spirit can do that. It is not by might or deeds but by the Spirit. The church has long taught that it is only through the sacraments will the favour of God be bestowed upon a believer, and that the sacraments are the mysteries of God that the Apostle Paul was talking about. The sacraments are not the keys to give understanding about God's cosmic plan for the universe and the unmerited favour that underpins it, but the Holy Spirit is.

The Catholic Church has used the sacraments as a means of tethering the believer to the institution, not as a means of tethering the believer to the Holy Spirit. But this is not the only deceptive practice it has inflicted on Christianity. Its institutionalised charter teaches that the only means by which one can receive God's favour is through the entirety of truth that has been revealed only to the Catholic Church. They profess that the Catholic Church is the only church that has received God's truth. What arrogance. They then name that entirety of truth as being the Bible, but only the one that the Catholic Church gave the world, the sacramental rituals, but only the ones that the Catholic Church gave the world, especially their way and meaning of Eucharist, and the hierarchal ministry of priests and Bishops but only those of one church, the Catholic Church. And it all comes back to the early Catholic fathers ego inspired Doctrine of Petrine Supremacy that I spoke of in Chapter 3. As the Old Testament God rightly said, "thou shalt have no other God's before me," so the New Testament self-appointed guardians of Christianity, the Catholic Church says, "thou shalt have no other church before us."

Other church organizations in a less dogmatic way do also promulgate that it is through partaking of the sacraments known in some churches as communion or the Lord's Supper that we are given power to overcome the enemy through God's Grace and implies that this is the only way. This is not correct. Jesus said that we shall receive power when the Holy Spirit has come upon us; the Apostle John said the Holy Spirit is with us, meaning leading us, but shall be in us. In us why? To psychologically guide us; to guide our mind, to transform our thinking processes and to set a guard around our renewed mind giving us all the power necessary to enable us to withstand the continuous onslaught of the ego mind thought processes.

I have spoken at various times throughout this book on how the church has institutionalised the Christian faith taking it from a revelatory engagement with God the Spirit into an institutionalised connection with God, a religion that honours God through pomp ceremony and ritual but its heart, its character and true nature, is far from God's nature and character qualities. Here's my simple point. Grace is not favour received through participation in a ritual; neither is Grace a group of Godly character qualities. Grace is not a thing, Grace is a force. Grace in Biblical history has always been a force of the Spirit of God, and that creative energetic force is the Holy Spirit herself, the Spirit of Wisdom and Truth.

"Grace is not a character quality that God displays in His attitude towards His children. Grace is not about us having our physical needs met through ritualised petitioning, but rather it is about us having our spiritual necessities accomplished. Grace is a spiritual energetic force, the creative aspect called the Mind of God, given to us by Jesus to sustain us and to lead us home."

Here's the thing. Grace the Holy Spirit is not only with us but also in us as we read in the Book of John. She is "with us" to lead us and redirect us if we stray from the path of holiness, and she is "in us" to guide us into all Wisdom and Truth. This then in the present moment defends our inner and outer self, giving us the peace and freedom to transition to higher levels of consciousness. Those are the two primary activities of this feminine creative force of God in fulfilling her role in the Atonement process. That is why Jesus sent her. The Holy Spirit in the first instance redirects or leads humanity back to God, by taking us forward into higher levels of consciousness or awareness of God via the Cross of Crucifixion. That is the "with us" part of her role that John spoke of. Then after our "at the feet of the Master experience", our cross experience, she then comes to abide continually in us, to transform us and to lead us home. That is the "in us" part of her role that the Apostle John spoke of.

The Holy Spirit being "with us" in the first stage regenerates the Soul by leading us out of the psychological wilderness of a life without God, and then comes to reside "in us", to live in the temple of our Soul where the Mind of Christ is in residence; to teach us the ways and will of God, to deal with any issues we have relating to our ego mind existence during our previous life in the wilderness, and to support us in any issues we may now have in our new Spirit led life existence whilst continually guarding our heart and mind against ongoing attacks. In doing these things she quietly in a comforting manner instructs us in all Wisdom to enable our thought processes to be so transformed as to remove all ego mind blockages, and to cosmically gently jettison us forward from collective unconsciousness to collective consciousness and finally to universal consciousness. Then we are ready to go home.

We see a picture of this process in the Old Testament with the Holy Spirit the force of Grace appearing in the form of a fire by night and a cloud by day leading Moses and his people through the wilderness of Egypt and out into the Promised Land, which is a type of analogy of the Atonement journey. The Holy Spirit is the Spirit of Grace that led Jesus into the desert. She then enabled Him to overcome the antagonistic attack of the ego mind, led Him back out of that wilderness, enabled Him to endure the cross, and it was the Holy Spirit who then took Jesus home. Jesus was not taken home to His inheritance through a religious ritual. Every aspect of His Atonement journey was achieved through His willingness to be led and guided by God's Spirit. There are numerous examples in the Bible of the Holy Spirit the Force of Grace in Her role as the active component of the Godhead leading and guiding, whether that be leading someone though something or leading someone out of something, taking them to a greater level of spiritual awareness as part of that person's spiritual evolutionary journey.

When John Newton and William Cowper penned the words and music of Amazing Grace it was a song of thanksgiving for the Holy Spirit the Spirit of Grace who had guided John psychologically out of an ocean of despair that his ego mind had imprisoned him in, causing him to "change his mind" about taking his own life. He said in the song, "I once was lost but now I'm found was blind but now I see". It was the Holy Spirit that opened his spiritual eyes that he might see. Straight after this event it was the Holy Spirit the Spirit of Grace who paved the way for him to be safely brought home to England, who guided him physically home, and then subsequently led him to the foot of the cross. In contemplating these two events he wrote, "how precious did that Grace appear the hour I first believed."

It was the Holy Spirit the Spirit of Grace, who had led him out the realm of the collective unconscious into the realm of collective consciousness, whereby he was able to see clearly the wrongness and inhumanity of his wilderness involvement in the slave trade, and it was the Holy Spirit who subsequently transitioned him into a state of universal consciousness, a state of awakening, a Spirit led life. All these things led John Newton to believe with an unshakeable conviction that as the Holy Spirit the amazing Spirit of Grace had brought him this far, similarly the amazing Spirit of Grace would take him all the way to his eternal home; and so he was thus able to conclude his song of praise to the Holy Spirit with the following words, "through many dangers, toils and snares I have already come, 'twas Grace that brought me safe thus far and Grace will lead me home."

> "At all times in the history of humanity when there has been seemingly uncontrollable disorder and chaos in play, causing pain and suffering to many, a secret wisdom has sprung into action to dissipate that darkness of humanity's Soul with its glorious healing and comforting light. That is the true essence of the Holy Spirit, the energetic force of Grace."

"Mind is the master power that moulds and makes, and man is Mind, and evermore he takes the tool of Thought, and shaping what he wills, he brings forth a thousand joys and a thousand ills. He thinks in secret, and it comes to pass and his environment is but his looking-glass."

James Allen from his book "As A Man Thinketh."

Life in The Spirit Living a Balanced Life According to God's Universal Laws

TWELVE

Ruby Altizer Roberts was born on April 22nd 1907 and died at her home in Christiansburg Virginia on May 24th 2004, aged 97 years. Ruby was an American writer and a very social person, a woman who regularly hobnobbed with artistic people and Hollywood stars. Being a prolific writer of poetry and verse she became the first female poet laureate of Virginia. She is remembered apart from her literary achievements as a woman with a personality as bubbly as a spring, a delightfully gregarious woman whose favourite pastime was to twice a day walk downtown from her suburban home dressed in a large colourful hat, carrying a sun umbrella, chatting with people as she walked, and stopping periodically to smell the occasional flower along the way. Ever noticeable in her literary writing portfolio was a love for the poetic verse. During her daily walks, Hardee's on Roanoke Street was one of her favourite places to stop, to rest her feet and to have some creative thinking time. Here she could often be seen breakfasting with old friends, or simply having some alone time and then ordering a biscuit and gravy to go.

From there, with a renewed sense of enthusiasm and vigour, she would most times go immediately home to write poems and short verse as well as short stories on family history, whilst sitting on her bed, tapping with two fingers on her electric typewriter. There were no computers in those days. She also wrote a variety of children's books some with spiritual overtones, a popular one amongst the locals being The Story of Buzzy Bee. It was the tale of a mean-hearted little bee who eventually repents of his bad deeds and changes his ways. It was often used in the local Sunday School classes in Christiansburg. Being quite gifted during her literature-writing lifetime she wrote some beautiful prose and poetic verse. In her book Look Down at the Stars, a memoir of her friendship with a man named Walter Bowman Russell, a writer, artist and sculptor, she wrote this verse about him.

"He dips his pen in golden flame of truth, he moulds a thing of beauty from dull clay, his eyes are closed to all that seems uncouth, he tunes his life notes to a silvery lay. He conquers all ills and holds no thought of death, nor fears the feel of clay or worm or clod, but gives forth love with every moment's breath, and knows this truth that he is one with God."

Ruby's friend Walter Bowman Russell (May 19th 1871 to May 19th 1963) who she wrote this verse about, was amongst other things a painter, sculptor, author, musician, composer, scientist, champion ice skater and lecturer, and in many ways a spiritual teacher and philosopher. In his work as a scientist he pioneered two of the greatest discoveries in his era, the isotopes in hydrogen and two of the elements used in the atomic bomb. He was once described as a man who was so cosmically aware of his own existence, that everything he brought forth in his chosen field of endeavour bore witness to the Light of God within him.

Glenn Clark, the founder of C.F.A. International, a global outreach of creative Christian living, an English College Professor, successful athletic coach, and author of numerous articles and books on the spiritual life, was a man who believed with all his being in the creative power of the human heart and the creative spirit within every human being. His life was totally devoted to helping his fellow human beings discover that creative spirit within them. Glenn was a fervent believer in the cosmic power for creative change embedded deep within the heart and soul of all human beings, regardless of their socio-economic background. In his work as an author he widely researched successful people and wrote about many, including Walter Bowman Russell. He once wrote of Russell after interviewing him whilst visiting his apartment, that Russell was a man so centred in his own cosmic consciousness, the power that enables one to think clearly and to subsequently create, that his life could not possibly be limited to one creative field alone. As seen in Russell's list of occupations above, he was not wrong.

Glenn Clark aptly described Russell as a man who had truly discovered cosmic consciousness, the creative secret of the universe. His viewpoint was confirmed as we look back on the life of Walter Russell and see what he actually did accomplish in his 92 years of existence on this earth, especially in the field of the creative arts witnessed in the many beautiful paintings and magnificent sculptures he produced in his lifetime. Twice Russell was a guest in the White House both as a painter of Presidential portraits and as a sculptor of Presidential busts.

However his early working years were not what you would describe as being easy. Russell voluntarily left school at ten years of age to start his working life due to family financial difficulties, which even in those days at such a young age was not a common event. But at all times as his work effort, output and ethic evidenced, from the beginning of his working life he seemed to possess an imbedded conviction that every human being has unlimited potential to achieve whatever they wish, if they are able to tap into the creative energy source and life force resident within them. He was once heard to say that anything can come to a person who trusts in the unlimited help of the Universal Intelligence, but went on to add, as long as one works within the "laws of the universe" and always gives more to others than they expect, doing it cheerfully and courteously.

He was in the first fifty years of his life an accomplished author, architect, music composer, painter and scientist. His paintings were exhibited around the world winning many awards. In his work as an architect he designed and built millions and millions of dollars worth of buildings in New York, and is known as the originator of the concept of studio apartments. At around 56 years of age he decided to add sculpturing to his list of creative achievements never having done it before. Amongst his many works he sculptured lifelike busts of Thomas Edison, of Franklin Roosevelt, and of other notables such as Mark Twain, General Douglas

MacArthur, George Gershwin, and Charles Goodyear. His Mark Twain bust so impressed literature notables such as Rudyard Kipling and George Bernard Shaw that they convinced the British Government to put it on display in the Victoria Embankment Gardens in London. George Bernard Shaw is most known as being the author of a book titled Pygmalion, which was subsequently adapted into that well-known play and movie My Fair Lady.

Glenn Clark once when speaking of Walter Russell told of how in an interview with him he became convinced that not only was Walter a firm believer in the cosmic evolutionary journey of this universe, but was convinced without a doubt that the world would need to suffer in order to understand the simplest of the universal cosmic principles, it being the unity of man with man and the unity of man with God, and that it is only through this unity that the world will become a better place. Russell firmly believed that humankind must first reap the harvest of its own seeds of hate, selfishness and greed that it had been sowing for centuries, before it would ever come to a true understanding that the universal laws of God, including the laws of balance and unity, all play an inevitable and inescapable part in the evolution of society. The Apostle Paul spoke of this principle of unity when addressing the people of the city of Ephesus.

I spoke in the previous chapter of the lyrics of the song Turn, Turn, Turn, written by the renowned singer songwriter Pete Seeger, and the lyrics of its main verse, "to everything there is a season and a time for every purpose under heaven, a time to be born, a time to die, a time to plant, a time to reap," which came from the Old Testament Book of Ecclesiastes. Russell too believed in the veracity of those words. He did not have any regrets about his fame as a sculptor coming too late in life. In his mind the age of fifty-six years, which was his age when he commenced sculpturing, was of no consequence, for to him there is a time for every purpose of God, a pre-ordained time that is not of our choosing, but rather it is of the universe's choosing. The reward of an easier more pleasurable lifestyle or an early retirement was not at the forefront of his mind as he commenced each creative undertaking. To Russell he was simply doing what universal consciousness desired him to do at that particular time in his life, and because of this he was assured in his heart that all would be well.

You see age was of no consequence to him. He was once heard to say, "great men's lives begin at forty the same age when the mediocre man's life ends." He believed fervently that whilst the world would say that we grow weaker and slower and less able to achieve as we grow older, that there is in fact no time limit or age limit on creativity. He believed that the wisdom and genius within a human being remains an ever-flowing fountain of creative achievement if we allow it, until the very last breath we draw. This was evidenced in his own life where it was said that in his lifetime he produced a quality and volume of work the equivalent of what six men might produce. When once asked the question did he ever get tired from all the masses of work he produced, he was quick to inform the questioner that creative energy, the thought energy of Universal Intelligence, meaning the Mind of God, is constant, forever balanced and never lessens.

Over these last few years I myself have come to believe the truth in Walter Russell's answer, clearly seeing that it is we ourselves who bring tiredness and sometimes illness into our lives through the introduction of unbalanced protocols and wrong prioritising. That as we immerse ourselves in the play of personhood (Chapter 1), and in specific thinking patterns or you could say as we embrace and entertain our sometimes wrong hereditary personality patterns, (Chapter 7), we create an energy flow imbalance, which then results in feelings of tiredness and anxiety. But our life source within, the creative energy source that keeps us alive and animated, the Holy Spirit, never tires. If we are generating negative energy it is not coming from the creative life source within. She, meaning the Holy Spirit, has neither the concept of negativity, failure, mediocrity nor the notion of tiredness present in her.

It is necessary for us to understand that we are the problem, we with our conflicting thought patterns create psychological imbalance, that ultimately manifests in mental and physical imbalance, the feeling of being drained of energy, for as a person thinks in his or her heart or mind, so they become. That is one of God's Universal laws. It is always first the thought and then the feeling, first an unbalanced state of mind, then an unbalanced state of body. Would it not be just logical then that if we adjust our thinking processes to tap into the creative energy source of the Spirit, the Mind of Christ, that is completely "balanced" in line with God's Laws of the Universe, that this must then influence our spiritual life, our mental life and our physical life to such a point that the millions of petty trivialities that would continually flood our mind and thus short circuit our physical energy system never have the opportunity to do so. I think it would.

For Walter Russell the achievement of balance was not an optional extra in his functional life. Maintaining balance in everything was an absolutely essential priority even in his own personal time management. In his work as an author, painter and sculptor he would never work for any more than two hours at any specific time. The concept of maintaining balance was also evidenced in all his business dealings, in that every deal he was involved in had to be a win win for both parties or he just would not proceed with it. There had to be the correct and equal measure of integrity on display from all participants. He did not proceed simply because its outcome would create a life of ease for him, or a handsome profit for one singular participant, this was not at the forefront of any thought processes he engaged in.

Even his entry into the world of architecture was not born out of an ego driven desire to build something that looked spectacular, or to sell something to make enough money to create a life of ease for himself. He entered into the world of architecture having never studied it, simply because being an artist himself, he saw the need for his fellow artists in New York to have somewhere small to live as well as to work so as to save on living expenses, and to be able to use that space, a type of worry free zone you could say, to create something lasting. Thus the concept of studio apartments was brought into the world, the name itself "studio apartment" coming from the combined terms art studio and apartment living.

In his work as an architect his thought process was always centred on achieving the correct balance between give and take, which saw him apply that principle in developing the property concept of co-operative ownership and then introduce it into the market. Real estate operators came along later and through self-interested greed, defiled that universal principle. They defiled the universal law of balance by putting profit before people. The value for all people side of the transaction never entered into the equation at all for them. They violated the universal law of balance by minimising the quality of the product and maximising the profit, rather than always prioritising and respecting the creative thought that underpinned the product. In the process of behaving this way they milked every operation for themselves leaving all liability with the client. This saw most of their buildings eventually go under financially. But not so with Russell. Through the application of the law of balance in all his contractual arrangements, every construction Russell built is still profitable to this day.

When the potential for wealth or self-gain, in particular easily gained wealth comes into the picture it is highly likely that imbalance will also enter the fray, because the ego mind if one follows it will always align itself with the lower and baser instincts of humanity, favouring personal gain over ethical behaviour, and will battle to achieve that, to tip the balance. For the unregenerate mind, as long as it can justify to itself the legality of what it is are doing, ethics will not enter the picture. But earthly legality is not heavenly legality. Did Walter Russell make money? You bet he did. But it was always obtained under the umbrella of ethical behaviour. When the potential for wealth or some sort of self-gain enters into the game of life, whether that game is politics, business and yes in religion also, it is highly likely for most people that imbalance will enter the picture also, and due to the unrenewed ego mind's influence, the imbalance will always favour wealth over integrity towards others.

The Catholic Church has an estimated wealth of more than $30 billion and this is only the amount of its net worth with regards to its ownership of properties including churches, schools, presbyteries, hospitals, nursing homes, office buildings, tennis courts and telephone towers. Let alone the billions of dollars believed to be stashed in the Vatican vaults, which came out of the Vatican's unholy alliance with Nazi Germany during World War 11 as the Nazi party appropriated the gold and fortunes of the Jewish people and other conquered nations around Europe and handed them to the Vatican for safekeeping. Each successive Pope has reached millionaire status, those same Popes who are seen at various times patting the heads of little children, whilst simultaneously condoning their bishops cover up of priestly paedophilia, and who are regularly seen in media shoots touring the world condemning society's indifferent attitude towards poverty whilst their church sits on billions of dollars of assets.

When Jesus in speaking to His disciples said, "it is easier for a camel to go through the eye of a needle than for a rich person to enter the Kingdom of God," He was not saying it is impossible, but simply that it is more difficult. Why? Because the ego mind will always favour the temporal over the eternal, the visible over the invisible. Subsequently an attitude of approaching life from its creative aspect with a desire to create something that will give back to humanity and withstand time, adopting a balanced approach, is replaced with a desire simply for ease of living in the present moment. The need for ease replaces the need to create and so any potential for a person to positively influence others in this short life and to leave a non-perishable legacy after they have passed is lost. Ironically though in death all that has been accumulated is lost anyway, because as the saying goes you can't take it with you.

This ability to live life from its creative aspect rather than from a "what will this do for me "aspect, is very noticeable in those involved in the arts and entertainment industry, both creative industries in their own right, with some artists and musicians continuing to create for years and years regardless of any monetary gain for their efforts. And whilst in the short term they never achieve monetary success, they continue to embrace the creative thoughts that come their way in an attempt to turn them into lasting legacies. They continue to create as their inner thoughts or creative spirit within wells up to a state of overflowing and is released into the universe in some kind of lasting form. That same creative principle is part of the functioning aspect of the Mind of God. Just because so many human beings through their selfish desires cause so much destruction in the world God does not say well that's it, no more babies, there's too many of them that are growing up and turning into walking talking disasters. God continues to allow the principle of creation and the universal law of creativity to work.

The famous artist Vincent Van Gogh, whose creative instincts and abilities were beautifully poetically remembered in the lyrics of the song Vincent by singer-songwriter Don McLean, never earned a living from his work, and was often destitute and close to starvation. The story is told that his brother came to visit him once and found Vincent lying on the dirt floor of a shack with no heat and close to death from hypothermia and starvation. He had given away his boots, coat and warmest clothes to people in the parish church who had less than him. In his lifetime he produced more than 2,100 artworks, including 860 oil paintings and more than 1300 watercolours, drawings, sketches and prints. One of his paintings called the Vase, which was simply a vase with fifteen sunflowers in it, was sold in 1987 for 82 million dollars. Vincent, who made no money in his lifetime from his creative works, continued to dig deep into that creative spirit and paint on, even when at the point of starvation. That is how powerful creative thought energy is.

True reality, that which endures and lasts, is born out of a balanced thought process. The created things in our lives are first conceived through thought and are subsequently brought to life or manifest after this, as did the concept of studio apartments with Walter Russell. All the world class sculptures he successfully produced and all the music he composed and all the books he wrote were conceived in the first instance from a creative balanced thought process, they were not just all momentary rational mind thought bubbles. Similarly, but equally important for us to understand is that all those things that we would group together under the banner of failure, things like angry emotions, poor choices, bad deeds, deceptions, disease and division are all conceived in an unbalanced thought process also. Thought creates the good, the bad and the ugly that we experience in life.

Everything starts with a thought. This world was created out of a creative thought in the Creative Mind of God. If the mind is out of balance the thought will be out of balance and the manifestation will be unbalanced. Even the original creation of this world first appeared in thought form in the Mind of God as we see in the Book of Genesis, which tells us that the Spirit was brooding, as it looked out over the darkness. To brood is to be engaged in a deep state of thinking. The whole continuum of first creation came out of the balanced thought processes of the Mind of God, and then was given to the creative agent of God, known as the Spirit of God, or more commonly as the Holy Spirit, for expression, to manifest God's thoughts into form. To take a little literature licence to demonstrate this and to show how this principle or law of creative balance was used in the creation of the universe, let me paraphrase the first few verses in the Book of Genesis Chapter One.

"Here is the story of how, in the very beginning, God created the heavens and the earth. It was all about creative balance. The earth and the heavens did not exist; there was only darkness and dark waters in an empty silent void. However the Mind of God existed and was hovering over this void, brooding over the emptiness it saw, and a thought came, let's do something about this. So God spoke a creative word "let there be light," and the creative Spirit leapt into action and light appeared. Then God thought again, wait a minute, this light is mixed with the darkness that was already there, so let's "balance" that out and separate them both. And it happened, the Spirit once again leapt into action and when She showed it to God, God said, that's good, that's very good, and God gave the name Day to the light and Night to the darkness, and then gave His approval."

A similar process happened in the rest of the creation story and it was all about balance. The Mind of God through the Spirit created a right measure of balance between light and darkness, between lands and seas, between the seasons each lasting three months, between animals that walk, animals that swim and animals that fly, and eventually to achieve the right balance in the human species the Spirit of God created a man and a woman. Balance was the key element involved in the complete creation of the world and as such is the key element that must be appropriated in the functioning world we live in. Life is all about creating something that lasts and creating that same something under the umbrella of balance, and if your thought process is out of balance then your life will be out of balance, and open to some measure of chaos, whether mild or manic depending on how much out of balance it is.

There is an ancient Zen concept that embraces the principle of balance. It simply says, "hurry slowly," which when first read might seem rather strange. How do you go fast slowly? The Anglo Saxon terminology for it is "hasten slowly." It refers to us creating a balance between thinking and doing. It's about making sure our thinking doesn't outpace our doing. Most people rush about every moment of their waking lives continuously doing things, which also involves continuously thinking things, because first comes the thought, I must do this, and then comes the action, the doing of that thought thing. The doing is always desperately trying to keep up with the thinking. People's bodies are not only rushing about doing physical things, their minds are continually rushing about doing thinking things, and tiredness and that feeling of being drained of energy comes not from the doing as most people think, but from the continuously increased level of thinking that initiates the doing. People say, "I'm just so tired I've been so busy doing things." No, it should be, "I'm just so tired I've been so busy thinking of things to do and then doing as many of them as I can fit in." The root cause of the problem is always in the first instance too much thinking which includes "over thinking things," which is in itself a form of worry potentially producing mental anxiety that then causes tiredness.

Here's my point. Inner awareness or intuitive thought arises out of a state of "mind stillness" not out of a state of "mind haste," mind stillness being sometimes described as a state of presence. Since everything created or accomplished first emerges as a thought, it is in the ego mind's best interest in its desire to keep people psychologically separated from God, to take away any opportunity for you to achieve some sort of balance between the temporal and the spiritual so as to create something that lasts. It is in the best interests of the ego to keep your rational thought processes or your ego mind functioning at full throttle to distract you from the spiritually aware state you are meant to live in, and take away the peace and joy that comes out of the state of awareness or presence.

Most of us have either tried to meditate at some time in our life or at least know of the existence of meditation as a discipline. The art of meditating works to achieve energy balance in a person's life and it is all designed around the concept of stillness of the mind. It is designed through breathing techniques to bring about a cessation of thought, to still mind activity so as to bring the inner essence into balance with the outer doing, and this then creates a physical and mental feeling of calmness in mind and body, which produces health benefits physically and mentally. It does this by removing blockages in the chakras or energy systems in the body. But here's my point and this is where many people miss the big plus of meditation. The stillness of mind or the cessation of thought that occurs in the meditation process opens up a psychological pathway for the entrance of spiritual thought if you want that. Most Eastern practitioners want that when they perform the discipline, most Western practitioners merely do it for the calmness of body and mind it brings.

What is the most common reason that sees most Western people give up meditation after attempting it for the first time? Most if asked would say, I just couldn't focus, my mind kept wandering. Of course it did that's why you are meditating, to train it to stop. That's like a baby standing up for the first time to try to walk and then when falling down saying, "naa, this walking stuffs not for me, I keep falling down." If you take the spiritual totally out of the meditating picture the ego mind has been given a free pass to mess with you. It doesn't have to necessarily be a religious experience, but there must be a measure of balance and openness towards both the physical benefits and the spiritual benefits. Remember even in the process of the mediation discipline, we are attempting to create something that was not previously there, whether that be physical calmness or spiritual awareness. Meditation is a creative discipline.

We see in the Bible in the genealogy of Jesus that in His humanity Jesus was a direct descendant of King David. If you read the history of King David in the Old Testament you will see that he lived by all appearances a tumultuous life, which would appear on the outside to be one totally out of balance with normality. Wars, adultery, you name it King David experienced it. Yet as history records he was even in the most tumultuous of circumstances always able to tap into the will, the way, and the thought processes of God. The secret of his being able to hasten slowly through all these things that confronted him I believe was in his capacity to embrace a meditative stillness which took him into God's presence, and merely being in God's presence is both physically, mentally and spiritually energising. This brought balance back into his life.

We see this in some of King David's writings in the Book of Psalms and in particular in what is known as the Psalm of Psalms or the Psalm of David where it says, "The Lord is my shepherd I shall not want. He leads me beside the still waters and in doing so He restores my Soul." To restore one's soul is to restore a state of right-mindedness, of balanced thought processes. We go from a state of not just being focused on what the rational mind would tell us about what is going on around us, but we balance that with what our spiritual mind, the Mind of Christ within, desires to say to us through the Holy Spirit. The Holy Spirit, the Voice of the God Mind came to David in his moments of meditative stillness and the Holy Spirit comes to us in our moments of physical and mental stillness, whether that be in the discipline of meditation or whether it is when we are sufficiently familiar with the process to enter into it at will; to enter into a state of awareness whenever we want, to activate it as an act of our own will.

Remember the Spirit is never not with us; it is our ever present energetic life source. We just allow other mind chatter to crowd it out, to talk over the top of it. As the Apostle John said, the Spirit is with us and the Spirit is in us. All the ugliness in the world, all the violence in the world, all the hate and prejudice in the world arises in the first instance out of wrong thought processes, from people taking the unbalanced approach of thinking what's right for me and what's best for me, rather than the balanced approach which is what's right for us and what's best for us. In many cases particularly in the areas of political and social ideology the ego driven unbalanced thought process seeks to align itself with those of similar unbalanced thought processes resulting in similar unbalanced intent. So we see gangs formed, we see groups formed, we see movements formed, political parties formed, religions formed, we see nations aligned with nations of similar unbalanced thought processes, all joining together to fight their common cause, whilst unknowingly aligning themselves with the ego's goal of division and destruction. If you refer back to Chapter 6 The Origins and Nature of Goodness and Evil I speak of the ego mind as always being bent on the destruction or crucifixion of the Christ Mind or the God Consciousness of the individual or society.

Thought or the thinking process is ultimately the source of all reality in the person or in society, whether that reality is categorised as balanced or unbalanced. How you think manifests the reality you produce. This is a universal principle or law that controls everything that materialises in this world whether tangible or intangible both good and bad; first the thought, then the resultant action that proceeds from the thought, then the manifestation of that resultant action. That is the creative principle of thought energy. Neither the individual nor the world will ever function at its optimum potential until the individual and then the collective gets their thought processes balanced right. People say we just want world peace or we just want equality and then go out and attack those who they blame for their sense of inequality, only further reinforcing inequality and prejudice and psychological imbalance. Ironically but in accordance with God's Universal law they create what they are trying to remove because of their unbalanced thought process. There will never be outer peace until there is inner peace. Inner peace is achieved only by getting the inner thought processes right.

Many people do achieve this but many more don't. Just watch the news and you will see that most don't, for their unbalanced thought process will always lean towards favouring their own wants and desires and not the desires of others. You may probably even find yourself saying out loud as you witness the manifestations of unbalanced thought processes, "what were they thinking?" The answer would be, "nothing balanced." Some will try and justify in their rhetoric that they are thinking of the other person as they take up this cause or that cause, but this is not the truth of it. Their thought process is simply favouring someone else's thought process or belief system that either aligns with theirs and gives them some sort of emotional or psychological connection, because to get involved makes them feel good about themselves, which brings it back to self-gain and self-interest, but it is not about truth.

Does that mean we should not get involved in things we believe in? No it doesn't. But if our manner of involvement, particularly if it is of an antagonistic or combative nature creates a deeper divide, a greater measure of disunity, it profits everyone nothing, and is merely playing to the interests of the ego mind of the universe, feeding angry and combative personality patterns into the collective unconscious of the universe. I spoke of this in Chapter 7 in relation to Jung's work in analytical psychology, the theory of psychoanalysis that focuses on the concept of the existence of a collective unconscious, and the importance of balancing opposing forces within the personality that emanate from this collective unconscious. Walter Russell whilst taking a balanced approach to life was not what you would call a religious person, but he certainly was a believer in God as the Creative Source of the universe and in the Universal Laws of God that underpin and sustain the universe of which the Law of Balance is one.

In an attempt to describe simply the purpose of these Universal Laws of God, I would say that their purpose in existing is to process and arbitrate every human thought that is projected into God's universe and then in accordance with the Universal Law that is applicable to that thought create a result. In other words every thought you throw out into the universe gets processed through a Universal Law of God and that Universal Law determines its outcome. That is how the Law of the Spirit that oversees Universal Law, which Jesus introduced into the world, operates. For instance if one of the Universal Laws of God is "give and it shall be given unto you," when you think and act in a giving way it shall be returned to you in like kind, at some time at some place. If you begin to give whether in thought or deed, the Universal Law of Giving emanating from Universal Consciousness, will go into reciprocation mode to return to you in like kind.

It matters not whether your thought is good or bad, it only matters that it is thought energy, and it will return back to you in like kind. Good thoughts will return in kind and equally bad thoughts will return in kind. Universal Law does not determine the morality of your thought it simply returns it back to you in the same form. It's a creative law that just works. If you are kind then kindness will be returned to you in some way or another. Whether someone thinks you deserve it or not does not enter into the equation. If you behave badly in some way or form bad behaviour will eventually be revisited upon you. Everything in this universe is created out of thought energy and whilst energy cannot be destroyed it can take form and can change form. Scientists will confirm this. It's outworking is sort of similar to the principle or Law of Karma in Eastern Religion but not quite the same.

So with Walter Russell saying he was a believer in the Creative Source known as God whilst not being a religious person, how then does a belief in God and a life lived in accordance with God's Universal Law differ from being a religious person involved in institutionalised religion?

This is how. Institutionalised religion is based on a Supreme or Superior Being having control of your life, and in its teaching focuses on your obedience to that Being and obedience to that Being's representative who the institutionalised church sees themselves as. This type of thinking is based on Old Testament theology incorporating Old Testament law and practice known as the Law of Sin and Death. In its practical outworking religion teaches that the controlling aspect of God's nature has been delegated to the church hierarchy and the church hierarchy implements it in the form of dogmas, doctrines and creeds, or whatever other man inspired laws the particular church you are involved in has put in place to control to some extent your spiritual experience. It is basically saying that obedience to God is witnessed solely in your allegiance and obedience to the church and its rules and regulations.

This type of institutionalised religious thinking and process has prejudged everyone as imperfect and fully sinful and in need of some measure of continual control to get them back on the right track and to keep them on the right track, and the church sees itself as the arbitrary implementer and enforcer of the level of control needed. The Catholic Church is the biggest proponent of these institutionalised practices. Quite the opposite of living under institutionalised religion is the principle of living under God's Universal Law, spoken of in the Bible as the Law of the Spirit of Life in Christ Jesus. Universal Law has pre-judged you as being exactly the opposite of how institutionalised church law has judged you. The Law of the Spirit of Life in Christ Jesus has pre-judged you as being perfect and sinless, so it never condemns or punishes you in any way, nor seeks to control you. It pre-judges you as sinless because of the Atonement of Jesus. However it does allow you free will to punish yourself if you so choose, but it does not seek to control you and stop you.

"How does this self -punishment come about?"

Without going into a deep dialogue about the creative thought energy process, which is how God's Universal Law works, let's just say that in the first instance people punish themselves through their own thoughts. If you psychologically punish others with your angry thoughts then anger will be returned to you in some form, not necessarily by the person who has been the subject of your anger, but it will be returned to you. Institutionalised religion says God will punish you for your angry thoughts, Universal Law says you punish yourself through your angry thoughts or behaviour. It's the "as you give so shall it be given unto you" principle at work. God doesn't punish us for being unforgiving, or bitter or mean or whatever else we do in thought or deed that causes offence against another, we bring similar things upon ourselves, because like produces like. That's how Universal Law works.

Universal Law is the functioning component of the Law of the Spirit in the New Testament and is spoken of in the Bible as having come into play to replace the Old Testament Law of Sin and Death, which was the "God will punish you if you are naughty" principle at play, that institutionalised religion still subtly uses.

The particular Universal Law at work here in terms of like producing like is the Law of Reciprocity. The Law of Reciprocity is the law that determines that something, some event, condition or circumstance is received back at all times without fail based on what it is that is broadcast into the universe and applies equally to physical events as to thinking events or thoughts. The Law of Reciprocity has the power to trigger feelings of indebtedness in us even when faced with an uninvited favour and irrespective of us liking the person who executed the favour. It is the Universal Law that states that whatever is sent out into the Cosmos, what modern day science refers to as the Unified Field, whatever is sent out in the way of energy or vibration through the resonance of your thoughts, emotions and actions, will manifest outcomes in the physical world, outcomes that unfold in your life based on whatever is given or broadcast out by you through these thoughts, emotions and actions.

This is how the spiritual Law of Forgiveness works. We ourselves only receive forgiveness in accordance with the measure of forgiveness we impart. This principle is hidden in the Lord's Prayer and most people miss it. Jesus in teaching the Lord's Prayer as it is called said we are forgiven our own trespasses to the same measure that we forgive those who trespass against us. In the Gospel of Mark in the New Testament we see Jesus saying that when you pray if you have anything against anyone forgive them first. Why? Jesus answered this question with the words, "so that your Father in heaven may forgive your sins." Don't ask God to forgive you if you hold unforgiveness in your heart towards anyone. Jesus was saying that doesn't work. Here's the thing. The underlying premise of the Atonement process that psychologically reconnects us back to God is that forgiveness is universal and not exclusive. To forgive is to look past. That's what God did for us, that's what Christ on the cross did for us. God looked past all the screwed up things we've done.

Forgiveness is a powerful force, meant to be given to all for the unification of all, for the restoration of peace in all relationships both spiritual and physical. If you have ingrained unforgiving thoughts lurking in the recesses of your mind they will subtly hinder you in all areas of your life. It is an outgoing also of the law of cause and effect. In order for there to be an effect in your life there has to be a cause, for cause and effect are both intrinsically operationally linked. There cannot be one without the other. It's the way this illusionary world operates. If you attack you will be attacked. If you give it will be given unto you. If you forgive you will be forgiven. True success comes about by focusing on the effect and not the cause. Deal with yourself instead of focusing on the thing or person that caused the effect, commonly known as playing the blame game.

This was a key component of Jesus' ministry. Forgiveness is a powerful energetic catalytic force for spiritual growth and a key component of God's Universal Law. I have included some tips on how to go about addressing unforgiveness if it exists in your own life at the end of the book. There is a powerful emphasis on forgiveness in the Bible because without forgiveness there is no peace and peace is the evidence of a Spirit lived life. When we deliberately withhold forgiveness from someone, perhaps in a sub-conscious effort to punish them, we are embracing an antagonistic attitude towards that person, a combative attitude, which comes from the ego mind not the Spirit led mind, and we are embracing hostility, the opposite of peace. Without peace you cannot function in the Kingdom of God, and so the ego mind wins.

We can all become great creators in life including in the area of a peace filled co-existence with all, through using this creative God energy that is upheld by Universal Law or alternatively we can become mediocre creators by not valuing it. The measure we get back will always be in accordance with the measure we put in. Any return on any investment is always in accordance with our level and intensity of desire and subsequent setting of intention. The true architect of all power to create is the energetic life force called the Holy Spirit within us as witnessed in the words of Jesus who said "ye shall receive power when the Holy Spirit has come upon you." The true meaning of those words being that as we engage with the Holy Spirit then the energetic creative force necessary to make possible that which previously was not possible becomes available to us.

Walter Russell believed that every person can multiply his or her own ability through a continuous recognition and realization and use of that energetic force to create something that was previously not in visible existence, the force that is resident in all human beings regardless of one's religious, social or financial status. He believed that when we fully understand that our thoughts can if we want them to, become primarily an extension of the God kind of thought, then in that instant nothing is impossible and unachievable. He once said, "I believe that such a constant realization ennobles one automatically, one's stature becomes greater, one's steps become more elastic, one's aura becomes more powerful, causing other people to see that Light in one's eyes which attracts people to Him who gave it." To me that is what Jesus truly meant when He described Himself as the Light of the World and when He encouraged us all to be witnesses for His Light.

For those readers who have embraced a lot of what of I have shared in this book but may be asking themselves, well where to from here, I have included as previously mentioned in the final pages a list of Daily Spiritual Practices that I incorporate into my own personal daily spiritual routine, none of them specifically time consuming, but all things I see as helpful in moving forward spiritually. They are easy to implement disciplines that when cultivated and subsequently morph into regular habits will not only promote Holy Spirit engagement in your daily routine but in doing so bring Her life-changing creative power into your life through the outworking of God's Universal Laws, the Laws of the Spirit of Life in Christ Jesus. Be blessed in your endeavours.

> "Mastery of life is not all about self-determination as many have led us to believe. True mastery of life is all about surrender to the true balance between our state of humanness and our state of consciousness, for in essence they are both intrinsically combined but we have wrongly come to believe that they are separate."

CONCLUSION

"The most beautiful and profound emotion we can experience is the sensation of the mystical. It is the power behind all true scientific discovery."

Albert Einstein

Throughout this book I believe I have not strayed too far from its original intent, that being to give the reader a greater understanding of what is known as the Atonement process. The Atonement process being the core element of God's Universal plan for the redemption of humanity, its overall purpose being to reconnect us psychologically with God, resulting in our re-establishing an ongoing and meaningful dialogue with the Holy Spirit as God's plan for the universe progressively unfolds in our life and in the lives of those around us. I have tried to lay the contents out in a way that the finite mind would find it reasonably easy to understand, but acknowledge that a lot of what I have discussed in this book would be relatively new to many people.

In these current times I believe that people are looking for answers rather than just the divisive opinions that we see coming forth particularly on social media, and I trust in some small way I may have provided some answers. To the finite mind so much of the world may seem chaotic, out of control and potentially unfixable, but I cannot go along with the last assumption that it is unfixable. I have an immovable conviction that God's Universal plan for the redemption of humanity still stands strong and is right on track, that the agent of God's plan the Holy Spirit knows what She's doing, and that the cosmic processes God has set in place and the cosmic forces He has marshalled to accomplish the plan will continue to move humanity forward through its spiritual evolution. For midst the chaotic state that exists in this world we must always remember as God's Word says, that when the enemy comes in like a flood, the Spirit of God will lift up a standard against him.

As I have reviewed the manuscript these last couple of months midst the trying times the world is experiencing as a result of the Covid-19 pandemic, I have never been more convinced of the message within the book's pages being so totally relevant to these times that we are living in right now. At the same time I still believe with absolute certainty that even if there were no pandemic as was the situation when I commenced writing this book back in 2019, the message within its pages and the spiritual concepts I have spoken of would not be any different, for these are eternal truths which do not alter according to external temporal circumstances.

In this present day I am also filled with absolute optimism for the ongoing successful evolutionary journey of humanity, because as I said in my quote at the end of Chapter 11, at all times in the history of humanity when there has seemingly been uncontrollable disorder and chaos in play, causing pain and suffering to many, a secret wisdom has sprung into action to dissipate that darkness of humanity's Soul with its glorious healing and comforting light. That is the true essence of the work of the Holy Spirit the Spirit of Grace as she leads and guides humanity to a higher level of consciousness, fulfilling Her Divine role and purpose as the Comforter, the Spirit of Wisdom and the creative agent of God.

The conclusions I have reached about God's plan for humanity and the way of its progression are not born out of logic and reasoning, as are so many spiritual assumptions we see in so many books. As I look back on what I have written I am firm in my mind that my thoughts do align with the thoughts of many people of both Eastern and Western religion who have gone before me, whose thoughts were intuitively in sync with the cosmic principles by which this universe operates, understanding that had come to them similarly as it did to myself from a deeper level of consciousness, a deeper level of awareness and knowing. Much of what I have written has come after being uploaded to my conscious awareness in the early hours of the morning, as I sat in contemplative silence seeking guidance before commencing to write what I believe was my Spirit designated task of completing this book.

At some stage in my spiritual journey, I can't remember exactly when it was, I made a major shift from a mental state of knowing that I was a child of God with a singular goal of getting to heaven in the afterlife, to a state of inner knowing that I am an immortal spiritual being right now, clothed in a physical body, living in an illusionary world, undertaking a series of illusionary activities that in the main are of no consequence to who I really am. It was an unshakeable understanding of what humanity's eternal purpose really is. At some stage in my life I heard an undeniable inner voice informing me that for most of my existence thus far I had been leading a life based on a false visible premise, and also on a false religious or spiritual premise, a premise centred mostly on the principles of logic and reasoning and the so called wisdom of man. However through God's graciousness I was able to embrace this realization and to hand over the past to He who is greater than all our past and present circumstances and experiences.

Similar to so many people of the Christian faith, I had up until that time lived my whole life in a state of determined personhood with a God over there and me over here attitude, believing however at the same time that if I really got into trouble and couldn't find my own answers through logic and reasoning God was still in my vicinity in my peripheral spiritual vision you could call it, close enough for me to be able to reach out to Him if I had the need, but only if logic, reasoning and self-determination appeared not to work. Rather than being a necessary guide for a true and complete spiritual journey through eternity, and the author and finisher of my faith, God was merely a God of convenience for me.

I have spoken of this state of mind throughout the book as a state of psychological separation from God and a psychological separation from everything that God's universe contains. This is how it was for me. For myself there was no sense of oneness with the universe to be seen or found in any of my mental meanderings save the odd time when I sat on a quiet beach at dusk watching the sun slowly setting and the evening shadows drifting across the seascape, simultaneously asking myself the question, is this all there is or is there more? But sometimes even just for a split second in these quiet moments of reflection I caught a glimpse of God's Grace and peace, not realising until later that this was the Comforter at work, She who moves in silence to meet us at our point of questioning as well as our time of need. Later seeing that this was the fragrance of the Spirit wafting across my sensory perceptions saying "everything's going to be alright, be at peace."

I remember at one stage in my search for spiritual truth reaching into the world of science and scientific achievement, to see what some of the greatest scientific minds of past and present generations were saying about the spiritual evolution of humanity. I came across one scientist who felt very comfortable both in his scientific expression and in his spiritual beliefs. His name was Albert Einstein. Einstein was one of those rare scientists who successfully managed being in the world but not of the world as Jesus encouraged us to be in the Book of John. Albert Einstein was a scientist who revolutionised modern physics. He was awarded the Nobel Prize in 1921 for his discovery of the Photoelectric effect, which formed the basis of Quantum Theory. Einstein believed that a human being is a part of a universal consciousness, a part of a whole, but that in a kind of optical delusion of his own consciousness he experiences his life as somehow separate from everything else.

I discovered in my research a statement made by Einstein which revealed that even though he appeared to be a scientific genius totally enveloped in the world of science and scientific thought, his thinking went much deeper than this. Einstein in fact valued the cosmology of the universe far more highly than he did the awards and accolades given him for his scientific opinion and achievement. One of the few overtly spiritual statements he made that confirmed this to me and has stayed with me for many years was when he said, "the most beautiful and profound emotion we can experience is the sensation of the mystical. It is the power behind all true scientific discovery." Einstein felt strongly that this illusionary lifestyle we create born out of our own perceptions and our lack of knowledge becomes a prison of personhood for us, and that every individual's task in life is to free themselves from this confined and restrictive state of being by widening our circle of compassion and love through embracing all living creatures, all of nature, and the whole of humankind. He believed that by embracing our universality and our interconnectedness we unleash our unlimited potential for creative expression.

How or why Einstein came to believe this we may never know, because it does not appear that at any stage of his life as a scientist he had a Damascus moment as we see the Apostle Paul, formerly Saul of Tarsus had in his lightning bolt conversion to Christianity on the road to Damascus, or as people like the modern day teacher of spirituality Eckhart Tolle revealed in his book The Power of Now. For myself there was no Damascus type moment either when I transitioned from a state of outer knowing to a state of inner knowing, from a state of being locked into the world of logic and reasoning to a state of being locked into the Mind of Christ, the God Mind, so please do not hope for some sort of spectacular spiritual awakening event to occur, that is just the ego mind at work. How you transition does not matter, what matters is that you do transition. Please do not try to sensationalise your evolutionary journey, just quietly surrender to its evolution. For myself as it is for many people I just quietly transitioned, although I believe it progressed relatively more quickly when I consciously decided to, as an act of disciplined habit continually reject all ego thoughts that crossed my mind and as I started to engage continuously with the Holy Spirit.

For those who may be caught up in "the world of religiosity" as I call it, which does include an evidence-based philosophical manner of thinking similar to the world of science, I simply say this; accept what was, accept what still may be, but above all else desire more for the future. At the same time set your intention as to what your spiritual expectations are but be not anxious for tomorrow. Intentional desire, not just wishing and hoping, is the catalyst that can bring change into your life. Intentional desire is thought energy that when pursued is constantly released into the thought energy of the universe which is the creative Heart of God. But use it only to desire more of God for it is a powerful thought process that has destroyed many lives when used in a type of covetous way. The ego mind knows this and uses the thought energy of desire against humankind by introducing covetous thought patterns into our minds, which then motivates and directs us towards covetous behavioural patterns. Life becomes focused on getting rather than giving.

The Bible says that God Minded people use desire to obtain truth. They seek first the Kingdom of God knowing that in doing so all good things will be added unto them. Desire deeply a greater understanding of the things of God and the things of the Holy Spirit and you will be moved in the right direction. To this end I would recommend a study course or simply as reading material a book titled A Course in Miracles, which some readers may be familiar with. The book is not tied to or aligned with any particular religious institution. A Course in Miracles places particular emphasis on the function of the Holy Spirit. It is long and detailed but if approached slowly in a focused deliberate manner chapter by chapter it will be quite helpful. Simply because you have been yoked to a particular religious organization all your life does not diminish your potential for a higher level of understanding or a deeper level of consciousness.

This modern world we live in over recent decades has shifted from a state of spiritual aspiration to a state of material and status accumulation, in a misguided belief that he who has the most toys wins, and that must change if we want to hasten our own spiritual transition and do our part in humanity's spiritual evolution. But to everything there is a time and a season. The current period of humanity's evolution might in the present moment seem to some to be at a crisis point, but in many ways it is no different to many other crises the world has witnessed in the past. It is important to understand however that in times like these lower levels of emotional and mental tolerance and balanced thinking come into play, usually evidenced in the emergence of radical ideological movements formed sometimes out of a certain individual's emotional pain but more often than not in truth galvanised out of a certain individual's ideological ego driven ambition. This when done in an attitude of intolerance only reinforces the innocent individual's existing emotional pain and introduces more collective pain. Discord, divisiveness and disunity are not part of God's plan for humanity.

For those task minded readers who say well where to from here, or I understand what you are saying, but what do I need to do right now that might be helpful in my spiritual journey, I have included some simple spiritual practices or pointers at the end of this chapter that you may find helpful. The important thing though is that these pointers are not taken to the extreme and thus become another ritualised routine that we think we must do in order to make gains spiritually. The routines themselves if adopted won't make you more spiritual or enlightened, but to adopt any of them in particular the aspect of Holy Spirit engagement and thought correction or mind renewal, will demonstrate a willingness to embrace spiritual aspiration and inspirational change and it is the willingness and desire and not the method that is the catalyst for change. Spiritual practices per sae do not make us more holy or enlightened, the Holy Spirit does that as she responds to our openness for change.

These pointers are the same ones I do as part of my daily spiritual, psychological and physical wellbeing regime. If you do adopt any of them and perhaps get into some sort of routine and then for whatever reason miss the mark in terms of consistency, the most important thing to remember is not to condemn yourself, judge yourself, or feel guilty, for the Holy Spirit does not see guilt. All the Holy Spirit sees when She looks at you is the guiltless Christ within you. Guilt thoughts are not God chastising you; they always come from the ego mind, for if the ego mind can continuously envelop you in guilt it is its way of attacking the Atonement process set in place by Jesus thus hindering your personal spiritual transitioning. So be firmly convinced as we read in the Book of Philippians that God who has begun a good work in you, with your display of willingness will complete it, even if at times you feel you have fallen short of the high expectations you may have of yourself.

As I touched on in the Introduction to this book, we have been given an opportunity through Christ's gift of the Holy Spirit to come to a perfect understanding of what human existence, our life as we call it, is all about, and to be gently and patiently guided to our ultimate eternal destiny. She is our guide in all of this and we have a choice to make, which the Book of Deuteronomy in the Bible refers to as a choice between Spiritual Life and Spiritual Death. The Voice of the Holy Spirit is the voice of Spiritual Life, and the murmurings and disruptive mental interference of the Ego Mind is the voice of Spiritual Death. If we are listening to both, which most people are, Christians and non-Christians alike, it is in Bible terminology known as being in a state of double mindedness, which generates an emotional lifestyle alternating at various levels of psychological or mental disturbance, this then being reflected in our physical and emotional life at various levels of tiredness and anxiousness, ranging in intensity from mild anxiety to off the charts extreme depression and fatigue.

Unlike the voice of the Ego Mind the voice of the Holy Spirit does not command, does not demand, and does not reprimand. If you are experiencing difficulties in life the Holy Spirit will not condemn you or seek to control or attack your sense of self-worth or make you feel guilty. If that is going on rest assured it is not God trying to teach you something. As I also said in my introduction if you have purchased this book looking for stimulating theories or interesting ideas or intellectually inspired religious debate or discussion, or a new serious set of practices you can implement into your life, you will not find them here. The words in this book are really no more than signposts. However I am hoping my words will point you in the direction of what practices are in the best interests of your attaining a higher level of conscious awareness and deter you from those practices and habits which are not conducive to this, and similarly which beliefs are in your best interests to maintain and which beliefs may simply have been a waste of time for quite a period of time.

We are given the Holy Spirit for edification and ongoing enlightenment and guidance. The Comforter, the Holy Spirit gently leads you in the right direction to the right choices. We must arrive at a point of knowing Her, not just knowing about Her, including how She moves and goes about doing what She does, and to do this we have to have what I mention throughout this book, some sort of communicative relationship and dialogue with her. I have included in this book all that I see as both relevant and necessary for both of these things to happen. Be blessed in your spiritual endeavours.

DAILY SPIRITUAL POINTERS AND PRACTICES

1. **Always greet the new day with gratitude, with some sort of gratitude dialogue.**

The day should always be greeted with a "Good Morning God" attitude and not with a "Good God it's morning" attitude. Starting off the day with positive intent engages Universal Law and makes all our goals easier. Our thought process has to be aligned with God's thought process from the get go, which is, "in everything give thanks for this is the will of God concerning you." (1 Thessalonians 5:18 and Colossians 3:17.)

I have attached my personal morning prayer of Gratitude and Intent that takes only 5 or 6 minutes to complete.

2. **At every opportunity engage with the Holy Spirit, talk to the Holy Spirit in your mind.**

Commit your day to the guiding Hand of the Spirit. Talk to the Spirit if you need to make an important decision. Seek guidance. If you practice it regularly enough it will eventually become an automatic response in any situation similar to a child who has an imaginary friend they continually converse with. It does not have to be some sort of disciplined prayer routine, just quiet, relaxed, silent or audible conversation. Cast your cares upon the Holy Spirit because She cares for you. That's why She is called the Comforter.

3. Live life deliberately focused on everything that comes into your life.

If you are talking to someone give him or her your full attention. If you are doing something give the task your full attention. Fully engage with everything that comes before you. This will minimise the opportunity for you to get lost in trivial and wasted thought. Give the present moment your full attention. Live life deliberately and not just accidentally as most people do.

4. Take some time, at least once a week, to get "lost in stillness."

What do I mean by that? Take time out from the inner and outer noise of the universe and spend time with the stillness of the universe. You may decide just sitting quietly breathing rhythmically or meditatively is what you need to do. Or take a walk at the beach and drink in the peace, or a walk in the park, or just a walk down the street, but not in this instance as a means of exercise, rather as a means of observing in a non-judgemental way the universe you live in, the goings on around you.

5. Take time occasionally to deliberately examine your thoughts, to observe your thoughts.

It does not have to be a regimented routine just do it when you think of it. You will be amazed at how many trivial and useless thoughts you entertain all the time. Just occasionally stop, step back and become 'the observer' of your current thought and it will surprise you how much you are living through your mind thinking about past events or future scenarios and expectations, usually with some regretful or anxious connotations. Then immediately say to yourself or out loud if you can, "my mind holds only what I think with God, a child of God can suffer nothing, I am that child." Actions like this are all part of the renewing of the mind process, which is the key component of the Atonement process.

6. Take a moment every day to deliberately forgive someone.

During the day at any particular time you think of it take a moment to deliberately and sincerely forgive someone, any one that comes to mind. At first you will find yourself choosing only those who you have minimum psychological discomfort with, then as you progress you may or should deliberately move on to the more difficult ones. It is a powerful spirituality influencer, an energetic force for not only your good but for the good of the beneficiary of your forgiveness. I spoke of this principle in Chapter 12.

7. Go for a brisk walk and take some deep breaths as you do

Develop a habit of getting some sort of exercise daily. It has all kinds of health benefits mental and physical. Does not have to be strenuous. Does not have to be of the Arnold Schwarzenegger type. Just a brisk 30-minute walk will suffice. Remember life is all about finding balance in everything.

Some Simple Tips To Help One Rise Above Ego Mind Identification

1. PAY ATTENTION...Listen to the voice in your head continuously.
2. PAY ATTENTION...To repetitive thought patterns.
3. PAY ATTENTION...To your current emotional state, your feelings.

It will surprise you how many trivial, destructive or negative thoughts you filter through your mind impacting on your emotions.

AS YOU DO THIS

Recognize that there is a voice there and here I am listening to it, or recognize that there is an emotion present and here I am feeling it. Don't try and fight it just observe it, like a teacher in a classroom who gives an occasional glance in the direction of a misbehaving child whilst saying nothing.

DON'T

1. DON'T dwell on the thought or feeling.
2. DON'T analyse the thought or feeling to see where it's coming from.
3. DON'T judge the thought or feeling.

JUST OBSERVE IT

1. Watch the thought almost in a way letting it know you are watching it but not embracing it.
2. Observe and feel the emotional energy it produces inside of you. Identification with the mind gives it energy; observation of the mind withdraws energy.
3. Try to avoid conversations with others that push for an opinion on or a judgement against some particular situation or person. These things are all manifestations of the ego mind.

"Remember thoughts and emotions feed each other. If we continually entertain a particular thought we give it energy, spiritual energy, power to create after its own kind. If we reject that thought with words or thoughts like "my mind holds only what I think with God," or "I am as God created me, the son (or daughter) can suffer nothing, I am that son," (or daughter) then we will de-energise, deflate and destroy the thought and it will eventually disappear totally."

When the thought is gone the emotion goes with it, and the energy that is withdrawn from your mind will turn into peace filled presence. Life will physically and emotionally feel a whole lot easier to navigate.

MORNING I AM PRAYER

A Prayer of Gratitude and Intent

The following is my early morning wake up discipline that I have been carrying out every day without exception for around eight years now to the point where I pretty much know it off by heart. It is a combined affirmation of gratitude and prayer of intent. Gratitude and Intent are both powerful energy forces that operate according to Universal Law and over time can have a powerful impact on your life.

Gratitude, the word itself, comes from the Latin root *gratus,* and *gratus* is also the root of related terms such as "Grace," the subject matter in Chapter 11. It's Proto-Indo-European root *gwere* means "to praise, to celebrate, to be in contact with the Divine." In the renowned neuro-scientist, author and spiritual teacher Deepak Chopra's article titled "Sowing Seeds of Gratitude to Cultivate Wellbeing," the co-authors reference clinical studies that prove the positive effects of gratitude on the recovery of patients with symptomatic heart failure. Science had been providing for many years now clinical proof supporting what many religions and spiritual traditions have been predicating for eons, that gratitude does you good. In his article Deepak also draws a powerful association between the physical and mental wellbeing that comes from an ongoing attitude of gratitude and the subsequent development of a higher level of spirituality.

Intention is the starting point of all our dreams and is an energetic force within itself that fulfils our needs. Everything that happens in life begins with an intention thought. The sages of India observed thousands of years ago that our life is shaped and impacted on by our desires which intention comes forth from. The classic Vedic text known as the Upanishads declares, "You are what your deepest desire is. As your desire is, so is your intention. As your intention is so is your will. As your will is so is your deed. As your deed is so is your destiny." Jesus said,, "Desire first the Kingdom of God, and all the things you need shall be added to your life."

The morning prayer can be recited out loud or read slowly and silently to oneself, or you can do as I did if you have a computer, record it with pauses between each main point enabling you to play it and repeat that section out loud, play the next section and repeat it out loud etc. It takes about five or six minutes each morning but you will find over time it will be the most valuable six minutes of your day that you will ever spend. Try to keep focused on each part of the prayer as the morning mind does have a tendency to drift out of immediate focus into thoughts about the day ahead. The prayer covers many areas that we have discussed in this book including Holy Spirit engagement, our thought processes, the Mind of Christ, the intuitive mind and the rational mind, creativeness, forgetting the past, forgiveness, achieving balance, embracing stillness and having respect for our body our instinctively operating earthly vehicle.

I am grateful Lord of the universe for today. I am grateful today for who I am, I am grateful today for where I am, I am grateful today for everything I have, and I am grateful for what I am doing right now. I am grateful for the Holy Spirit who you sent. Holy Spirit I align my will with your will for my life and ask that you would today guide my thoughts, guide my will, guide my reason, guide my intent and guide my actions and behaviours that they be in accord with God's will for my life and the part I will play in God's will for humanity.

I am grateful Holy Spirit to open my eyes today, I am grateful for another day to live my life, for a new start. I am grateful to feel the breath in my lungs and the beating in my heart. I am grateful Holy Spirit for today, for the opportunities in the next twenty-four hours; I welcome the chance to do something amazing and creative with the day today. I choose to make the most of today, I energise my thoughts, I focus my intention, I remind myself of how far I've come and believe that I will go the distance today to whatever goal or vision I have in mind. I remind myself of achievements accomplished successfully and channel my focus to today only and the present moment only that I might make the most of the next twenty-four hours and not be bothered as to what comes after this.

I am grateful Holy Spirit for this body and vow to treat it well today. To eat well, to nourish it well, hydrate it, exercise it, stretch it, move it and relax it. I am grateful for the Mind of Christ within me, for my intuitive mind and my rational mind and vow to use them both well, to focus on learning to applying knowledge gained, to reflect, and to hold myself accountable. I place my rational mind in subservience to my Christ Mind. I commit to staying humble, I agree to talk and think well of others and myself and to channel my focus in conversation only to the positive. I commit to let go of wasteful thinking, to let go of dwelling on the past where there are no more lessons to be learned, to let go of fear and anxiety of the future and instead focus on what I can control, my own actions and my own thoughts, my own reactions and my intent.

I am grateful Holy Spirit for the people in my life, those who are supportive and those who I in some way have learned from. I take a moment to remember all the small and great things done for me; there is so much to be grateful for. Whether something simple like a door held open, a smile from a stranger, or the gift of time and attention from another. I am grateful Holy Spirit for what I give myself, the time to reflect alone in stillness, to clarify my thoughts and to remind myself to press on. I am grateful for the courage I have to do what feels right instead of following the crowd, balancing listening to others and my own rational mind and listening to my intuitive voice, the voice of the Holy Spirit within me.

I am grateful Holy Spirit for the basics, to breathe, to eat, to sleep and to move. I remind myself that not everyone has these basics; I remind myself that I am privileged to have them. Today is all I have and I promise to use my time well. I am grateful for this day these twenty-four hours, I am grateful for the unlimited potential that lies inside of me. I promise to use my time well, to use my thoughts feelings and actions well, to be clear on my intent, to be flexible and adaptable, and to respond with good grace to life's unexpected events.

I commit to work towards being the best that I can be today, to realise my unlimited potential, to continue with my goals, to stay strong and ignore distractions, and to let others negativity just pass by. I refuse to feed or entertain my own doubts, I commit to being the best that I can be today, from thinking to clarifying intention, from clarifying intention to taking action, with the time energy and resources available. To be the best in heart, mind body and spirit for myself and for others, to give the best of myself as I focus and set intention, as I clarify my vision and next action steps, I am grateful dear Holy Spirit for today and I am ready for today. Thankyou, thankyou, thankyou for today.

> "Accept what was; accept what still may be, but above all else desire more spiritually, for desire is the catalyst that can bring change into your life. Desire is thought energy that when pursued is constantly released into the thought energy of the universe the cosmic enabler of the Creative Spirit of God."

Recommended Study or Reading Material

A Course in Miracles - Foundation for Inner Peace

Available on Amazon

www.ingramcontent.com/pod-product-compliance
Lightning Source LLC
Chambersburg PA
CBHW071854290426
44110CB00013B/1139
9780987622815